Behold the Men

Behold the Men

An introduction to critical theologies of masculinities

Edited by

**Robert Beckford
and
Rachel Starr**

scm press

© Editors and contributors 2025

Published in 2025 by SCM Press
Editorial office
3rd Floor, Invicta House,
110 Golden Lane,
London EC1Y 0TG, UK
www.scmpress.co.uk

SCM Press is an imprint of Hymns Ancient & Modern Ltd
(a registered charity)

Hymns Ancient & Modern® is a registered trademark of
Hymns Ancient & Modern Ltd
13A Hellesdon Park Road, Norwich,
Norfolk NR6 5DR, UK

All rights reserved. No part of this publication may be reproduced,
stored in a retrieval system, or transmitted,
in any form or by any means, electronic, mechanical,
photocopying or otherwise, without the prior permission of
the publisher, SCM Press.

The editors and contributors have asserted their right under the Copyright,
Designs and Patents Act 1988 to be identified as the Authors of this Work.

Scripture quotations are from New Revised Standard Version Bible: Anglicized
Edition, copyright © 1989, 1995 National Council of the Churches of Christ in
the United States of America. Used by permission. All rights reserved worldwide.

British Library Cataloguing in Publication data
A catalogue record for this book is available
from the British Library

ISBN: 978-0-334-06123-6

Typeset by Regent Typesetting

Contents

1	**naked bodies (introduction)**	**1**
1.1	Missing bodies	1
1.2	Behold the Men – *uhuru wise* (2022)	5
1.3	Male, men and masculinities	7
1.4	Using this book	9
1.5	For reflection, conversation and action	10
1.6	Bibliography	10
2	**earthed bodies (becoming men)**	**12**
2.1	Introduction	12
2.2	#BlackWomenMatter: Theological anthropology and toxic masculinity – *Robert Beckford*	20
2.3	For reflection, conversation and action	28
2.4	Bibliography	28
3	**displaced bodies (mission)**	**32**
3.1	Introduction	32
3.2	Mission and Men – *Carver Anderson in conversation with Robert Beckford*	41
3.3	For reflection, conversation and action	47
3.4	Bibliography	48

4 broken bodies (resisting sin) — 50

  4.1 Introduction — 50
  4.2 Dead Man Stalking – *braveslave* — 56
  4.3 Incel and the Goddess – *uhuru wise* — 57
  4.4 Resisting sin: Seeing masculinities and violence through the cross – *Will Rose-Moore* — 58
  4.5 For reflection, conversation and action — 65
  4.6 Bibliography — 65

5 bodies of Christ I (the man Jesus) — 69

  5.1 Introduction — 69
  5.2 Contextualizing Christ – *Chris Greenough* — 73
  5.3 The temptations of masculinity: a rude Buddhist-Christian theology of toxic seductions – *Bee Scherer* — 81
  5.4 For reflection, conversation and action — 93
  5.5 Bibliography — 93

6 healing bodies (seeking salvation) — 97

  6.1 Introduction — 97
  6.2 Models of salvation and masculinities – *Carlton Turner, in conversation with Rachel Starr* — 100
  6.3 Dinosaurs will roar and Eagles must soar – *braveslave* — 111
  6.4 For reflection, conversation and action — 113
  6.5 Bibliography — 113

7 bodies of Christ II (church) — **115**

- 7.1 Introduction — 115
- 7.2 Penetration, prescription, appropriation: A risk assessment for (white, straight) male ecclesiologists – *Al Barrett* — 123
- 7.3 Weakness and strength: living within the paradox – *Donald Eadie* — 131
- 7.4 For reflection, conversation and action — 137
- 7.5 Bibliography — 137

8 resistant bodies (pastoral care) — **140**

- 8.1 Introduction — 140
- 8.2 Conversations on Dalit masculinities – *Raj Bharat Patta* — 146
- 8.3 Transformative solidarity across people of diverse genders – *Karl Rutlidge* — 150
- 8.4 For reflection, conversation and action — 155
- 8.5 Bibliography — 155

9 receptive bodies (liturgy) — **158**

- 9.1 Introduction — 158
- 9.2 Worship: composting male epistemologies and other knowings – *Simon Sutcliffe* — 164
- 9.3 For reflection, conversation and action — 173
- 9.4 Bibliography — 173

10 created bodies (God)   **176**

    10.1 Introduction   176

    10.2 Masculinity and the *imago Dei*: learning how to be a man – *Michael J. Leyden*   183

    10.3 For reflection, conversation and action   191

    10.4 Bibliography   191

11 connected bodies (community)   **194**

    11.1 Introduction   194

    11.2 'I have sought you and I have found you.' Queer African masculinity in the hagiography of Late Antique Egypt – *J. A. Robinson-Brown*   195

    11.3 For reflection, conversation and action   205

    11.4 Bibliography   205

Index of Biblical References   207
Index of Names and Subjects   209

1

naked bodies (introduction)

1.1 Missing bodies

Men have discussed and debated the relationships between God, humanity and the world for centuries. But men's bodies have often been absent from such conversations. This book seeks to encourage men who are interested in talking about God and faith to bring their bodies into the conversation. While it is primarily focused on Christian traditions and themes, it does not presume faith, but only an interest in reflecting – individually or with others – on what it means (theologically) to be a man in Britain today.

Prompts – Robert

The African American Hebrew Bible scholar Randall Bailey introduced me (Robert) to the critical relationship between men's bodies and scripture in the early 1990s. On a visit to the Queen's Foundation for Ecumenical Theological Education in Birmingham, where I was working as a tutor in Black Theology, Randall conveyed a story about his experience teaching Paul's description of the body of Christ (1 Corinthians 12) to church groups in the USA. Towards the end of the class, after an analysis of the scriptures, Randall would ask the parishioners gathered to consider why Paul's 'body of Christ' had no genitalia. The question was generative; he wanted the class to think more critically about what Paul says about men's body in his corpus. Did Paul have a problem with men's bodies? Furthermore, in the present, how did masculinity, sexuality and power collude in the Christian tradition to simultaneously centre some men's bodies and marginalize others?

Struck by Randall's line of thinking, I began to contemplate the construction of Black men's bodies in cultural and Christian traditions. Inspired by Black British cultural studies and their emphasis on the politics of representation (Hall et al. 2013), my initial reflection on the subject, 'The Maasai have a point: Black male sexual representation and Christology' (Beckford 1998, pp. 61–78), expresses a desire for representing Jesus as fully (sexually) human, as a counterpoint to the sanitized images produced in much of British contemporary Christian art at that time. I hoped that by deconstructing the meaning of the body of Christ in all its diversity, complexity and toxicity (Black) Christian men could reflect critically on our bodies.

There was criticism from the Black Church. A more daring earlier version of the book chapter, published as 'Does Jesus have a Penis?: Black Male Sexual Representation and Christology' (Beckford 1996), led some people in the church to question my gender identity as just raising the question of how Black Christian bodies navigate the world was, to them, profane. There is a socio-historical backstory that explains the criticism. Much Black Christian thought on the body is underpinned by colonial Christian thought, traditional ideas of masculinity, bodily purity and spiritualized theological reflection. In sum, Black people asking questions about the Christian body always risks a challenge to the legitimacy of the white colonial body politic.

At times, I have been complicit. Much of my work has involved reflecting on the surface of the Black Christian body, the epidermis or attire (e.g. Beckford 2009). As a consequence, I have also neglected how my reflection played into traditional models of masculinity by evading questions of power, coercion or control of women's bodies. Therefore, I come to this book as part of a journey of recapturing the radicalism for transforming thinking expressed in 'The Maasai have a Point'.

Prompts – Rachel

My (Rachel) journey towards this book began while studying in Argentina where, though neither Roman Catholic nor Argentinian, I was welcomed into the community of *Teologanda*, a Roman Catholic women theologians' network. In a context in which women still struggle to access theological education, *Teologanda* is a vital space for discussions around gender and power in the church. At their conference in 2008, I went along to a panel exploring masculinities, having already begun to explore different models of masculinity in relation to my research on domestic violence, asking how certain models, often those promoted by the dominant church, work to increase the risk of violence occurring. I was aware of feminist theologians' work on gender roles and relationships but hadn't yet encountered theological discussions on what it might mean to be a man until that panel, where I met Larry José Madrigal Rajo, a Salvadorean theologian, activist and community educator. For several decades, Larry has supported work across Central America in helping men reflect on their experience and gender expectations. These workshops, in which the complexity of bodies, emotions and relationships are honoured, try to untangle the deep connections between dominant models of masculinity and violence (Bird et al. 2007; Madrigal and Reyes 2007). Larry's work and friendship have been life-giving to me, and to many.

A second prompt was my experience of teaching critical theologies of gender at the Queen's Foundation for Ecumenical Theological Education in Birmingham. When male students asked: 'What should I read about masculinity?' I struggled to identify an accessible resource that explored masculinities from a critical, theological perspective. I wanted a text that would apply the same kind of questioning and insights present in feminist, womanist and queer theologies, to the experiences and expectations that shape men within Christian traditions. Which models of masculinity are healthy for men, their faith journeys, and their relationships between men, women and people of diverse gender identities? How does theology recognize and explore the diverse experiences of being a man? How are sex and gender identities shaped by ethnicity and colour, sexuality, class, age, health and disabilities? Significant theological work has been done by men marginalized by some aspect of their identity such as race, colour or sexuality; sometimes exploring masculinity, but other times leaving it unexamined. While there are a vast number of guides to men's spirituality, many of these, as we explore within the book, require men to conform to dominant models of masculinity, marked by control, aggression, self-reliance, and a denial of the complex relationships with and between bodies (Gelfer 2009). In contrast, within biblical studies sustained and in-depth conversations around models of masculinity within the Bible have been taking place for several decades (Smit 2017); with male biblical scholars often tasked by feminist colleagues to do the work. Will Moore's book, *Boys will be Boys, and Other Myths. Unravelling Biblical Masculinities* (Moore 2022) offers an accessible way into these conversations, and we see *Behold the Men* as sitting alongside Will's book.

Process

The idea for *Behold the Men* emerged in 2018, while I (Rachel) was staying at Gladstone's Library in north Wales. I remain grateful for conversations with Richard Sudworth and other Queen's colleagues at that early stage, which helped me to develop my thinking. And I am even more grateful to Robert for his willingness to co-edit the book, and the energy and commitment he brings. Robert's questioning of the assumptions that I've made repeatedly as a white middle-class woman, and his encouragement to make deeper and broader connections, have been vital. To work alongside a colleague such as Robert, who is so keen to help people ask deep questions about identity, relationships and power, who is realistic about the challenges of injustice, yet confident about human agency and ability for change and transformation, is a gift.

It has been a further delight to work with so many insightful, committed male theologians who make the book such a rich resource. Our contributors identify as Black, Brown, Asian and white; Indian, British, Caribbean, English, African, Welsh and more; able-bodied, with a disability; trans men, queer, non-binary, straight; Pentecostal, evangelical, Methodist, Anglican. The West Midlands features prominently: Robert is from Coventry and Rachel from Wolverhampton, and both of us are connected to Queen's in Birmingham, as are several of the contributors. We want this text to speak from and to British contexts, but a legitimate criticism would be that much of what we talk about is more focused on England than Scotland or Wales.

Much theology undertaken by men has worked to ignore, deny or limit bodies. In recent decades, most (but not all) feminist, womanist, queer and disability theologies have placed the body central to the theological task. And the body has been a significant focus for critical masculinities studies also. This book seeks to join these wider conversations, while not attempting to engage with all aspects and debate. Our primary focus remains to ask what it means to do theology as someone whose body is designated male at birth, and/or who identifies as a man, and/or who is living in spaces between their sex at birth and their gender identity.

In our earliest conversations about the book, we talked about the importance of the body. While we cover shared ground with some systematic theology texts, we made a conscious decision to begin not with God but with human bodies, specifically, men's bodies. Each chapter places bodies central to the discussion: naked, earthed, displaced, broken, of and in Christ, healing, resistant, receptive, created and connected.

Alongside a diversity of experiences, the book is textured in style and approach. There are some formal academic pieces, and some more reflective writings. There are lived and imagined conversations. There are poems scattered through the text. We hope that this gives a sense of the different styles of theology through which it is possible to explore masculinities.

Within the chapters that follow, readers will encounter a range of theological perspectives on masculinities, with contributors beginning from varied expectations, taking different approaches, asking a range of questions, and offering diverse perspectives. We hope this feels invitational rather than excluding, although we recognize some tensions present within the different voices.

Many contributors – alongside colleagues such as David Tombs – tested out their contribution at the *Behold the Men* conference held online in October 2021. The conference was well attended and received, with fabulous contributions and discussions that shaped this book. We remain grateful to all those who contributed, to colleagues who helped with organization, technical support, and chairing reflection groups, and to Queen's and SCM Press for their support for the conference and this book.

The poem that follows was written as part of the process of exploring what it might mean to *Behold the Men*. We are grateful for this and the three other poems offered. uhuru wise and braveslave are two aliases of A. D. A. France-Williams. He is the author of *Ghost Ship: Institutional Racism and the Church of England* (SCM Press, 2020). You may hear Azariah on BBC Radio 2's *Pause for Thought* or BBC Radio 4's *Daily Service* where he is a regular contributor. As well as being a Visiting Scholar with Sarum College in Salisbury, Azariah is a public speaker, retreat leader, singer and poet who enjoys clowning and wild swimming.

1.2 Behold the Men – *uhuru wise* (2022)

The queer, non-binary,
trans man, transgressive
is disruptive, to the electable
man.

The cowboy, square jawed,
with stolen, delectable land.

BEHOLD THE MEN

He has a woman on each arm,
or at the end of each fist.

That 'man's man' is dying
and he will not be missed.

The rabble rousing Rabbi,
the Palestinian Jew.

He took up the fight, with the bullies,
he lived, and spoke the truth.

Love was his mission, the baton
is now passed on.

Will we make a decision, to continue
the prophets' song?

The song of repentance, calls the
shame riddled men of Anon.

The song, and this dance, says,
'You are loved, and with us you belong.'

Therefore, 'Behold the Men',
the eunuch, the mystic,
drag queens with pristine rouge lipstick.

To those with outer bruises,
from rough hands using stop and search.
To those with inner bruises,
from prejudice and hate, preached at church.

Stand if you can, sit if you need,
reach out, hold our hands,
as together we are freed.

1.3 Male, men and masculinities

In this section, we offer an introduction to key terms used throughout the book, while recognizing that language is fluid and our use of these terms across the book is not always consistent.

Male, female and intersex refer to how a person's sex is assigned at birth, a process that is not always as clear cut as we might assume. Sex classification relies on 'chromosomal, hormonal and anatomical characteristics' (Killermann 2020), and these different aspects of the body may relate in complex ways. For a long time, sex has been understood as binary (male or female), but in reality, sex is much more of a continuum, as the term intersex recognizes (Edley 2017, Killermann 2020).

Men, women and non-binary people refer to gender identity and expression, which exist along a continuum. An individual person's gender identity and expression may also change over time. The term men includes cis men and trans men. *The Genderbread Person* is a resource developed by Sam Killermann to help groups explore the diversity of ways in which we might think about gender identity, gender expression, sex, sexual and romantic orientation (for a more detailed discussion see Thatcher 2020). Gender refers to socially constructed roles (expected norms, roles, etc.) and therefore what it means to be a man varies greatly over time, between different cultures and societies. As the World Health Organization notes, 'Gender is hierarchical and produces inequalities that intersect with other social and economic inequalities.'

Masculinity describes characteristics, qualities and behaviours associated with being a man. These vary greatly across time and place, cultures and societies, families and individuals (for an overview, see Smiler 2019). Therefore, it is more accurate to speak of multiple masculinities, as class, ethnicity and colour, nationality and sexual orientation interact with gender. That said, many people believe that the model of masculinity with which they are most familiar is the only way in which it is possible to be a man. This results in attempts to fix masculinity according to a particular pattern or model.

In this book, we, like many other writers on masculinities, make use of Raewyn Connell's concept of hegemonic or dominant masculinities (Connell 2005 [1995]; Connell and Messerschmidt 2005). Hegemonic masculinity:

> means the pattern of social conduct by men, or associated with the social position of men, which is the most honoured, which occupies a

central position in a structure of gender relations, and which helps to stabilize an unequal gender order as a whole. Especially, hegemonic masculinity confirms and enables the social and economic advantages of men *in general* over women. Crucially, this pattern of masculinity is distinguished not only from femininity, but also from the subordinated or marginalized masculinities that exist in the same society. (Connell 2020, p. 17)

Connell's work helps make visible that there are many different forms of masculinity, which differentiate men from women and non-binary people, and from each other. These different forms of masculinity change and develop all the time, and the ideal or dominant model of masculinity differs across different cultures and societies. In every context, however, there is a form of hegemonic masculinity, which men are penalized for not achieving. Most men do not achieve the dominant form of masculinity. Connell identifies subordinate masculinities that relate to men who challenge the assumptions of dominant models (e.g. queer masculinities); marginalized masculinities that relate to men who are marginalized on the basis of some aspect of their identity (e.g. Black masculinities); and complicit masculinities that relate to men who appear to support the ideal model even if they do not achieve it themselves (Edley 2017).

From the late twentieth century within many western societies, one dominant model of masculinity is sometimes referred to as 'the manbox' (David and Brannon 1976). This model defines masculinity as: non-femininity; striving for success and status; independence including emotional independence; risk-taking and aggression (Edley 2017; Smiler 2019). We note:

> In the West, the man box is the hegemonic form of masculinity today. Men who demonstrate the greatest level of adherence to this definition of masculinity receive the greatest level of societal benefits. These men typically come from the demographic majority groups: white, heterosexual, upper class. (Smiler 2019, p. 47)

One of the main aims of this book is to make visible the diversity of masculinities, recognizing that men are often pressured to perform a certain type of masculinity, which works to deny the reality of who they are. JJ Bola describes the importance of removing the mask and celebrating the 'beautiful variations of manhood and masculinity' (2019, p. 73). Making visible the diversity of ways to be a man is in itself liberating, as is evident in Derek Owusu's collection, *Safe – 20 Ways To Be A Black Man In Britain Today* (2019).

Finally, we note Joseph Gelfer's (2016) exploration of the development of masculine identity. He notes a move from an unconscious masculinity where the dominant model of masculinity and gender relationships is accepted unthinkingly; through concern that masculinity is under threat; a recognition of how gender functions in relation to power; an awareness of the fluid nature of identity; to moving beyond masculinity, while still recognizing its social impact. As with other models of identity development, Gelfer sees these as overlapping stages, through which men might move back and forth.

1.4 Using this book

How might you use this book? Inspired by Serene Jones and Paul Lakeland's *Constructive Theology: A Contemporary Approach to Classical Themes* (2005), we offer the following way through:

- Each chapter begins by mapping out some of the questions and conversations taking place, asking how these might be developed.
- In the second part of the chapter, one or two contributors offer a more focused exploration of the chapter theme.
- At the end of each chapter are questions for reflection and action, individually or with others.
- We recognize that reading and discussing some of the themes explored in the book might be difficult and painful. We encourage you to be attentive to your own need for space or support. Alongside your existing support networks, some organizations you may find helpful are: the Samaritans, the Campaign Against Living Miserably (CALM), Stonewall, HOPE not hate and the Open Table Network.

We hope this book will make visible some of the many creative conversations that are already taking place around masculinities, perhaps not always explicitly or theologically, but there, waiting to be discovered. We ask: What are the theological questions that we might ask about masculinities? And what resources already exist both within theology and in other disciplines? We hope this book will function as an encouragement to male theologians, church folk and others to take these questions further.

1.5 For reflection, conversation and action

1 Why are men's bodies often missing from theological conversations?
2 What are some of the experiences, insights and questions you bring to this conversation?
3 With whom would you like to have conversations about the themes explored in this book?

1.6 Bibliography

Beckford, Robert (1996), 'Does Jesus Have a Penis? Black Male Sexual Representation and Christology', *Theology & Sexuality* 3(5), pp. 10–21.
Beckford, Robert (1998), *Jesus Is Dread: Black Theology and Black Culture in Britain*, London: Darton, Longman & Todd.
Beckford, Robert (2009), 'Black suit matters: Faith, politics, and representation in the religious documentary', in Anthony B. Pinn, *Black Religion and Aesthetics: Religious Thought and Life in Africa and the African Diaspora*, New York: Palgrave, pp. 135–51.
Bird, Susan; Delgado, Rutilio; Madrigal, Larry; Bayron Ochoa, John; and Tejeda, Walberto (2007), 'Constructing an alternative masculine identity: the experience of the Centro Bartolomé de las Casas and Oxfam America in El Salvador', *Gender and Development* 15(1), pp. 111–21.
Bola, JJ (2019), *Mask Off: Masculinity Redefined*, London: Pluto Press.
Connell, R. W. and Messerschmidt, James W. (2005), 'Hegemonic Masculinity Rethinking the Concept', *Gender and Society* 19(6), pp. 829–59.
Connell, R. W. (2005 [1995]), *Masculinities*, 2nd edition, Cambridge: Polity Press.
David, Deborah Sarah and Brannon, Robert (eds) (1976), *The Forty-Nine Percent Majority: The Male Sex Role*, Reading MA: Addison-Wesley Publishing Company.
Edley, Nigel (2017), *Men and masculinity: The Basics*, Abingdon: Routledge.
Gelfer, Joseph (2009), *Numen, old men: Contemporary Masculine Spiritualities and the Problem of Patriarchy*, London: Equinox.
Gelfer, Joseph (2016), 'The Five Stages of Masculinity: A New Model for Understanding Masculinities', *Masculinities and Social Change* 5(3), pp. 268–94.
Hall, Stuart; Evans, Jessica and Nixon, Sean (2013), *Representation*, 2nd edition, London: Sage Publications.
Jones, Serene and Lakeland, Paul (2008), *Constructive Theology a Contemporary Approach to Classical Themes*, Minneapolis MI: Fortress Press.
Killermann, Sam (2020), 'Comprehensive* List of LGBTQ+ Vocabulary Definitions', https://www.itspronouncedmetrosexual.com/2013/01/a-comprehensive-list-of-lgbtq-term-definitions/ (accessed 27.9.24).

Madrigal, Larry and Reyes, Francisco (eds) (2007), *Reimaginando las Masculinidades: Revista de Interpretación Bíblica Latinoamericana (RIBLA)* 56.
Moore, Will (2022), *Boys will be Boys, and Other Myths: Unravelling Biblical Masculinities*, London: SCM Press.
Owusu, Derek (2019), *Safe – 20 Ways to be a Black Man in Britain Today*, London: Trapeze.
Smiler, Andrew M. (2019), *Is Masculinity Toxic? A Primer for the 21st Century*, London: Thames and Hudson.
Smit, Peter-Ben (2017), *Masculinity and the Bible: Survey, Models, and Perspectives*, Leiden: Brill.
Thatcher, Adrian (2020), *Gender and Christian Ethics*, Cambridge: Cambridge University Press.
World Health Organization 'Gender and health', https://www.who.int/health-topics/gender#tab=tab_1 (accessed 27.9.24).

2

earthed bodies (becoming men)

2.1 Introduction

In Genesis 2, God creates human beings from dust and breath. The word used of the first person roughly translates as 'earthling' – from the earth (Trible 1978). Genesis 2 teaches that humans are created out of dust, to care for the earth to which they will return. And, when the first murder occurs, it is the earth that both receives and bears witness to the violence.

In her reading of Genesis, Brigitte Kahl (1999, 2001) identifies two patterns running through it. The Eve pattern explores how women work with God to bring about life, despite the death-dealing efforts of men. And the Abel pattern is a working out of the question Cain asks of God: Am I my brother's keeper (Genesis 4.9)? It takes the length of Genesis for the brothers, of whom there are many, to correctly answer this question for themselves: Yes, a brother is a brother's keeper. Yes, to be a brother is to care for each other, not to compete or kill. Cain's murder of Abel is a failure to be a brother. He is sent away from the possibility of being a brother (never to know Seth), from his family, land and home, from the place of belonging.

This chapter explores these same questions and concerns for men today. What relationship should men have with the earth out of which they are formed? How might men live well towards death, the return to earth? And, what does it mean to be a brother, to live well with other men, women and non-binary people?

In every time and place, there are many different models of masculinity. Here we focus on three that are visible in Britain today, and which, in various ways, are also present in the life of the church. These models, which are shaped by ethnicity, colour, sexuality, class and age, are: the successful man; the family man; and the wild man. By selecting three broad models, all of which we want to nuance and critique, we do not wish to limit expressions of masculinity but rather use these dominant models to explore some of the questions and challenges facing men in Britain today, and to prompt a critical conversation around masculinities within the church. To conclude this first part, we consider what it might mean to return to the field with Cain and Abel, asking how men might be encouraged to live authentic, vulnerable lives, in which mutual dependence is recognized and celebrated, peace and justice sought, and both the limits and possibilities of human life on earth are honoured.

In the second part of this chapter, Robert Beckford explores how, within the history of theological anthropology, some bodies have been protected, while the goodness and dignity of others has been denied. He returns to the beginning of Genesis to explore what it means to be made in the image of God. He then asks how womanist biblical interpretation might offer further resources to challenge toxic masculinities in both Bible and church. Robert is a practice-based theologian who researches across diverse media texts.

Dominant models of masculinity in the life of the church

Christian theologies have much to say about what it means to be human (World Council of Churches 2005). There are some points of agreement: humans are created, mortal, made in God's image; and some areas of debate: humans are fundamentally good, tragically flawed or both; humans are equal in dignity, or not; human identity and relationships are fixed, natural, or fluid and full of future possibilities. When gender, sexuality, ethnicity and colour are introduced into the discussion, the debate only increases, with Christians holding diverse and contradictory views about human identities, roles and relationships.

In recent decades, many churches have explored their teaching and practices in relation to gender, either seeking to establish more equitable forms of relationships; or, conversely, retreating into an (imagined and idealized) past in which gender roles and relationships are fixed according to patriarchal, heteronormative models. The relationship between Christianity and dominant models of masculinity, has, however, been largely unexamined (Smit 2019). As such, Peter-Ben Smit (2019) argues, much of the church has legitimated hierarchical, violent models of masculinity.

Various ecumenical organizations have undertaken work on reshaping masculinities from a faith perspective. These recognize the impact of faith beliefs on understandings of gender roles and relationships.

Tearfund, for example, uses biblical stories in its training programmes, seeing in the Bible resources to challenge patriarchal norms, gender injustice and gender-based violence (Deepan 2017). Similarly, the World Communion of Reformed Churches' training programme uses the Bible to help men reflect on their roles, health and relationships in the context of their faith (Sheerattan-Bisnauth and Peacock 2010). Both these examples are programmes designed to encourage gender equality in the church and society, and which recognize (to an extent) that dominant models of masculinity need to be challenged for men's own health and wellbeing, and in the face of gender-based inequality and violence.

While there is much to be commended from such programmes, we wonder if a more radical approach is needed. What if the church undertook a more sustained and critical analysis of dominant models of masculinity, instead of assuming them? We turn now to explore three broad models of masculinity present within contemporary Britain, asking how they are present within the church and how they might be resisted (for a fuller discussion of these and related models, see Gelfer 2009).

The successful man

'Normative notions of masculinity are strongly tied to youth and to heterosexuality, to physical and sexual prowess, to economic production' and, we would add, to whiteness (Slevin 2008, p. 37). In this section, we explore two overlapping versions of this model: the financially successful man and the physically and sexually successful man.

In contemporary Britain, men's identity continues to be strongly connected to paid work (Kummer 2022). To be a man is to work, to earn money, to provide. Although there have been significant shifts within the nature of work in western contexts over the past century, qualities associated with white middle-class men continue to be valued within commercial sectors – driven, decisive, demanding of self and others (Roberton and Shand 2020). The pressure to succeed in the workplace – whether for the company, to increase or maintain status among peers, or to provide for the family – increases the risk of heart attack, high blood pressure, drug and alcohol dependency, mental illness, suicide. If to be a man is to work (and be successful at it), older men, unemployed men and financially or otherwise unsuccessful men might feel – or be judged – as 'less of a man' due to their lack of participation in the public workspace and lack of ability to produce or earn (Tarrant 2020; Slevin 2008).

A second model of the successful man is that of the active, muscular man, who conquers the gym or wilderness (Edley 2017). While some forms of work, such as farming, mining or construction work, or military service, still require a physically strong body, many other forms of work undertaken by British men today do not. Yet, pressure to achieve a lean, fit body – and the status gained through this work – remains. For some marginalized men, for example, young, unemployed men, control over their bodies through exercise and diet may be one of the few ways to gain status as a man (Ravn and Roberts 2020). Men – especially younger men and gay men – are expected to care about their appearance to a much greater extent than in the past. We note how Black men are often celebrated (and constrained) as athletes (while their achievement is often denied through the framing of their achievements as due to 'natural' talent or physique). While the body itself is the primary focus of control, men's bodies may also be used to dominate others – on the pitch, in business meetings and especially in the bedroom. Popular men's health magazines promote performance-driven masculinity (Van der Watt 2016) achieved through 'hard gymnasium exercise, diet, the development of brain power, and capital investment' and with the aim of 'sex and the seduction of women' (Louw 2012, pp. 165–6).

Despite its beginnings as small, struggling communities, the church is not immune to the lure of success. Western churches are often overly keen to attract and promote (young-ish, white, middle-class, presumed heterosexual) men. If men are understood to bring status to the church, the church is unlikely to question or challenge men's status. Many churches in Britain today appear overly concerned with what might be understood as success: numerical and financial growth; media image and branding; a desire to 'grow younger' as the Church of England has stated. Secular notions of sexual success may be limited through the church's restriction of sex to within marriage, but heterosexuality and virility are certainly celebrated within many churches. For some churches, individual financial success is seen as a legitimate outcome of conversion and discipleship (e.g. the prosperity gospel movement); while others might talk of blessings of family and career that come through faith. Yet other parts of the church are resistant to a focus on success, recognizing the gift of a declining – even dying – church; of small acts of everyday faithfulness; of a community made up of misfits and stragglers.

The family man

A focus on the family, and the family as the space from which men may gain status and respect – from male peers and wider society – has become increasingly central to western models of masculinity. Although there are many different models of family life and roles, men have long been expected to provide for the family. Historically, in western contexts, this role was carried out at a distance from the family, with the husband or father figure associated with absence and authority. Today in Britain there is an increased expectation that men will be present within family life. New fathers often express anxiety and confusion about their role – how to be both present for partner and child but also continue to feel responsible as financial provider (Baldwin et al. 2019). It was notable that during the covid-19 pandemic, many middle-class men in Britain had to adjust to working from home, and thus be 'confronted with the demands of care' present in the daily family routine (Kummer 2022, p. 123).

The family man model is central to dominant Christian understandings of masculinity, with most churches encouraging, through practice, culture and teaching, a focus on (heterosexual) family life and wellbeing, and with many placing men firmly at the head of the family unit. New Testament texts reflect significant struggles within the early church over household order: Were Christians to confirm to a patriarchal, enslaving model, or discover a different model of family life? For much of the history of the church, patriarchal, enslaving models won out. More recently, some sections of conservative evangelicalism have reframed patriarchy as 'servant leadership' calling on men to focus on the family, and be willing to make sacrifices for the good of the family, to bear the burden of leadership and responsibility (Du Mez 2020). In other parts of the church, there has been a gradual, but sustained move towards more egalitarian, democratic models of family life (Starr 2018), in which roles and responsibilities are not defined by gender.

The wild man

The modern 'wild man' as a concept is most clearly linked to Robert Bly's book, *Iron John* (1990). Bly argued that the safety of contemporary western society – including the church – had caused men to forget their true nature. He proposed that deep within all men lies a complex, wild masculinity, and that men needed to find their way back to this authentic self. Bly promoted wilderness retreats to help men leave behind their busy schedules; and allow themselves to be spontaneous and honest about their desires, including their sexual desires. Of course, for many marginalized men, contemporary western society has never been safe or secure; the model assumes white, middle-class identity. Indeed, as Kristin Du Mez observes about the USA conservative evangelical context: 'With a few exceptions, Black men, Middle Eastern men, and Hispanic men are *not* called to a wild, militant masculinity. Their aggression, by contrast, is seen as dangerous, a threat to the stability of home and nation' (2020, p. 301).

The mythopoetic movement sought to re-establish what it perceived to be traditional, patriarchal models of family life, and especially the relationship between fathers and sons, which modern society was understood to have ruptured. As Mark Pryce (1993) and Joseph Gelfer (2009) have both observed, this return to an imagined past involves a reassertion of male dominance. Whether intentionally or not, the wildman, along with associated models – iron man, king, warrior – centre masculinity around violence and power.

Second, the risk taker. In this version of the wild man, which is more visible in contemporary white British society, wildness is expressed through a lack of care. Such models of masculinity suggest a real man regularly drinks large amounts of alcohol, eats unhealthy food, drives recklessly, and practices unsafe sex (Ravn and Roberts 2020). In Britain, men are expected to – and do – drink more than women, and in more damaging ways (Patterson et al. 2016). Men's lack of self-care, connection with their emotions and networks of support result in men being three times more likely than women to be at risk of suicide (Samaritans 2017). Cultural and peer pressure on men to be (hetero)sexually active, either within a committed relationship or in casual hook-ups, increase the risk of sexual violence for women, non-binary people and marginalized men. And as Kenny Monrose (2020) notes, Black men continue to be framed as sexually promiscuous and as violent, resulting in increased risk to their own wellbeing, especially where poverty and racism prevent them from achieving masculine status through other means.

Despite the dominant church's long history of concern over physical pleasure, alcohol (in some traditions) and, especially, sexual activity outside (and even within) marriage, support for this model of risk-taking masculinity can be found in some Christian traditions. Kristin Du Mez (2020) observes how, from the early 2000s, conservative white evangelical movements in the USA promoted increasingly aggressive forms of masculinity focused on action, power, danger, and the need for white men to protect family and nation (often defined in exclusively white terms), and control women. Leaders such as Mark Driscoll at Mars Hill Church celebrated men's aggression, competitiveness and wildness – and instructed women to submit to men, including sexually (French 2021).

Many Christian traditions are fearful of sex, resulting in a culture of silence and shame, and a failure to promote sexual health, and just, loving sexual relationships. Christian anxiety over gender identity and the sanctioning of LGBTQI+ identities and sexual practices continue to damage the health and wellbeing of many men, women and non-binary people. Yet in Britain today, especially among younger people, there is increased acceptance of gender fluidity and a diversity of sexual identities and practices. Perhaps the task of the church here is to listen and learn from the reality of people's experiences, concerns and desires. As Edley (2017) notes, despite the rhetoric, men are often anxious about their bodies and sexual activity, often feeling vulnerable during sex and longing for intimacy and mutual respect with their partners. How might the church make space for men to 'talk [honestly] about sex – all the good things and the bad things that may be' (to quote Salt-n-Pepa, 1991)?

Controlling men

All three of these models are shaped by a desire to control. The successful, 'self-made' man, through discipline and hard work (it is claimed) achieves the goals set by dominant models of masculinity: wealth, knowledge, power and respect. He is in control of his own life and able to control those around him. The family man exercises a more subtle form of control. He works to establish a family and provide for them. The family man seeks to be in control of himself, to ensure he acts in ways that are best for the family, and, to a certain extent, although this is far less the case in much of Britain today, is expected to control his household. Risk-taking men at first glance appear to demonstrate a lack of control or care towards their bodies. However, this disregard may perhaps be a form of disciplining the body – a means of pushing themselves to the limit, of demonstrating an ability to bear pain or uncertainty.

In the final section of this introduction, we explore alternative models of masculinity which seek to restore connection between body and mind, between men, women and non-binary people; and between humans and the earth.

Embodied men

The dominant church has long sought to distance itself from the body (Copeland 2009). It has focused on the spirit and soul, reason and rationality over bodies, emotions, desires and death. It has sought to control and discipline the body, most especially the bodies of women, Black and Brown bodies, queer bodies. As Jarel Robinson-Brown comments,

> The Black Queer body in the Christian community so often takes the place of [the] scapegoat – heterosexual Christians, having identified the location of 'sinfulness' in bodies other than their own, rid themselves of their need for grace and forgiveness, leaving the Black Queer body apparently in need for redemption of which the heterosexual has no need. (2021, p. 94)

Since theology was for a long time done by men (and still is in some contexts), and since white heterosexual men have often assumed and overlooked their bodies ('for some theories of masculinity the body is antithetical to the very idea of being a man', Edley 2017, p. 64), much theology has failed to engage with the body. But, again, to quote Jarel Robinson-Brown, 'if we want to be set free from the entanglements that our fear of the body has led us into, we must trust more what our bodies really tell us when they experience freedom, pleasure and love' (2021, p. 95).

One of the first twentieth-century theologians to engage explicitly with the body was James B. Nelson (1978, 1992). Nelson focused on men's bodies, and specifically bodies designated male at birth, asking what we might learn about strength and vulnerability by paying theological attention to male genitalia – the phallus or penis. Nelson argued that it was vital to overcome binary divisions between body and spirit, sexuality and spirituality, etc. His insights continue to be relevant decades on.

Most theologies of the body have been undertaken from positions of marginality, with many feminist, womanist, queer and Black theologians beginning with their lived, embodied realities. Such theologians have noted how bodies have been classified and ordered, often resulting in attempts to control the body (Copeland 2009). They have underlined the importance of engaging with the lived reality of physical bodies – which can be sites of pleasure but also trauma (Copeland 2009; Moore 2009; Pinn 2010). Specifically, Darnell L. Moore (2009) warns that doing theology from Black bodies is a painful, messy process, which often results in encounters with violence, pain and trauma.

What might an embodied, earthed theological model of masculinity look like? And how might the church encourage men in its practice? Such a model of masculinity would begin by recognizing that men are bodies and souls – bodysouls – and must find ways of accepting and valuing their whole self (Louw 2012). It would encourage men to engage with the complexity of their bodies, lives and stories: to listen to their bodies that speak of trauma and grief, violence and pain, joy and hope. It would make space for fluid notions of sex and gender identity, roles and relationships. Queer theologies have much to offer here (Gelfer 2009). An embodied earthed model would support men in discovering and expressing their emotions, to understand that to be human is to be finite and vulnerable (World Council of Churches 2005, Louw 2012). It would bear witness to the relational nature of humanity, that all humans, men included, can only exist in relationship (World Council of Churches 2005, Anderson 2020). As Phyllis Trible (1978) observed on reading Genesis 2, the first human is not gendered, only becoming so through the creation of a second person, a partner. Gender is relational, and thus to be a man can only be understood in relation to other men, women and non-binary people; in relation to the wider world; and, for people of faith, in relation to God. Finally, such a model would challenge men to work for justice, equality and inclusion (Baker-Fletcher 1996; Anderson 2020).

2.2 #BlackWomenMatter: Theological anthropology and toxic masculinity – *Robert Beckford*

What does it mean to be a man made in the image of God and how can this likeness provide an alternative to toxic masculinity? Much depends on what we understand to constitute the divine imprint on men's bodies and the meaning and emphasis of toxic masculinity. In Western Christian thought, there is no singular divine 'stamp' to contend with, and thus, in pursuit of a solution, early theological wrestling with this question took place through a series of unhelpful binary oppositions. Classic theological compartmentalizing of the world between humans and the rest of creation, and dividing of the body and soul, contradicted the holistic, unifying impulses in both the Bible and those present in many indigenous spiritualities encountered during the so-called age of (western) expansion. Modern theology has sought to correct these binary oppositions by focusing on the 'self' and contended with human identity as a consequence of history, culture and socialization (Kärkkäinen 2021).

Yet, even these new formulations have been a source of controversy, as some histories, cultures and societies have been considered superior to others. What is at stake in theological anthropology, then, is the foundational issue for all theological reflection – the (in)ability to see-act on all bodies as equally reflecting the divine.

It is imperative to foreground Black women's experiences of toxic masculinity. We often forget that the contemporary resurgence of the movement against the sexual abuse and harassment of women was (re)originated by survivor and activist Tamana Burke. Burke coined the phrase 'Me Too' on social media in 2006, to signify this discourse against sexual violence, and the hashtag #MeToo became central to highlighting the continued problem of sexual assault, especially against Black and Brown women. These (neo)origins of a longstanding criticism were suppressed in the post-2014 appropriation of the discourse by predominantly white women, therefore marginalizing the long history of harassment and rape culture faced by Black and Brown women (Burke 2017). By foregrounding Black and Brown women's experiences, I am seeking to reconnect criticism of toxic masculinity with the original concerns of Black women.

A theoretical tension exists between theological anthropology and toxic masculinity – the two primary discourses in the subtitle of this contribution. Theological anthropology contends that all humans are made in the image of a triune God, that all humans possess the *imago Dei*; conversely, toxic masculinity describes a range of negative, destructive masculine performances that distort, undermine and destroy the full humanity of *all* people. Yet, as is explored in this book, insightful analysis raises serious questions about the source of toxic masculinity. Its origins are not outside of the Christian tradition but inscribed within it. All of which means that we must contend with *the Bible as a site of contested masculinities*. Furthermore, depending on our tradition, to resist toxic masculinity – as this must be our goal – we may find our answer somewhere on a spectrum between revision of the tradition and abolition of it. Abolition does not mean rejection, but a desire to 'cast out' the oppression (beast), destroy it and build something new in its place.

In what follows, I want to move from the particular to the universal and, by way of exploring Black perspectives on theological anthropology and toxic masculinity, contour some of the factors that prevent us from valuing all bodies. My ambition is not to provide concrete indictable answers to the question but instead, gesture towards practices that may help us resist oppressive thinking and doing, that result in the devaluation of all bodies that do not identify as cis men. Methodologically, this contribution weaves together data from autoethnographic experience and insights from Black, feminist and womanist theologies.

Positionality

Let me begin by positioning myself within this matter. After all, no theologian approaches the task devoid of context, history or culture – all coalesce in theological reflection and therefore, the best we can do is to 'out' our biases in the search for greater reflexivity, refusing the Eurocentric theological myth of total objectivity. Asking an African Caribbean man, raised in late modern postcolonial, post-industrial, inner-city Britain, to write about theological anthropology comes with a set of discrete presuppositions. Two defining realities inform my social context as part of this conversation. These are: theological anthropology's history of anti-blackness, and my own collusion with toxic masculinity.

First, whiteness informed theology and anthropology have not been kind to African Caribbean people. With few exceptions, inside of these hegemonic discourses, the idea of Black people being fully human is a relatively new idea (Copeland 2009). Africans in the Caribbean encountered Christian theology as an oppressive, white supremacist system in which Black people occupied a lower rank on the scale of human maturity. As Caribbean philosopher Sylvia Wynter demonstrates, white western man was the archetype of being human and conversely, Black people, a subcategory (Mignolo 2015). Anthropology is equally problematic. As African American theologian J. Kameron Carter (2014) reminds us, this academic discipline emerged coterminous with the European establishment of the colonization of Black and Brown peoples in the so-called New World. Indeed, anthropology legitimates early forms of racial hierarchy and cultural chauvinism. Hence, for Carter, theology and anthropology are codependent because 'theology spiritualizes anthropology's racial hierarchy' (2014, p. 176). How can we mitigate these problematic traditions? I propose that we 'out' this history by foregrounding the fact that all formulations of theological anthropology are a power/knowledge play (Gordon 1980). Therefore, we must always consider who benefits and who loses out from any particular articulation of what it means to be human.

Second, I must confess that I have interpolated images of toxic masculinity. I have been ideologically 'hailed' in an 'Althussian way', that is, I have believed I have a choice about how I construct my masculinity when, in reality, I am just internalizing preexisting ideas. Projecting back, the indoctrination starts early. Like many men of my generation and demographic, the teaching we imbibed at church and home established a view of women's bodies as less than, and thus subordinate to, men's bodies. Nowhere was this viewpoint more poignant than in readings of the Fall narrative in Genesis 3. I sat through numerous Sunday School lessons, which, with the best of intentions, reified sexist ideas of male and female roles and furthermore folded the Fall into femininity so that it came to be synonymous with 'Eve's sin' (Storkey 1994). Armed with this gendered reading, we men collapse(d) masculinity into male headship and leadership, consequently, legitimating male authoritarianism or toxic Black Christian masculinity. Toxic masculinity in Black churches produces epistemic and physical violence. Epistemic violence is a form of knowledge oppression, that is, 'a forced delegitimating and sanctioning repression of certain possibilities of knowing, going hand in hand with an attempted enforcement ... of other possibilities of knowing' (Garbe 2013, p. 3). A good example is the refusal to ordain women to the highest offices in the church (see article 'Church of God says women can't be bishops' 2010). Predicated on a patriarchal reading of the New Testament, all-male leaderships refuse diverse interpretations of gender roles in order to legitimate patriarchal church structures. Epistemic violence legitimates physical violence. This relationship is identified in the stories of Black women published in one of the first books to tackle intimate partner violence in the Black British church context: *Walk in the Way of Love: Ending Domestic Abuse in Black Majority Churches in the UK* (2018, see Kanyeredzi 2020).

To account for my personal limitations, I will seek to reverse the Black church trajectory in the hope of challenging it by foregrounding the discrete experience of violence towards Black women. As African American womanist scholar M. Shawn Copeland (2009, pp. 29–38) reminds us, it is in Black women's experiences that we find a history of struggle against multiple forms of violence based on divisions of race, class and gender. My argument is this: the best way to understand and counter the problematic relationship between these two discourses (theological anthropology and toxic masculinity) is through the corrective work of womanist biblical scholars. Not content with identifying toxicity in the Bible, they also critically correlate the sexual abuse of women in the Bible with violence and exploitation against Black women in the present. But their studies do not end there. They foster practices of resistance and re-existence that are helpful for developing a non-toxic or empowering masculinity. All of which is extremely useful for developing a womanist-inspired empowering or non-toxic masculine identity.

Imago Dei

Theological anthropology concerns itself with what, in the Christian tradition, it means to be human. Intriguingly, despite the importance of this question (after all, salvation history has much to do with what it means to be human) there are few places in the Bible that delineate the facets of the image of God. An inordinate amount of theological speculation has filled the lacuna (Cortez 2010). While disputes exist on what areas are central or marginal, a consensus arises in four basic categories of thought and action. These are: likeness; sex, gender and ethnicity; sin; and Christology (Jones and Lakeland 2008).

The likeness of God describes how humans reflect God (Cortez 2010, pp. 17–27). Likeness can be thought of in a variety of ways that theologians categorize as structural, functional or relational. Structural likeness describes human capacities, such as rational thought and free will. Human freedom and responsibility mean that humans are capable of decision making and complex thought. Presupposing that only humans are endowed with these capacities among all of God's creation, on this basis, humans are made in God's image. Yet, there are fissures between freedom and responsibility. Sin distorts what it means to be human (Copeland 2009).

The functional likeness of God refers to what humans do to reflect the divine image. Specifically, the powers that humans have that the rest of the created order does not. Such as having dominion (Genesis 1.26) or stewardship over creation, and thus being God's representatives on earth (Cortez 2010, p. 20). Just like structural likeness, functional likeness also carries a history of exploitation. Dominion should not be understood as domination of the created order, but sadly, this view has not always been taken seriously in European Christian history. In the last five hundred years, theological claims of dominion have supported the colonization of Africa, enslavement in the West Indies, and many diverse forms of racism. Compounded by sexism, it is evident that as womanist theologians have argued, the Christian tradition has been far too easily complicit with intersectional structures of oppression (Moore 2023, pp. xv–xviii).

The relational approach to likeness views the image of God as neither structural nor functional but about living in community; after all, God in Genesis 1 is a relational being; thus, humans are made to be in relation with God, each other and the whole of creation (Cortez 2010). Yet again, all these relationships are distorted due to sin, separation and violence.

In theory, then, the image of God is a powerful democratizing and inclusivist ideology. It underlines the unity of the human species and the created order. But the repeated failure in human history to value all people, especially visible in the Western experience of Black women, makes clear that the egalitarian vision of theological anthropology must be fought for (Dadzie 2021). What then is the source of this distress? Is the sin of toxic masculinity a failure to live up to the dictates of the Bible, or is the Bible also culpable? The latter is underlined in womanist scholarship.

Toxic biblical masculinities

Womanist interpreters seek to identify, confront and offer alternatives to biblical toxic masculinity and its contemporary implications. Two important texts are: Renita Weems (1995), *Battered Love: Marriage Sex and Violence in the Hebrew Prophets*; and Ericka Shawndricka Dunbar (2022), *Trafficking Hadassah: Collective Trauma, Cultural Memory, and Identity in the Book of Esther*.

According to Weems, today's toxic masculinity (and related sexual violence) can be connected back to images of divine abuse of women in the prophetic texts, which construct images of God in relation to the abuse of women's bodies. The biblical tradition is complex, with the Hebrew Bible reflecting contradictory attitudes towards women. On the one hand, sexual violence against women is understood to signify human failing, deserving of the severest of punishments including capital punishment (Genesis 34.25). On the other, there are narratives that appear to accept, even legitimate violence against women (Genesis 19). Weems seeks to reveal and resist such violence. In her work on the prophetic texts, she concludes that the prophet's use of violent and misogynistic metaphors contributes to the sexual pathologizing and brutalization of women's bodies in the present. The toxic metaphors of the prophetic texts have real life consequences in the ministry and teaching of all churches.

Ericka Shawndricka Dunbar's reading of the book of Esther implicates a distorted image of God in the sexual exploitation of Black women. Dunbar unearths a tale of gender-based violence and sexual exploitation in the text, making visible the sexual trafficking of girls by the imperial court. Dunbar identifies how this ancient story connects to violence against women through history. She connects the transporting of women across national boundaries in Esther to the sexual trafficking of

Black women during the transatlantic chattel slave trade. And the attitudes that legitimated transatlantic chattel slavery's sexual trafficking continue into the present, specifically in the stereotypical objectification of Black women's bodies. Such stereotypes legitimate violence against Black women in the modern world, ensuring the failure of legislators and law officers to adequately protect them. There is a British resonance to this tragic modern outcome. In 2022, the case of 'Child Q', a 15-year-old Black girl-child stripped-searched by police after she was wrongly suspected of carrying cannabis at her school, further heightened awareness of state-sponsored violence and the vulnerability of Black girls, even in spaces where they are supposed to be safe (Nickolls 2022). In response to such violence, Dunbar argues that communities of faith must challenge biblical texts that support violence and sexual exploitation. Like Weems, she asserts that 'some stories cannot or should not be redeemed' (2022, p.120).

Empowering Resurrection

Where do we discover a more progressive empowering masculinity? Are there alternative representations and narratives in the Bible to the oppressive ones identified by womanist biblical scholars?

Some womanist theologians invite us to revisit the life of Jesus as a guide for a template for a positive masculinity. This approach does not emerge solely from the Bible, but also from the lived experience of Black women. First-generation womanists, for instance, underlined how the story of Jesus was empowering for Black women throughout history (Grant 1989). Even if their faith in Jesus did not lead to their immediate liberation, they found ways of operationalizing the story for their survival and elevation in ways that were otherwise foreclosed (Douglas 2019). Some narratives of Jesus present an alternative representation of masculinity. Take for instance, Jesus' encounter with the woman accused of adultery (John 8). Here the toxic judgements present in other biblical accounts are turned on their head, and there is a different focus on wellbeing and restoration. Jesus implicates men's sinfulness in any sexual sin, and by extension in the exploitation of women's bodies. Second, Jesus, rather than being silent on the inherent contradictions at play, 'outs' the hypocrisy of the sexual ethics at play and reinstates the full value of the woman's body. In these two moves, Jesus' opposition to patriarchy's toxic masculinity are made legible. But not all commentators agree that the Jesus narrative is free of patriarchal, toxic masculine features. Will Rose-Moore argues that not all of Jesus' encounters with women rate highly on the non-toxic masculinity scale (Moore 2022, p. 154). Rose-Moore, alongside other theologies of liberation, identifies the resurrection as generative for radical human transformation. He proposes that this Jesus event can redeem toxic masculinity. Through the cross and resurrection, an all-powerful god is made vulnerable, divested of gender norms and power based on the traditional masculine/feminine, powerful/weak binaries. Consequently, it is in the liminality and power of resurrection that we find a way for men to enter Christ's non-toxic empowering masculinity (Moore 2022, p. 155). In other words, to be possessed by the same Spirit that raised Christ from the dead makes the renewal and transformation of individuals and societies possible (Douglas 2021).

If we are all indeed made in the image of God, we must disavow toxic masculinity as a feature of the likeness of God. The racialized origins of the #MeToo movement nurtures an interest in confronting the sexual exploitation of Black women's bodies. The Bible contains numerous incidents and images of misogyny and sexual violence, but also identifies a radical confrontation with toxic norms. In womanist theology, the life of Jesus demonstrates what bell hooks (2004) termed 'a longed-for manhood'. Yet, for other theologians, it is in the resurrection event that new possibilities for being human as radically inclusive beings are realized. Ultimately, whether we feel there is enough in the Bible to work with (reform) or that we need to find alternative sources and traditions (abolition) both have the same *telos*, to overcome the sin of toxic masculinity by abolishing gender discrimination in the church and society and engaging with Jesus' alternative model of being human.

What are the several implications of these insights for those seeking to challenge and overturn the patriarchal norms that govern much of (Black) church life? First, pastors and ministers must be challenged to educate themselves on the influence of toxic masculinity in their theologies and ministries. As mentioned above, much of what passes for theological anthropology in the Black Church context and probably beyond this demographic is still informed by 'whiteness' (Carter 2014, p. 178). Equally important is to address issues of toxic masculinity at the foundations of Christian education – Sunday School. Content, pedagogy and theology must oppose toxic masculine normativity in the Bible and Christian culture. This ambition will require a radical commitment to creating, sourcing and developing new materials and a new educational approach. It is also vitally important for churches to train congregations and even appoint qualified individuals to support victims of intimate partner violence and other manifestations of toxic masculinity. Ultimately, what is preached, taught and modelled has a profound impact on how we model what it means to be made in the image of God.

2.3 For reflection, conversation and action

1 With which character do you identify in the story of Cain, Abel and Seth? Why?
2 Which, if any, of the models of masculinity described in this chapter resonate with your experience, either within or beyond the church? What have you found helpful and what have you found harmful or limiting about them?
3 How might men engage well with feminist and womanist biblical scholarship and theology?

2.4 Bibliography

Anderson, Herbert (2020), 'A Theology for Reimagining Masculinities', *Concilium 2020/2: Masculinities: Theological and Religious Challenges*, pp. 25–36.
Baker-Fletcher, Garth Kasimu (1996), *Xodus: an African American male journey*, Minneapolis: Fortress Press.
Baldwin, Sharin; Malone, Mary; Sandall, Jane and Bick, Debra (2019), 'A qualitative exploratory study of UK first time fathers' experiences, mental health and wellbeing needs during their transition to fatherhood' *British Medical Journal Open* 9(9), e030792.
Bly, Robert (1990), *Iron John: A Book About Men*, Ringwood Victoria: Element.
Burke, Tarana (2017), '#MeToo Was Started for Black and Brown Women and Girls: They're Still Being Ignored', *Washington Post*, 9 November 2017.
Carter J. Kameron (2014), 'Humanity in African American Theology', in Katie G. Cannon and Anthony B. Pinn (eds), *The Oxford Handbook of African American Theology*, Oxford: Oxford University Press.
'Church of God says women can't be bishops', *The Christian Century* September 7, 2010, https://www.christiancentury.org/article/2010-08/church-god-says-women-can-t-be-bishops (accessed 26.9.24).
Connell, Raewyn (2020), 'Men, Masculinity, God: Can Social Science Help with the Theological Problem?', *Concilium* 2020/2, pp. 13–24.
Copeland, M. Shawn (2009), *Enfleshing Freedom: Body, Race, and Being*, Minneapolis MN: Fortress Press.
Cortez, Marc (2010), *Theological Anthropology: A Guide for the Perplexed*, New York NY: T & T Clark International.
Dadzie, Stella (2021), *A Kick in the Belly: Women Slavery and Resistance*, Brooklyn NY: Verso.

Deepan, Prabu (2017), *Transforming Masculinities: A Training Manual for Gender Champions*, Teddington: Tearfund.
Douglas, Kelly Brown (2019), *The Black Christ*, 25th Anniversary edition, Maryknoll NY: Orbis Books.
Douglas, Kelly Brown (2021), *Resurrection Hope: A Future Where Black Lives Matter*, Maryknoll NY: Orbis Books.
Du Mez, Kristin Kobes (2020), *Jesus and John Wayne: How White Evangelicals Corrupted a Faith and Fractured a Nation*, New York NY: Liveright Publishing Corporation.
Dunbar, Ericka Shawndricka (2022), *Trafficking Hadassah: Collective Trauma Cultural Memory and Identity in the Book of Esther and in the African Diaspora*, Abingdon: Routledge.
Edley, Nigel (2017), *Men and masculinity: The Basics*, Abingdon: Routledge.
French, David (2021), 'Why a Masculine Ministry Rose and Fell: Learning the Lessons of Mark Driscoll's decline', *The French Press*, 8 August 2021.
Garbe, Sebastian (2013), 'Decolonization of Knowledge: On the Criticism of Epistemic Violence in Cultural and Social Anthropology', *Austrian Studies in Social Anthropology* 1, pp. 1–17.
Gelfer, Joseph (2009), *Numen, Old Men: Contemporary Masculine Spiritualities and the Problem of Patriarchy*, London: Equinox.
Gordon, Colin (1980), *Michel Foucault: Power/Knowledge: Selected Interviews and Other Writings 1972–1977*, New York NY: Pantheon.
Grant, Jacquelyn (1989), *White Women's Christ and Black Women's Jesus: Feminist Christology and Womanist Response*, Atlanta GA: Scholars Press.
hooks, bell (2004), *We Real Cool: Black Men and Masculinity*, New York NY: Routledge.
Jones, Serene and Lakeland, Paul (2008), *Constructive Theology a Contemporary Approach to Classical Themes*, Minneapolis MI: Fortress Press.
Kahl, Brigitte (1999), 'And she called his name Seth (Genesis 4.25): The Birth of Critical Knowledge and the Unread End of Eve's Story', *Union Seminary Quarterly Review* 53(1–2), pp. 19–28.
Kahl, Brigitte (2001), 'Fratricide and Ecocide: Re-reading Genesis 2–4', in Dieter T. Hessel and Larry L. Rasmussen (eds), *Earth Habitat: Eco-Justice and the Church's Response*, Minneapolis MN: Fortress Press, pp. 53–70.
Kanyeredzi, Ava (2020), *Domestic Abuse and Black Churches: A Research Overview*, Black Church Domestic Abuse Forum, https://bcdaf.org.uk/vlogs (accessed 26.9.24).
Kärkkäinen, Veli-Matti (2021), 'Classical Approaches to Theological Anthropology', in Mary Ann Hinsdale and Stephen Okey (eds), *T&T Clark Handbook of Theological Anthropology*, London: T&T Clark, pp. 11–23.
Kummer, Armin M. (2022), 'Cracks and Care: Pastoral-theological Reflections on the Gender Implications of the Covid-19 Pandemic', *Journal of Pastoral Theology* 32(1), pp. 116–31.
Louw, Daniel J. (2012), 'Marketplace Masculinities Within the International Public Arena of Global Media: Towards a Christian Spiritual Approach to Male Embodiment and "Genital Ensoulment"', *International Journal of Public Theology* 6, pp. 159–82.

Mignolo, Walter (2015), 'Sylvia Wynter: What Does it Mean to be Human?', in Katherine McKitrick (ed.), *Sylvia Wynter: On Being Human as Praxis*, Durham NC: Duke University Press, pp. 106–23.
Monrose, Kenny (2020), *Black Men in Britain: An Ethnographic Portrait of the Post-Windrush Generation*, London: Routledge.
Moore, Darnell L. (2009), 'Theorizing the "Black Body" as a Site of Trauma: Implications for Theologies of Embodiment', *Theology & Sexuality* 15(2), pp. 175–88,
Moore, EbonyJanice (2023), *All the Black Girls are Activists: A Fourth Wave Womanist Pursuit of Dreams is Radical Resistance*, New Jersey NY: Row House Publishing.
Moore, Will (2022), *Boys Will Be Boys and Other Myths: Unravelling Biblical Masculinities*, London: SCM Press.
Nelson, James B. (1978), *Embodiment: An Approach to Sexuality and Christian Theology*, Minneapolis MI: Augsburg.
Nelson, James B. (1988), *The Intimate Connection: Male Sexuality, Masculine Spirituality*, Philadelphia PA: Westminster Press.
Nelson, James B. (1992), *Body theology*, Louisville, KY: Westminster/John Knox.
Nickolls, Lauren (2022), 'Child Qu and the Law on Strip Search', UK Parliament, https://commonslibrary.parliament.uk/child-q-and-the-law-on-strip-search/ (accessed 26.9.24).
Patterson, C., Emslie, C., Mason, O., Fergie, G. and Hilton, S. (2016), 'Content analysis of UK newspaper and online news representations of women's and men's "binge" drinking: a challenge for communicating evidence-based messages about single-episodic drinking?' *British Medical Journal Open* 6(12), e013124.
Pinn, Anthony B. (2010), *Embodiment and the New Shape of Black Theological Thought*, New York NY: New York University Press.
Pryce, Mark (1993), *Men, Masculinity and Pastoral Care* (Contact Pastoral Monographs 3), Edinburgh: Contact Pastoral Limited Trust.
Ravn, Signe and Roberts, Steven (2020), 'Young Masculinities: Masculinities in Youth Studies', in Lucas Gottzén, Ulf Mellström and Tamara Shefer (eds), *Routledge International Handbook of Masculinity Studies*, London: Routledge, pp. 183–91.
Robertson, Steve and Shand, Tim (2020), 'Men, Health and Medicalization: An Overview', in Lucas Gottzén, Ulf Mellström and Tamara Shefer (eds), *Routledge International Handbook of Masculinity Studies*, London: Routledge, pp. 360–370.
Robinson, Victoria (2020), 'Masculinity and/at risk: the social and political context of men's risk taking as embodied practices, performances and processes', in Lucas Gottzén, Ulf Mellström and Tamara Shefer (eds), *Routledge International Handbook of Masculinity Studies*, London: Routledge, pp. 488–97.
Robinson-Brown, Jarel (2021), *Black, Gay, British, Christian, Queer: The Church and the Famine of Grace*, London: SCM Press.
Sheerattan-Bisnauth, Patricia and Peacock, Philip Vinod (2010), *Created in God's Image. From Hegemony to Partnership. A Church Manual on Men as Partners: Promoting Positive Masculinities*, Geneva: World Communion of Reformed Churches and World Council of Churches.

Slevin, Kathleen F. (2008), 'Disciplining Bodies: The Aging Experiences of Older Heterosexual and Gay Men', *Generations: Journal of the American Society on Aging* 32(1), pp. 36–42.
Smit, Peter-Ben (2019), 'Sustainable Masculinity in Ecumenical Perspective: The Pilgrimage of Justice and Peace', *Ecumenical Review* 71(1–2), pp. 84–100.
Starr, Rachel (2018), *Reimagining Theologies of Marriage in Contexts of Domestic Violence : When Salvation is Survival*, London: Routledge.
Storkey, Elaine (1994), 'Atonement and Feminism', *Anvil* 11(3), pp. 227–35.
Tarrant, Anna (2020), '"Maturing" Theories of Ageing Masculinities and the Diverse Identity Work of Older Men in Later Life', in Lucas Gottzén, Ulf Mellström and Tamara Shefer (eds), *Routledge International Handbook of Masculinity Studies*, London: Routledge, pp. 192–200.
Trible, Phyllis (1978), *God and the Rhetoric of Sexuality*, Philadelphia PA: Fortress.
Van der Watt, J. (2016), '"BIG, HARD and UP!": A Healthy Creed for Men to Live by?', *HTS Teologiese Studies/ Theological Studies* 72(2), a3105.
Weems, Renita J. (1995), *Battered Love: Marriage Sex and Violence in the Hebrew Prophets*, Minneapolis MI: Fortress Press.
World Council of Churches (2005), 'Christian Perspectives on Theological Anthropology', Faith and Order Paper 199.
Wynter, Sylvia (2003), 'Unsettling the Coloniality of Being/Power/Truth/Freedom: Towards the Human, After Man, Its Overrepresentation – An Argument', *CR: The New Centennial Review* 3(3), pp. 257–337.

3

displaced bodies (mission)

3.1 Introduction

Are churches places where men feel at home, and should they be? There is a persistent anxiety that men have been displaced from church – because the church, it is argued, has become too sentimental, or because women are seen to have overstepped gendered boundaries, moving into positions of leadership within the church. Yet (some) men continue both to be present and to hold power in the church. In this introduction, we ask whose bodies have been displaced by the church, and consider how churches have sought to make space for (certain types of) men.

Following this overview, in conversation with Robert Beckford, Carver Anderson reflects on his experience of working with young Black men in Birmingham. Carver is a Pentecostal pastor, ministering within the New Testament Church of God, as well as across ecumenical networks. He is cofounder of Bringing Hope, an organization supporting people impacted by crime, serious violence and other challenging social concerns. In his experience, the church needs to meet young men where they are; be both respectful – and questioning – of their culture; and, most of all, to listen and offer practical support, as they seek a 'safe place' to belong.

Displacing bodies

Much of the dominant discourse around mission is concerned with bringing people into the church, or its sphere of activity, whether as converts or partners. Yet, in the history of western Christianity, what is evident is that many bodies have been displaced through mission activities. The western church's participation in systems and practices of enslavement, colonialism and imperialism, in cultural and religious destruction around the world, is well documented and, at last, beginning to be acknowledged (World Council of Churches 2012; Beckford

2014; Reddie and Troupe 2023). White western Christian men – and many women – have systematically removed men, women and non-binary people from their land, family, culture and religion. Black and Brown bodies have been beaten, bound and broken. Christian converts (an often violent process) have been, and continue to be, required to still their bodies and disconnect from their spirit and spiritual traditions (Pereira 2015; Turner 2020). Evangelism within colonial contexts has been a feminizing experience – with people of all genders required to submit, listen, learn from the white man (and, at times, the white woman). As Willie James Jennings (2020) observes, white Christian colonialism has resulted in a fracturing of self and story, a loss of land, memory and ritual; or as Robert Beckford (2014) suggests, a zombification of Black bodies. Jennings places dominant forms of white masculinity, which desire control of self and others, at the centre of the problem, calling for a restoration of bodies and souls, and a way of understanding faith that allows for questions, conversation and connection.

Contemporary mission studies and practice is diverse and inconsistent. The World Council of Churches statement *Together towards Life: Mission and Evangelism in Changing Landscapes* (2012), the *Five Marks of Mission* developed by the Anglican Communion (1984, with the fifth mark added in 1990), and the Methodist Church in Britain's *Our Calling* (2000) all indicate a shift towards a more integrated, holistic understanding of mission which brings together care of souls and bodies, including the body of the earth, and seeks to honour the work of peace and justice in all places. Similarly, Selina R. Stone (2023) identifies how, for progressive Pentecostal churches, social justice is central to mission practices. Yet, in many parts of the church, practices of mission and evangelism are still marked by violence, inequality, exploitation and deceit (World Council of Churches 2012). Competition and consumerism continue to shape mission practices in problematic ways, resulting in religious violence, abuse and division. Modes of mission that collude with unjust structures and fail to care for bodies, which seek to disprove the faith of others, and which require submission to a singular concept of religious truth, connect in various ways – hierarchies of control, binary thinking – with dominant models of masculinity.

Have men been displaced from church?

Across denominations and locations, more women than men regularly attend church (Francis and Village 2021; Zurlo, Johnson and Crossing 2023). In contemporary Britain, the lack of men in the pews or worship circle is in marked contrast to the predominance of men at Friday prayer at the mosque, and the continued visibility of both men and women within synagogues and other religious spaces. While studies suggest that women have always been more faithful church attendees, that men are less present in church is repeatedly framed as a crisis that requires radical, urgent action (Gelfer 2010). No doubt, the continued overall decline in church attendance in Britain adds to such concerns, resulting in fewer younger men (or women) attending church. Yet the picture is more complex than the headlines suggest. Within Black Pentecostal and other Black majority churches, there is a higher proportion of men, including young men (although still a majority of women). And in the past few decades, African and Eastern European Christian migrants have contributed to the growth of cultural or language-specific congregations and fellowships, in which men's attendance is higher – perhaps because these churches often strengthen men's national and religious identities in ways which support patriarchal models of masculinity and fixed binary gender roles, in contrast to those encountered more widely in contemporary Britain.

Concern over a lack of men in the church turns out to be concern over a lack of certain types of men. In the eyes of certain sectors of the church, not all men are created equal. Since the nineteenth century, in various guises, the muscular Christianity movement has promoted a physically active, sexually and morally pure model of white, heterosexual Christian masculinity. For churches influenced by this movement, only some men are desirable. The men's ministry movement (beginning in 1990s USA), while more ethnically diverse in its reach, has continued this tradition by focusing its attention on young and middle-aged, heterosexual men, with the potential to be active, successful leaders. Such prejudices extend beyond gender-specific outreach: a study of the Episcopal Church found that young men were more likely to receive additional affirmation for being at church from other members of the congregation (Lummis 2004).

If we were to ask why men choose not to attend church, we would encounter a variety of theories and related solutions. For some, the reasons are to do with secularization, and reflect the persistent decline of religious beliefs and practices in Britain. The church has to compete with other demands on men's time on a Sunday morning: catching up with paid work; time with family and friends in the midst of an increasingly demanding work culture; or participating in or watching organized sports. There are other spaces where men feel at home, even where they feel connected to a sense of the sacred or spiritual. Men spend time with other men, gain a sense of identity, community and purpose in a variety of spaces: at football grounds, down the pub; in the mountains, sea or allotments; in virtual spaces (gaming, social media). In many, but not all, of these spaces, men are in the majority – even to the active or unconscious exclusion of women and non-binary people.

Second, following David Murrow (2005), we might ask (if) *Why Men Hate Going to Church*. For Murrow and many others, men choose not to attend church because the church has become feminized, a term that has been used both to speak of women's increased religious activity, and of a more sentimental or pietistic faith culture, believed to be marked (varyingly) by emotional expression, irrationalism, vulnerability in worship and prayer, increased ritual practices, or a culture of submission (Pasture 2012; Francis and Village 2021). For some, more reflective styles of worship are framed as feminine, in contrast with more charismatic evangelical styles of worship, often led by a mic'd up (male) worship leader and band. Yet at the same time, the more sentimental lyrics and emotional expression of certain contemporary worship songs of such traditions are criticized as too feminine – with some men favouring rousing, triumphant hymnody, full of battle imagery and belief in an all-powerful God (Nyhagen 2021). A third reason offered for the lack of men in church is that Christian faith, with its focus on caring and community, its concern for the weak and marginalized, is more suited to women who are perceived to be more nurturing and empathetic (Lummis 2004; Nyhagen 2021). Here, Christian faith is understood to be in contrast with qualities associated with men within dominant models of masculinity – strength, independence, control.

And one more to conclude: for some men, church is associated with family life, and thus the private, domestic sphere which has historically been understood as women's space. A survey of Church of England laity found men to be more critical of the closing of church buildings during the covid-19 pandemic which resulted in the church moving into the domestic space: 'This significant change was exemplified when the Archbishop of Canterbury presided at the Easter morning eucharist for the nation from his kitchen table, and when the Dean of Canterbury Cathedral began to conduct the daily offices from the deanery garden' (Francis and Village 2021, p. 4). For some men, such a move represented a loss of authority, a retreat from what they perceived to be the more appropriate public space.

While, for whatever reasons, many men appear uninterested in church life, the church is not uninterested in them. Indeed, in some churches, there is significant focus on what men may desire from the church. Men's needs are placed central to the life of the church, it would seem, even when they are absent. And where men are engaged in church life, they are often expected and encouraged to take up leadership positions. Women continue to be prevented from ordination and leadership in the majority of church traditions, thus women make up the body of the church, but men the head (as we explore in a later chapter). In a study of a charismatic church in England, leadership opportunities were used to recruit and retain young men (Wignall 2016). Indeed, some studies suggest liberal churches – where women are more likely to be in leadership – seem to attract fewer men, whereas there is more of a gender balance within evangelical churches (Lummis 2004). Thus, a necessary question is: If a church makes space for men, what does that mean for the participation of women and non-binary people?

Beyond the sanctuary: men in church halls, basements and gardens

While, in most churches, there are fewer men than women at worship on a Sunday morning, men are present in spaces beyond the sanctuary. Caretakers and gardeners (voluntary or paid), treasurers and churchwardens: men's involvement in church is often focused on practical tasks, especially those that require endurance, strength, or professional skills.

There is another group of men who are to be found in church halls and basements across the country. These are men who come to the church out of need. Many churches host foodbanks, the need for which has increased dramatically over the past decade. While women are more likely to use food banks, young single men who are unemployed are also likely to turn to food banks (Prayogo et al. 2018). Alcoholism is higher among men in Britain and thus men are more likely to attend Alcoholics Anonymous or other recovery groups, many of which are hosted in local churches, such as the Methodist Church which has historically encouraged abstinence. Men make up the majority of prisoners in Britain – and men marginalized due to racial or economic inequality are disproportionately at risk of being imprisoned. Ex-offenders, who may have connected to the church through prison chaplains, may attend support groups at local churches as they seek to re-establish themselves in wider society. Young men involved in gang culture have been a focus for some local church outreach; for example, in London the faith-based organization Targeted Against Gangs (TAG) works with police to reduce gang violence. Meeting in church spaces, TAG runs conflict resolution and counselling programmes for gang members, seeking to redirect young men away from violence towards regular employment and more secure family and faith connections (Armstrong and Rosbrook-Thompson 2017). A further group of men increasingly present in British churches are refugees, asylum seekers or other vulnerable migrants who meet at church in order to learn English or to receive other forms of community support; and who may also choose to join the worshipping community.

Such activities raise questions as to the shape and purpose of mission among men. For Robert Beckford (2004), Selina Stone (2003) and others, a concern is that some Black Pentecostal churches (but the same criticism could be applied to many other churches in Britain engaged in welfare activities) fail to engage with underlying issues of social injustice and, by placing the burden of responsibility on individual men, do not integrate social and political activism into mission activity.

Separate spaces – men's ministries

Concern over the lack of (young, heterosexual, cis) men in church has resulted in the development of men's ministries or groups, that is separate spaces in which men might gather to explore and deepen their faith, offer mutual support and perhaps be equipped for leadership roles within the church (Gelfer 2013). Men's groups are varied, serving a range of needs. While some are spaces for critical reflection on models of masculinity, or offer support for developing life skills, such as parenting skills; others seek to attract or reassure men by celebrating dominant masculine interests, activities and concerns: sport, success at work and food (specifically the eating of red meat) (Gelfer 2010). Here, Christian values are folded into dominant models of masculinity, often with little critical distance or challenge.

The muscular Christianity movement of the nineteenth century saw churches promote physical fitness and team sports as a way of encouraging certain values and virtues among men. Sport was seen as a way of attracting men to Christianity and, as a result, churches founded gyms, cricket and football clubs. To take a Birmingham example, 'Aston Villa grew out of a cricket club established in the early 1870s by the members of a Wesleyan Young Men's Bible Class' (McLeod 2012, p. 101). In contemporary Britain, sport and physical activity remain a key element of men's ministry and outreach, with churches organizing friendly kick-abouts and, especially, days out walking. While some churches encourage mixed abilities and use sport to encourage friendship across cultures and genders; for others, sport continues to be framed as an activity for men, resulting in a lack of critical examination of gender stereotypes.

Sharing food is central to church life. Yet, it is often profoundly gendered, with (red) meat often used to attract men to targeted events (Gelfer 2013). In Britain, there is a strong history of Christian vegetarianism, and significant recent growth in the number of people choosing a vegan diet (although the majority of vegans are women). Nevertheless, in many white British church contexts, bacon continues to be symbolic of something that attracts men to church: men's (full English) breakfasts; or more informal offerings of bacon baps and cups of tea. Such associations of red meat and manliness are problematic. As Carol J. Adams' (1990) work makes visible, meat-eating has a long association with dominant models of masculinity, including models that generate violence against women and children. Similarly, Joseph Gelfer notes how the preparation and consumption of red meat by groups of men at church events serve as a symbol of men's dominance over nature and, through the sexualization of meat, as a symbol of sexual aggression towards women. Such insights make clear the need for churches to ask critical questions about how their own unexamined practices support dominant, violent models of masculinity.

A review of publicity for around twenty Christian men's groups or men's ministries meeting across England found such groups exist across a range of denominations (Roman Catholic, Baptist, Anglican, Pentecostal, Methodist and including groups connected to Catholic Man and Christian Vision for Men). Influenced by white conservative evangelical men's ministry movements from the USA, the majority of these groups appear to perpetuate dominant models of masculinity. There is a focus on: self-control (spiritual and sexual purity); leadership – the need for men to reclaim their rightful place within the church, nation and family; and success (career and connections). Activities include: sport, wilderness activities (plenty of muddy men), war films, full English breakfasts, curry nights and drinks down the pub. A few groups, notably those connected to Methodist churches, have a notably different tone, characterized by jigsaw puzzles, cups of tea and comfy chairs. These seem to target older men and focus on overcoming loneliness and isolation, as well as mental health in general. How might more churches offer men a nuanced, reflective and holistic space? One example comes from the Ugly Duckling Company, which produces a range of conversation cards. Its *Table Talk for Blokes* (2011) takes characters or expectations present within dominant models of masculinity and explores them through a series of questions: for example, challenging the 'lone wolf' figure, or asking what it might mean to make a difference in the world as a man. There is a focus on conversation and the possibility of discovering a range of ways to be a Christian man.

Evangelizing men

The belief that men have been displaced from church has resulted in a focus on attracting men to church. Mission and evangelism continued to be activities and conversations that are dominated by men – and, within white western church contexts, often attract (and sometimes generate) significant amounts of money. As we explore, a number of evangelizing programmes and methods perpetuate dominant models of masculinity in seeking to attract men.

The Alpha course was widely promoted in white British church contexts from 1998 into the early 2000s and continues to be offered by many churches. It seems an appropriate example, therefore, to consider. Alpha weaves together fellowship, conversation, prayer, praise and teaching (Hunt 2005; Tomlin 2013). A significant moment in the course is a weekend away which focuses on the Holy Spirit and in which participants are encouraged to be open to experiencing the Holy Spirit at work in them. Alpha thus brings together doctrinal discussion with an experience of community and embodied faith (Cottrell 2005). Studies suggest that participants on Alpha courses have reflected the demographic of British conservative evangelical churches: white, middle class, with women making up nearly two-thirds of participants (Hunt 2005). However, if there is one gender in which Alpha appears more interested, it is men, more specifically young, heterosexual men. Among the posters created for the national campaign in 1998, one read: 'Job, Flat, Car, Girlfriend, Season ticket to United. Still not Satisfied?' (Hunt 2005, p. 67). More recently, Bear Grylls features on promotional material for Alpha. And *Prison Alpha* (most prisoners are men) is a significant element of the Alpha industry (Hunt 2005).

Alpha both challenges and confirms dominant models of masculinity. Its attention to embodied, emotional faith encourages men to feel faith in new ways. And the experience of receiving the Holy Spirit is often described in ways that contrast dominant models of masculinity: surrender, submission, being guided and transformed. Yet in other ways, it conforms to such models. While the course is structured as a series of questions, and open conversation expressing doubts is encouraged, the answers are preset. The video talks given by Nicky Gumbel make it clear that the aim of the course is to come to know the 'truth' (Watling 2005). Graham Tomlin (2013) suggests Alpha is less concerned with proving the truth of Christianity than with offering an opportunity for a person to experience Christianity through fellowship, worship and prayer. Nevertheless, questions remain as to the extent to which Alpha perpetuates binary modes of thinking (right/wrong), and whether such programmes offer space for a diversity of understandings of Christian faith, and of Christian men's identity, especially since Alpha is rooted in white conservative evangelical traditions which often encourage conformity to dominant gender roles and relationships.

We end this introductory section by considering how conversion narratives are often constructed in binary modes, and ask whether they work to reinforce or challenge dominant models of masculinity. Christian conversion narratives often emphasize the problematic way in which masculinity was performed previously: via sexual activity, drinking and drugs, violence and sometimes crime. Conversion functions as a reframing of what it means to be a successful man: rather than respect won through force or fear, financial or sporting achievement, conversion seeks to reorientate men towards faith and family. Mark Elsdon-Dew's book, *Life Change: 16 Men Tell Their Extraordinary Stories* offers clear examples of such a narrative. In it, stereotypical male characters – violent criminals, sportsmen, explorers, successful businessmen – experience conversion that enables a break with addiction and violence, or a re-evaluation (but not rejection) of worldly success.

When describing conversion experiences, one study suggests that men favour 'metaphors that represented forms of adventure ... exciting physical or emotional activity or discoveries of some kind typically associated with fun and high energy [while women prefer] comforting and peaceful metaphors' (Knight, Woods and Jindra 2005, p. 121). Men tend to focus on themselves, mentioning few other characters, whereas women tend to identify someone other than themselves as the central character. Interestingly, while women are more likely to reflect on their failings, many men also include examples of failings in order to fit their conversion narrative into a redemptive arch (Knight, Woods and Jindra 2005). The baptism of Russell Brand by Bear Grylls in the Thames in 2023, following Brand being accused of sexual violence by multiple women, serves as example of how, when conversion is seen as an unquestioned 'good', there can be a lack of interrogation of the need for truth-telling, justice and lasting change.

In conclusion, while men are less likely to be in church, they continue to hold power in their presence and absence. If churches are to engage in more holistic, healthy forms of mission, they need to interrogate their collusion with unjust structures of inequality and oppression, including those perpetuated through adherence to dominant models of masculinity.

3.2 Mission and Men – *Carver Anderson in conversation with Robert Beckford*

Robert: So, the first question is: Is the church a male space? I'm thinking specifically about your experience as a New Testament Church of God minister, formerly National Youth Director, working now with a significant amount of Black men in the criminal and post-criminal justice system. So, what's your take on this? Is the Black church a male space?

Carver: From experience, the Black majority churches struggle to engage Black men or men *per se*, because the church, broadly, is feminized. So, there's certain expressions, thoughts and functions in worship, praise, sermons, also conversations that men struggle with. This is because they may feel judged, vulnerable, disconnected, especially those from an unchurched background. In effect, churches seriously struggle to engage and effectively support men in general and Black men more specifically. I believe there is an absence of a theology relating to men, which grapples with how churches respond to their concerns, challenges and interests. The notion of the *imago Dei* should be actively explored as to how it relates to men who may be hurting, fearful, vilified or just struggling with life. While Black men are not a homogenous group, there are some foundational needs regarding identity, belonging, respect, aspirations and hopes that are necessary to address.

Robert: How does that then compare with spaces where you find lots of Black men? So, if I go to the gym, it's packed with Black men. If you go to some of the social gatherings, you know, events, especially musical events, there are lots of Black men – African, African-Caribbean. Why is it that we can find men in these spaces but not in Christian places? What needs are not being met by the church?

Carver: 'Black brothers' will go where they feel affirmed, respected, liberated, safe and protected. This may be going to the gym or other social spaces. Of course, we know this is not the case for some, who may be in conflict with other groups or individuals, in community or prison. I believe it is important to view the needs and interests of men as they relate to body, soul and spirit.

Robert: It's true.

Carver: You know why? Because there's something about these three areas that offers us the opportunity to develop ways to engage and address the needs of men with approaches and activities that help them to develop healthy and positive choices and decisions regarding body, soul and spirit. So, churches don't exactly do that for men, which becomes a barrier and disconnector for many men. Men are seeking people and spaces they can relate to! That is why you will see men taking time and money to attend social functions that connect or speak to their realities. There's definitely something about relationality. Tupac Shakur, who died early, was someone who was relational in many ways, even if we may not agree with all his lyrical expressions – when people went to see him, it was rammed! Men were there because there was an energy and connectivity to what he had to say. I think spaces where men frequent are where there is potential for needs to be met. They may not understand the full rationalization relating to needs being met, but they will know what it feels like to be welcomed, affirmed and empowered. There's conversations, thoughts, challenges and interests that men grapple with on a daily basis. These may include conflict situations, family concerns, finance, health, trauma, employment, political issues and racism. So, we are faced with men, who may see church as a place where their stuff is not being addressed in any meaningful way.

I'm generalizing in one sense, but because of my own research and speaking to Black men who say, 'Blood, the church doesn't relate to me!' I continue to be concerned about churches that are inward-looking and may lack the spiritual and cultural competences to meet Black men at the point of their needs. Importantly, we want men to come into the church space, but we are not going into their spaces and community context.

Robert: So are you suggesting that mission to Black men should really be about meeting them in their spaces, rather than expecting them to come into what you described as the quite 'feminized' space of the Black church?

Carver: I think it's both. Once you enter in their space, you are more likely to understand their context a little bit more. I've done a lot in the community where Black men are concerned, which has included going to places and homes that have made me uncomfortable at times, where I have seen and heard challenging things. At the same time, I have relied on my faith, to support me to show compassion as I seek to address contextual needs. I don't think we've done enough to enter the spaces of Black young men to become more familiar with their thinking, conversation, perspectives and lifestyle choices.

Robert: Yeah, I agree. So, tell us then about the work that you're doing at the moment, specifically with men. How do you engage with men and what do you feel works in terms of your ministry? What do you do differently that allows you to engage with them, as a Pentecostal pastor?

Carver: I have not always been comfortable or competent in seeking to address the needs of Black young men and their families. Over the years I have been involved in challenging situations with their families, who are involved or at risk of involvement in activities, lifestyle-choices and behaviours that cause harm to themselves, or others, or their local communities. Inevitably, this has meant addressing issues that arise in the form of criminality, serious violence, use of weapons and negative group or gang activities. It is in the context of all this that we have developed a praxis, drawing on faith and public health principles in working with men in community and the prison context.

So, building a relationship with men who are unchurched, who have things that they're grappling with, is important. The men and their families we work with need to have a sense of trust in us and the work we do to support them. So, what we do in Bringing Hope (a Birmingham-based Christian charity) is to develop a relationship with men, where they are! We meet them at their point of interest, challenge, concern, uncertainties, fears and trauma. In our work, the currency of TRUST is crucial. It may take six, eight, nine months or a year before someone starts showing some positive indication that they trust us. I've got a number of men that I'm working with at the moment who call me *uncs*. So that is an endearing term from a street perspective, *uncs* or big man are indicators of being respected.

Robert: If there is such a big gap between where the church is at and where men are and the work that you're doing, then how can we possibly transform the church, so it becomes that kind of welcoming space? Can worship and ministry work in the same way? Because if you're dealing with men who are dealing with their brokenness, with the traumas that they've had within their lives, and if you've been in the criminal justice system – which is a form of torture, in terms of how prisons are run; it's torturous – can we then expect those men to go into a service where they begin with six or seven praise and worship choruses?

Carver: Let us do our best to understand how men function cognitively, when it comes to church, vulnerabilities and identity. For some who may enter the doors of church, the long praise and worship does not connect with them. Some sermons take no account of the realities of young Black men who only know the *code of the streets*.

When I came to this country from Jamaica in 1977, I was nine and I am now 66. So, I've done all the journey of understanding church, from childhood to being an adult now. I still remember when Sis Douglas, she's now 100, used to engage the children in fun things during the praise and worship in Sunday School. She was very relational and child orientated. It made us want to praise the Lord! It made us want to make noise and engage with the activities. This is a necessary model in our consideration to engage men in our churches; it's about how we create a space for development, learning and growth. Importantly, it needs to be co-produced. Co-production with men who are not Christians yet will help the church create a space. I think co-production is something that we don't do!

I believe we are in a critical period, where Black young men are disproportionately being categorized as 'hard to reach', problematic, violent, gang-associated, socially excluded, difficult and dangerous. This is why churches need to explore what it means to reimagine how we engage men who are struggling with some complex issues. Are churches asking the critical question about the lack of young Black men in their churches? For some men, there's a perception about the church being weak, feminized, wishy-washy, long, Bible-bashing and making a lot of noise. There are arguably stereotypes from church and non-church folks about the streets, community and the church. So how do we deconstruct that? We deconstruct that by having a conversation with each other in a safe space. Without a radical change in how we do church, I believe men will continue to be on the margins, especially the type of men Bring Hope engages.

Robert: I agree. So given that, what kind of men do you think are made welcome at church? Because there are many of us who do go. So how does it work then for those of us who are made welcome?

Carver: In general, I believe the type of men who are welcomed to churches are those who are compliant, responsive, reliable and balanced;

men who don't exactly rock the boat and are not challenging of the ethos of the church, its preaching, teachings and approaches. I am in full support of Black American civil rights activist John Lewis who said, when you see something that's not right, that's not just, you have a moral obligation to do something, say something. This notion should be encouraged, where men are empowered to express concerns in churches. It can be seen that churches encourage passivity of men, which is oppositional to men who may have lived a life of conflict, associated with the code of the streets and community activism. I have noticed that men who may have come from an unchurched context sometimes enter churches and fall into a passive trajectory because they feel that the pastor, the deacon, the elder, knows more than them. While this may not be the case, we have to commence the journey of seeing these men as assets. These are men with complex realities, who have something to offer to any church willing to co-produce initiatives, activities and programmes for Black men.

Robert: So how do you talk to men about their faith then? Is it storytelling? How does it emerge? Because if we have to find places, if we have to co-produce, how do we begin that process of talking about faith to men?

Carver: Firstly, it is important to commence the trust and relationship building journey, by hearing about what they have to say about their situation (positive and challenging). The conversations or discussions should also explore their understanding about spirituality, faith, morality and social concerns. From Bringing Hope's perspective, we may talk about notions of 'being loyal', which for some, may mean doing a long prison sentence for a friend, because one does not want to be seen as a snitch or sellout! Again, this is the code of the streets.

Importantly, I always seek to acknowledge potential trauma or pain of past or present issues. I also give my own story about how on 6th June 1977, like Saul on the road to Damascus, God manifested to me in a strong emotional and spiritual way, resulting in me being curled up on the floor in floods of tears! Some men would say, 'Boy, Carver, you get beat by God.'

As a Pentecostal, I firmly believe there's something about the spirituality that transcends just what I say – so I have to depend on the work of the Holy Spirit, the mediator, comforter and transformative force. Dietrich Bonhoeffer helps me here, with his total dependency on Christ, through faith. I mean, he was a martyr, wasn't he? I ask myself 'Carver, are you ready to give up all for Christ, in order to see greater divine and supernatural manifestations in church, community and prisons?'

I also reflect on David in the Bible who was said to be a man after God's heart, yet he failed and faltered at times. In the Bible there are stories that offer insights into the spiritual and emotional challenges of life, even though we are Christians. In effect, I do not offer false hopes to people who become Christians or are considering becoming one.

My approach to some individuals who talk negatively about the church or Christianity is to ask if they have ever read any part of the Bible towards understanding notions of faith, Christianity and spirituality. More often than not, the answer would be no! This then offers me an opportunity to develop a conversation about further understanding about grappling with the real essence of life, faith and morals from a Christian context.

Robert: How do we engage with Black men talking about faith? Where do we find sacred space for Black men? Where do people say this is sacred to them, where they feel at peace.

Carver: Well, recently I've been reading this book with a number of men, Myles Munroe, *The Fatherhood Principle*. The space was created for up to 25 Black men between the ages of 23 and 67 to explore issues relating to masculinity, fatherhood, trauma, fear, social challenges and spirituality. Conversations were transparent and without judgements. I have a motto when working with men: *come as you are*, even if you are in pain, doubt, confusion or are dealing with anger or relationship concerns. It is in the coming into a space together that the possibility of healing, support and transformation can emerge. The Rock New Testament Church of God in Birmingham, where I meet from time to time, is presently developing a safe space for men through their Men's Ministries activities. An aspect of my involvement with them is to explore what it is to self-reflect as a man and to develop approaches and actions that we account to each other for, as we seek to be men of activism and relevance relating to issues mentioned earlier.

As I continue to self-reflect and assess my impact and effectiveness relating to engaging and supporting men, the following questions help to sharpen my focus:

- How do my present practices, attitudes, mind-set and approaches support me to effectively engage and work with men?
- Do I understand what the key issues are, associated with being a man with complex issues and challenges?

- What further advice/understanding and knowledge do I require, for me to develop new and fresh ideas and tools to be more effective in reaching out to men?
- What are my inner fears, inhibitions, doubts and concerns about engaging men in community/church?
- How am I perceived?
- What issues may support/hinder my capacity to achieve my goals to be effective and relational with churched and unchurched men?

I am confident that, should leaders or churches decide to be proactive and intentional regarding reaching men, along with a coproduction approach, we can experience a fresh development with church and community working for the support and development of our men.

Robert: Amen. So, in closing, then, how would you summarize, if somebody was to say to you, Carver, what is your mission to men?

Carver: My mission to men is to be a relevant voice and, as Paul says, follow me as I follow Christ. So, I believe the character of Christ should be totally resident in how I deal with Black men or men *per se*. I will continue to seek to be a man of love, compassion, justice and hope; working to support men in and out of church to live positive lives. That they can be men that say, 'I can do all things through Jesus because I understand who I am, with all my flaws, with all my history, with all my contention.' But you know, there is a song: *Something inside so strong*, and I believe that's where it needs to be, Robert.

Robert: Fantastic. Thank you.

3.3 For reflection, conversation and action

1 How do you feel about the history or histories of western mission? What questions remain for western churches?
2 Why do you think fewer men than women attend church? Do any of the reasons given fit with your experience, either as someone who attends church, or not?
3 What story would you tell about your faith experience, or, about some other aspect of your experience, identity or commitments that has shaped you?

3.4 Bibliography

Adams, Carol J. (1990), *The Sexual Politics of Meat: A Feminist-Vegetarian Critical Theory*, New York NY: Continuum.
Anderson, Elijah (1999), *Code of the Street: Decency, Violence and the Moral Life of the Inner City*, New York: W. W. Norton.
Armstrong, Gary and Rosbrook-Thompson, James (2017), '"Squashing the Beef": Combatting Gang Violence and Reforming Masculinity in East London', *Contemporary Social Science* 12(3–4), pp. 285–96.
Beckford, Robert (2004), *God and the Gangs: An Urban Toolkit for Those Who Won't be Sold Out, Bought Out or Scared Out*, London: Darton Longman and Todd.
Beckford, Robert (2014), *Documentary as Exorcism: Resisting the Bewitchment of Colonial Christianity*, London: Bloomsbury.
Burns, Stephen (2019), 'Ordination Services, After the Abuse: Postcolonial Proposals', *Liturgy* 34(2), pp. 41–50.
Cottrell, Stephen (2005), 'Evangelism – Which Way Now? An Evaluation of Alpha, Emmaus, Cell Church and Other Contemporary Strategies for Evangelism', *Political Theology* 6(2), pp. 260–2.
Elsdon-Dew, Mark (2019), *Life Change: 16 Men Tell Their Extraordinary Stories*, London: Hodder & Stoughton.
Francis, Leslie J. and Village, Andrew (2021), 'The Pandemic and the Feminisation of the Church? How Male and Female Churchgoers Experienced the Church of England's Response to Covid-19', *Journal of Beliefs & Values* 43(2), pp. 207–16.
Gelfer, Joseph (2010), 'Evangelical and Catholic Masculinities in Two Fatherhood Ministries', *Feminist Theology* 19(1), pp. 36–53.
Gelfer, Joseph (2013), 'Meat and Masculinity in Men's Ministries', *The Journal of Men's Studies* 21(1), pp. 78–91.
Hunt, Stephen (2005), 'The Alpha Program: Charismatic Evangelism for the Contemporary Age', *Pneuma* 27(1), pp. 65–82.
Jennings, Willie James (2020), *After Whiteness: An Education in Belonging*, Grand Rapids CO: William B. Eerdmans.
Knight, David A., Woods Jr., Robert H., Jindra, Ines W. (2005), 'Gender Differences in the Communication of Christian Conversion Narratives', *Review of Religious Research* 47(2), pp. 113–34.
Knödel, Natalie (1997), 'The Church as a Woman or Women being Church? Ecclesiology and Theological Anthropology in Feminist Dialogue', *Theology and Sexuality* 7, pp. 103–19.
Lummis, Adair T. (2004), 'A Research Note: Real Men and Church Participation', *Review of Religious Research* 45(4), pp. 404–14.
McLeod, Hugh (2012), 'The "Sportsman" and the "Muscular Christian": Rival Ideals in Nineteenth-century England', in Patrick Pasture and Jan Art (eds), *Gender and Christianity in Modern Europe: Beyond the Feminization Thesis*, Leuven: Leuven University Press, pp. 85–105.
Murrow, David (2005), *Why Men Hate Going to Church*, Nashville, TN: Nelson.

Nyhagen, Line (2021), '"It's Not Macho, is it?": Contemporary British Christian Men's Constructions of Masculinity', *Journal of Men's Studies* 29(3), pp. 259–77.

Pasture, Patrick (2012), 'Beyond the Feminization Thesis: Gendering the History of Christianity in the Nineteenth and Twentieth Centuries', in Patrick Pasture and Jan Art (eds), *Gender and Christianity in Modern Europe: Beyond the Feminization Thesis*, Leuven: Leuven University Press, pp. 7–33.

Pereira, Nancy Cardoso (2015), 'De-Evangelization of the Knees: Epistemology, Osteoporosis, and Affliction, in Liturgy in Postcolonial Perspectives Liturgy', in Cláudio Carvalhaes (ed.), *Postcolonial Perspectives: Only One Is Holy*, New York NY: Palgrave Macmillan, pp. 119–23.

Pew Research Center (2016), 'The Gender Gap in Religion Around the World', https://www.pewresearch.org/religion/2016/03/22/the-gender-gap-in-religion-around-the-world/ (accessed 26.10.24).

Prayogo, Edwina, Chater, Angel, Chapman, Sarah, Barker, Mary, Rahmawati, N., Waterfall, T. and Grimble, George (2018), 'Who Uses Foodbanks and Why? Exploring the Impact of Financial Strain and Adverse Life Events on Food Insecurity', *Journal of Public Health* 40(4), pp. 676–83.

Reddie, Anthony G. and Troupe, Carol (eds) (2023), *Deconstructing Whiteness, Empire and Mission*, London: SCM Press.

Stone, Selina R. (2023), *The Spirit and the Body. Towards a Womanist Pentecostal Social Justice Ethic*, Leiden: Brill.

Tomlin, Graham (2013), 'Evangelism as Catechesis, Hospitality and Anticipation: A Study of the Alpha Course', *Christian Education Journal* 10(3), pp. 91–102.

Turner, Carlton (2020), *Overcoming Self-Negation: The Church and Junkanoo in Contemporary Bahamian Society*, Eugene: Pickwick Publications.

Watling, Tony (2005), '"Experiencing" Alpha: Finding and Embodying the Spirit and Being Transformed – Empowerment and Control in a ("Charismatic") Christian Worldview', *Journal of Contemporary Religion* 20(1), pp. 91–108.

Wignall, Ross (2016), '"A man after god's own heart": Charisma, Masculinity and Leadership at a Charismatic Church in Brighton and Hove, UK', *Religion* 46(3), pp. 389–411.

World Council of Churches (2012), *Together Towards Life: Mission and Evangelism in Changing Landscapes*, https://www.oikoumene.org/resources/documents/together-towards-life-mission-and-evangelism-in-changing-landscapes (accessed 26.9.24).

Zurlo, Gina A., Johnson, Todd M., and Crossing, Peter F. (2023), 'World Christianity 2023: A Gendered Approach', *International Bulletin of Mission Research*, 47(1), pp. 11–22.

4

broken bodies (resisting sin)

4.1 Introduction

In *T&T Clark Companion to the Doctrine of Sin* (Johnson and Lauber 2016), men discuss other men discussing sin: Augustine, Aquinas, Reinhold Niebuhr, Karl Barth, Paul Tillich, etc. Yet there appears little or no analysis of the specific ways in which men may sin, or the relationship between models of masculinities and how sin is understood. This seems surprising, since the possible connections are immediately apparent when we consider how sin is often understood as rebellion, selfishness or pride, attitudes that are somewhat encouraged by various dominant models of masculinity present in contemporary western contexts. Indeed, feminist theologians have argued that accounts of sin particularly fitting for men are those that focus on arrogance (having an inflated view of one's own worth) and greed (using up too many resources) or, to use more recent terminology: mansplaining and manspreading. Toxic forms of masculinity, which encourage men to prioritize their own needs and demonstrate self-sufficiency in meeting them, prevent men from finding their authentic, interdependent place in the world.

The first part of this chapter explores how dominant models of masculinity intersect with notions of sin. We argue that patriarchy, white supremacy and other intersecting oppressive ways of ordering society are forms of structural sin. We consider how a focus on self-interest and profit results in ecological destruction. We recognize how men often collude with other men, for example, in creating and sustaining rape culture. We note how dominant models of masculinity train men in violence. Finally, we ask how men might seek to be in solidarity with women and people of diverse gender identities, with the natural world and, at the same time, with themselves.

Two poems by braveslave and uhuru wise follow.

In the final part of the chapter, Will Rose-Moore explores how the crucifixion of Christ reveals both human sin and possibilities of resisting sin. He considers how masculine domination and violence might be understood as sinful; and asks how Christ's solidarity with suffering humanity might demonstrate alternative and liberative ways of being in the world. Will identifies as a bisexual (queer), cisgendered man. He is a PhD student in theology and is ordained in the Church of England. Will's book *Boys Will Be Boys, and Other Myths: Unravelling Biblical Masculinities* (2022) offers an accessible and engaging introduction to biblical masculinities.

Patriarchy as structural sin

Under the influence of liberation and other contextual theologies, there has been a shift in theological focus from personal (sexual) sin to structural sin; that is, from the policing of individual 'sinful' acts to the identification and analysis of systemic violence and inequality. Patriarchy, white supremacy, heteronormativity, neoliberalism and anthropocentrism have variously been described as forms of structural sin. While individuals remain responsible for their actions, they are understood to be caught up in sinful structures and patterns of relationship, perhaps able to resist, perhaps not – the television series *The Good Place* 2016–2020 explores how today's complex global economies and systems often result in everyday complicity with injustice. To offer a different example, Susan A. Ross in her analysis of clergy sexual abuse identifies how 'sin resides not only – although it is primarily – in the abuser, but also in the structures that have minimized the harm to victims, protected abusers and diocesan bank accounts, and discouraged victims and their families from pursuing redress' (2019, p. 642).

Roman Catholic ethicist Connor M. Kelly describes 'a structure of sin as an institution or collective practice that either socially idealizes or economically incentivizes actions seeking exclusive self-interest(s) at the expense of the common good' (2019, p. 301). The connections with dominant models of masculinity are evident: through competition, capitalism and consumption, men are routinely encouraged to prioritize their own needs – often framed as the needs of their nation, company, 'race' or family. Recent years have seen a rise in gendered forms of nationalism in Britain (and elsewhere) which present the nation as needing defending from external threats or internal betrayal, and (wrongly) suggest that it can be self-sufficient. The 'take back control' Brexit narrative played into dominant narratives of masculinity that prioritize control and self-reliance (Agius, Bergman Rosamond and Kinnvall 2020).

Whitney Bauman (2003) describes patriarchy as a hierarchy of order and value: moving from God defined as male, spirit and most valuable, to earth defined as female, bodily and least valuable. It is, he argues, 'a system that is oppressive for much of life on this planet' (2003, p. 52). Bauman observes how patriarchy intersects with the global market economy to prioritize the financial success of white western men, achieved through the exploitation of all other bodies, including the body of the earth. It is unsurprising, therefore, that white western men dominate climate change denial movements, since they benefit most from the unrestricted exploitation of materials (Hultman and Pulé 2020). Writing out of the experience of the covid-19 pandemic in El Salvador, Larry José Madrigal Rajo and Walberto V. Tejeda Guardado (2020) further observe how men are not encouraged to care for themselves, or see themselves as carers for others, and are permitted to be careless about their impact on their surroundings – so it is unsurprising that dominant models of masculinity discourage care for the environment.

Ecumenical Patriarch Bartholomew I and Pope Francis both identify environmental destruction as a form of (structural) sin. In a recent World Council of Churches publication, ecological sin is described as a failure to acknowledge the sacramental nature of the world, resulting in the exploitation of natural resources beyond what they can recover from, and a breaking down of the relationships that sustain life (Andrianos and Tomren 2021, pp. 152, 200). How, then, might individual men break with their participation in environmental sin? Martin Hultman and Paul Pulé (2020) argue that what is needed is not a return to the wilderness to become the 'wild man' – such spiritualities remain self-centred. Instead, men need to reconnect with the earth in more sustained ways, which honour the natural world and recognize their dependence on a multitude of other living beings. In Britain and, more specifically, Birmingham and the Midlands, the work of practitioners such as Sam Ewell, Al Barrett and Simon Sutcliffe (the latter both contributors to other chapters in this book) offer a more honest, grounded response to the earth.

As individuals, men can and do resist and reshape dominant models of masculinity, choosing to develop equitable, inclusive models of relationships, in which their own needs are given appropriate attention alongside the wellbeing of others. Nevertheless, patriarchy and related structures of oppression continue to be the context in which individuals, institutions and communities operate.

Rape culture as collusion

Rape cultures are characterized by aggressive, heteronormative models of masculinity that denigrate and objectify women, and present sexual encounters as adversarial, in the process making it more difficult for sexual partners to be clear about consent (McCabe 2018; Smiler 2019). Rape is further used as a means to oppress marginalized men: witness the long history of male rape within contexts of enslavement and today in prison settings and elsewhere (Curry 2017). Sex with women (and, sometimes, feminized men) is understood as a necessary means of performing masculinity, and something to which men are entitled. While individual perpetrators remain responsible for their actions, Megan K. McCabe explores how rape culture 'constrains the possibilities of being for men and women' and creates a context in which sexual violence is more likely to take place (2018, p. 650).

Elements of rape culture are visible within descriptions of the culture of Mars Hill Church, Seattle under the leadership of Mark Driscoll. In sexually explicit, confrontational sermons, Driscoll challenged men to take up their 'God-given' leadership role, in the church, nation and especially the home, where they should expect their wives to be sexually available to them (Johnson 2017). Driscoll's performance of toxic masculinity is well-documented, but many theologically conservative churches and organizations share similar teaching and patterns of behaviour. Within churches, rape culture is sustained by a fear of sex, a focus on purity, and the idealization of (heterosexual) marriage.

While many men do not fit – or want to fit – the dominant model of masculinity within their context, they may still find it difficult to recognize and challenge rape cultures. In a men's group, men might be encouraged to conform to a dominant model of masculinity, express misogynistic views and support other men against women (Smiler 2019). This can lead to men feeling conflicted about challenging friends or colleagues' problematic views or behaviour. Yet in so doing, they participate in the violence of rape culture. Indeed, McCabe (2018) argues that simply by living according to gender norms and expectations, individuals collude with sin because in so doing they perpetuate harmful stereotypes. Alongside a long-term commitment to ending patriarchy and other oppressive structures, McCabe explores how individual men might interrupt and expose sexual violence through the practice of solidarity. She comments:

> Solidarity makes demands of bystanders; it means working together to stand with those who are in danger by opposing and resisting the

kinds of tactics like blocking doors and pressuring drinks on women to foster their incapacitation. It requires calling out men who talk about such behaviors as if it is funny or socially acceptable. (McCabe 2018, p. 653)

Sinful acts

So far in this section, we have considered sinful structures and systems such as patriarchy and anthropocentrism; and collusion with sinful cultures and communities, such as rape cultures. In the final part of this introduction, we consider individual actions and responsibility. For much of the history of the church, the assumption has been that to talk of sin is code for sex. The greater the distance Christian theologians placed between the soul, spirit and mind, and the body, the more problematic sex became. Messy, uncontrollable, pleasurable, dirty – sex was banished from Christian discipleship and, even, for some theologians, from marriage. Prior to Vatican II, the focus of Roman Catholic moral teaching was on sinful acts and thoughts, especially in relation to sex (Keenan 2016). Sex was closely policed, requiring confession and penance. But Vatican II introduced a more holistic focus on the journey of discipleship and, alongside some other parts of the church, the Roman Catholic Church became increasingly aware of structural forms of sin.

That said, sex remains an obsession for parts of the church, with church leaders and thinkers from Orthodox, Catholic, Protestant and Pentecostal traditions concerned to limit sex to within heterosexual marriage and for the purpose of procreation. Church teaching and practices continue to have a negative impact on the wellbeing of women and people of diverse genders and sexual identities: limiting access to sexual and reproductive health care; invalidating gender and sexual identity; assuming a male domination, female subordination model of sexual activity; and legitimating men's control of women – by preventing or requiring women to be sexually active (Ross 2019; Agius, Bergman Rosamond and Kinnvall 2020). While heterosexual married men may appear to benefit from such teaching, the impact on their relationship with their sexual identity and lived experience is often limiting, shaming and harmful.

Feminist theologians such as Margaret Farley (2006) and Susan A. Ross (2019) argue that discussion of sin should not focus on specific sexual acts but rather on the quality of the relationship. Broken relationships generate violence (including sexual violence); sexual relationships should therefore be marked by justice and mutuality. Sinful acts are thus those marked by violence and injustice.

Men routinely commit violence. Men's violence is directed against women and non-binary people, other men and themselves; family members and strangers. Men's violence can be state-sanctioned, for example in a military context, or classed as criminal behaviour – with (predominantly young, poor, Black and Brown) men accounting for 95% of the UK prison population (Edley 2017). It can be cheered on – in sport; or denounced as shameful – 'hooliganism'. While it has been argued that men's violence is due to biological factors, most specialists believe men are socialized into violence (Longwood 2006), noting that many men do not commit significant acts of violence (Edley 2017). Writing from his own experience of growing up as a Black man in Britain, JJ Bola (2019) observes how violence is one of the few ways in which boys are taught to communicate their emotions or are allowed to have intimate physical contact with other men through play-fighting, and that a wide range of games and activities encourage boys to fight an enemy.

Men have more opportunities for violence. In Britain, privileged white men have amassed wealth and power over centuries. They are more able to cause economic, social, political and physical harm to other men, women and non-binary people. Men are expected to commit violence – and are often excused from it. Men use violence, including sexual violence, to gain status among other men. Disagreements between men often result in physical violence because it is difficult for men to find socially acceptable ways of 'backing down' when challenged (Edley 2017). Privileged white men are most likely to carry out mass murders, often motivated by a sense of betrayal that they are not as successful financially or sexually as they expected to be (Edley 2017; Smiler 2019). Men may carry out violence to mock or shame others, a feature of some contemporary models of masculinity that are marked by exclusive self-interest (Smiler 2019). Men who are marginalized due to colonialism, racism or class barriers may see violence as one of the few avenues for them to prove their masculinity – since other modes, such as financial success or social status are unavailable to them (Boonzaier and van Niekerk 2020).

The work of the Centro Bartolomé de las Casas in El Salvador offers one method of addressing men's violence and encouraging institutions and individuals to develop more just, equitable models of relationship (Bird et al. 2007). Recognizing that men are socialized to be violent, there is also recognition that cultural beliefs and practices change – and that even within a dominant model of masculinity, there are a variety of ways in which men perform masculinity, including in non-violent ways. The centre works with a wide range of institutions: from local government leaders to clergy to bus drivers. Male participants 'work to change their own habits and create alternative idea patterns, seeking to sustain deep and lasting change' and are equipped to encourage other men to reflect and move away from violence (p. 115). A key feature is helping men reflect on their experiences and express emotions non-violently. Another important element is for men to recognize their capacity for violence but to understand that other options exist. Yet, the organizers note, participants are often discouraged from continuing with the course by friends and family members, who view non-violent models of masculinity as shameful, even homosexual.

Dominant models of masculinity are harmful, including to those men who seek to live according to them. While individual men may find it difficult to break with these models, they often subtly resist adhering to them fully. Rather than disobedience, argue feminist and other liberation theologians, sin is better understood as brokenness, which results in the wounding of self and others and which requires healing, justice and renewal of right relationships. The recognition that people sin out of their strength (Keenan 2016) might enable men to see how that same strength provides possibilities for alternative modes of being and relating that overcome brokenness and dis-ease.

4.2 Dead Man Stalking – *braveslave* (2020)

Jean Vanier a gentle man, inspiring spiritual director, and an insidious sexual predator.
Both and, monster and man, when one version of him ended the other began. Deep pain
in the L'Arche community, their values to value the least of these, yet it turned out their
founder was the beast of these, but he is dead.

But his crimes are alive, his grime survives, his legacy from being canonized is demonized,
people cannot believe his mystical ploy, he played Jesus and demanded satisfaction, from the
women he supported his deceit garnered a reaction.

White man playing the Almighty, and teaching vulnerability, oh the irony stings,
L'Arche will survive because they became stronger than the flawed man, who
threatened the floor on which they stand, but he was no longer in command.

So when they fall they will rise, post trauma, shock surprise, and redeem his lessons though they no
longer trust his essence. The ravenous father who hid in plain sight, the adoring crowds drawn to
his light. But light obscures as well as reveals, a surgeon's knife can wound as well as heal.

Will men with power always feel immune, that their indiscretions are exceptions and won't
mushroom? Like Weinstein a white God preying on women, as Vanier prayed with women, both
were sinning and thought they were winning.

It has to stop. Wetoo cannot Fleetoo, we need to deal with Metoo, we cannot Betoo complacent
living adjacent to pain in our sisters, the scars on their souls, are inflicted by us if as bystanders. We
watch and wait, it may as well be our mouths vomiting hate, upon their bodies, our fingers tearing
them asunder, we invite God's wrath, prepare for heaven's thunder.

4.3 Incel and the Goddess – *uhuru wise*

Faceless keyboard warriors,
spewing aggressive avatars.
Puncturing, hacking inflicting,
knotted bloody scars.

Involuntary celibates, or incel,
a virulent internet virus of women haters.
The Adam who detests the Eve
of whom he is made.

It is himself he defeats,
as the repressed she in he,
remains unheeded, incomplete.
Alt-Right delete.

Atheists of the mother good,
forge a twisted brotherhood.
Fanatics who demand, it is understood,
that it is a man's man's world!

Yet in a world without the feminine,
humans are left with nothing, bitter void.
No recourse, but to slide in
the black holes rancid mouth,
all life destroyed.

Western men will never mature into their maleness
whilst denying the Ancient African Goddess.
Incel until you grow into your womanity,
toxicity is all we will see,
of your so called masculinity.

4.4 Resisting sin: Seeing masculinities and violence through the cross – *Will Rose-Moore*

Introduction

In this contribution, I question traditional ideas of redemption through the cross and consider what is often implicit in Christian assertions of salvation in terms of violence and masculinities. I re-conceptualize sin using Mark 15 as an example of the threefold flow of sin within which Jesus' male body finds itself entangled. I briefly overview some contemporary contextual theological accounts of sin from feminist and Black theologies. From this, I offer a reading of the cross as a place of male-on-male violence that calls for a rejection of redemptive suffering and demands resistance to sin in all its forms. The crucifixion account reveals that some masculinities involve (in)action and collusion with sin. There is, therefore, a need for a constructive and transformative theological approach to masculinities and redemption, that further recognizes contextual and social aspects of sin.

Conceptualizing sin through the cross

Traditional interpretations of the cross and sin vary remarkably (see Weaver 2011). Some see the death of Jesus as a triumph over evil (e.g. *Christus Victor*), others see his death as a ransom sacrifice for human sin or suggest Jesus dies on the cross in punitive replacement of humanity (e.g. penal substitution). Yet Jesus' crucifixion occurs not as a work of God but at the hands of other men. The brutality Jesus experiences is the result of the human flaw of sinfulness and epitomizes the worst of humanity's potential. His endurance of the cross though, despite possessing divine power to break free from its hold, shows that the Christ who is crucified chose to know fully the worst of human experience. In this act, God's commitment to an incarnation of grace and love is revealed: a God *in* and *as* humanity, even when suffering from the very worst of human actions (John 1.11). This is the transgressive, transformative, mature and vulnerable love of God (Robinson-Brown 2022, p. 81). This is a Christ in 'solidarity with the world's marginalized, even unto death' (De La Torre 2017, p. 66). This is a reality in the incarnate life of Jesus and, as David Tombs says, '[t]o say that Jesus could not have been vulnerable to the worst abuses of human power is to deny that he was truly human at all' (Tombs 2021, p. 22).

Johan Galtung (1969; 1990) talks of three types of violence – direct, structural and cultural. I will use this lens to explore three parallel categorizations of sin. First, sin can be direct and individual, as one acts harmfully towards another and inflicts wounds to a human's self. Second, sin can also be structural, whereby there are conditions in place that allow oppression against marginalized groups to occur more easily, including lessened human rights and the reduction of support. Finally, sin can be cultural: parts of culture can legitimize and normalize such violence. Misogyny, racism, queerphobia and so on, are just some examples of prejudice that have become embedded in many cultures, stunting human flourishing and God's good intention for creation.

We can see these different levels of sin and violence in the Passion narrative of Mark 15 (Thomas and Moore 2022). First, there exists a level of individual sin in Mark's account. Soldiers, as imperial agents, enact violence: physically controlling Jesus' body and where it travels (15.1), as well as stripping him (15.20), while others mock him (15.29–32). Simultaneously, Jesus finds himself among criminals, judged within an unjust political structure that allowed the crowds to decide his fate (15.11, 27). His death (and particularly his body) is used as a political weapon for the empire to scare and deter those who might be resistant to

Roman power (Tombs 2021, pp. 16–17). Finally, we can see the cultural aspect of a mob-like mentality (15. 8–15), whereby the criminalization and crucifixion of an individual can take place as if it is legitimate and necessary, whether rightly or wrongly.

Even though these are only a few examples from a densely packed passage, we can see how Jesus' body is passed around in continuous acts of sin, between individuals acting within wider systems and structures. They are entangled with one another, whereby individual sinful acts are independently driven, but dependent on the structural and cultural aspects that allow for them to occur and be normalized. Mark's Jesus 'ends his story like a tragic hero' (Wines 2023, p. 11). This is not least because of how crucifixion can be 'an especially effective way by which to humiliate and degrade a victim because its meaning is densely encoded with social and cultural values around gender, identity, power and conquest' (Reaves and Tombs 2020, p. 292). It is clear from this that Jesus could be seen to die a death of emasculating shame and humiliation, as a result of physical violence as well as social sin at many levels.

We should not fail to notice the integral dynamic of gender, and specifically masculinities, at play here. Many in history, as well as at present, die similar deaths to Jesus where the social meanings of bodies and identities are threatened. In some ways, Jesus' death is not necessarily unique. Feminist and Black theologies give us a glimpse of such contemporary instances. They can bear witness to the most vicious ways in which humans can act towards one another. When 'space is made' for hermeneutical approaches that better resonate with each of our own realities and experiences (Thomas 2022, p. 236), we see the pervasive reality of sin in different cultural contexts and settings, and especially its common intertwinement with toxic configurations of masculinity. Sin must be accounted for contextually.

For example, feminist readings of the cross have noticed the ways in which structures of patriarchy historically can be named as sin. Accounts of sin and salvation have often been male shaped (Saiving 1960) and readings of Jesus and his emphasized maleness have provided a normative Christology and soteriology that has excluded women (Ruether 1993, pp. 134–5). Women might therefore identify more with the crucified than the crucifiers (Crysdale 2001, p. 8), because of their shared suffering (Johnson 2017, p. 76). Rosemary Radford Ruether (1993) argues that sin 'exists precisely in the distortion of relationality' (p. 181), and so humanity must journey towards a 'consciousness of evil' that recognizes individual and social sins at work, especially the domination of women by men (pp. 183–92). Not only is this a human relationality, but when we suffer at the hands of one another 'God's glory is dimmed' too (Johnson 2017, p. 15).

Black theologians have also unveiled the resonance of the cross and its suffering. James Cone (2011) drew an association between the crucifixion of Jesus on the cross and the lynching of African Americans. For Cone, the Black Christ is 'God [who] becomes oppressed humanity' and rebels against structures of evil (Cone 2020, p. 128). Instead of sin being an act against God, Anthony G. Reddie (2020) reimagines sin as the tearing apart of the bonds of humanity, disuniting the bonds of community and fellowship, akin to Ruether's argument of relation distortion.

Reconciliation and the righting of relationships, then, is at the heart of resisting sin. Part of that reconciliation must be repentance for those actions and beliefs that cause inequality of power and a distortion of relationships. Contextual readings of sin reveal and denounce the sustained attempts of powerful men to dominate women, other men and other marginalized groups. The act of one human (or human system) reducing the humanity of another is sin at its worst, dishonouring God's own image.

If Jesus at his death is also considered 'worth less – or worthless' (Tombs 2023b, p. 68), then Jesus resembles (and even embodies) those considered worthless by society today and those who are often sinned against individually, structurally and culturally. Contrary to most doctrinal accounts of Jesus' death, there is no redemption in the violence inflicted on Jesus, or other individuals today: redemption is only that which 'promotes the full humanity' of God's children (Ruether 1993, p. 19), something that violence cannot achieve. Jesus' crucifixion is no less than 'murder' (Crysdale 2001, p. 9). To argue otherwise would give violence, and indeed its consequent suffering, a restorative or retributive function (Douglas 2015, p. 186). Even more palatable theologies still idealize a suffering that 'serves only to strengthen ... potential for victimization' (Johnson 2017, p. 267). In line with many contextual theological accounts, salvation is equally found in the life and work of Jesus, and some say his crucifixion should be seen as nothing more than the 'gross manifestation of collective human sin' (Williams 1993, pp. 166–7). It is in Christ's assurance of grace and forgiveness in the face of human sin and violence (Luke 23.34, 43), rather than in the infliction or endurance of violence, that redemption is found.

Naming the layered violence of the cross is critical for the construction of a contextual theology of sin that is attentive to certain established dynamics of masculinities. Men can be the perpetrators but also the victims of violence (Greenough 2021, pp. 8–33). Men oppress other men, as well as women and people of a diversity of gender identities from other marginalized groups (including those who identify as queer, those with disabilities and those of ethnic minorities) for reification of their own masculine status within the hierarchy of gender. They attempt to assert dominance through power and violence for their own proclamation of authority. Since hegemonic masculinities are not easily performed (Connell 2005, p. 79), most men will inevitably find themselves dominated by others even when they try to dominate. Masculinities are themselves in a complicated intersection of relationships encumbered by aspects of power and gender, and distorted by sin. Masculinities are always in-becoming, negotiated and transforming (Rose-Moore 2024). Corresponding theologies must be equally heterogeneous and contextual, then.

Resisting sin through the cross

In the face of humanity's sin, it can hardly be disputed that – regardless of which Gospel account we read – Jesus is emasculated by the Roman empire's control and torture of his male body (Moore 2021, p. 90; Moore 2022b). Jesus embodies an outpouring of himself, a kenosis of all status he could have had in the ancient world (Douglas 2015, p. 176), in order to be crucified in the most unmanly way (Moore 2021; Moore 2022a, pp. 142–53; Moore 2022b). There is not only a theological self-emptying, but a social one (Philippians 2.7). Jesus responds to humanity's sin in the torturous practice of crucifixion with a self-giving love for his own creation (O'Donnell 2018, pp. 122–5). Jesus exemplifies the generativity of love even in torture and death through self-giving. Rather than Jesus' suffering and death being understood as redemptive, it should be seen as exposure of – and thus resistance to – individual, structural and systemic sin (Girard 1979; 1986). Love is what remains – however wearily – in the face of violent sin, even through death (Rambo 2010).

I resonate strongly with Tombs' theology of the cross, which draws on feminist and womanist theological work and sees the cross not only as a site of violence and oppression but also as a call to work towards liberation. Rather than glorifying the crucifixion (Williams 1993, p. 167), or even 'glorifying' its interpretations (Moore 2022b), I suggest the cross gives witnesses an ethical imperative to release those who are 'crucified people' today (Sobrino 1982; Tombs 2023a). In Tombs' words, 'the proper task for Christians is not to glorify or romanticize the suffering of the cross but to resist the cross and find ways to take victims down from [their] cross' (Tombs 2023b, p. 7).

Individual men caught up in the systems that perpetuate male privilege and power are often complicit, if not active, in the violence and oppression acted against marginalized bodies. In this way, many men have fallen short of the glory of God (Romans 3.23) and have sinned through their action, as well as inaction; through their desire for hegemonic status as well as their complicity (Connell 2005, pp. 77–8, 79–80). The exposition of human sin in the Passion narrative is not only that Jesus ended hanging from a cross by the work of human hands, but that humanity also did not intervene as it went on. Complicity with sinful structures and systems, and cultural acceptance of inequality and injustice, are of equal reproach as individual actions of sin. Within patriarchal systems, most men benefit from the 'patriarchal dividend' (Connell 2005, p. 82), from the oppression of identities that do not present like them, whether they like it or not. For contemporary Christian men, rejection and resistance of the sinful violence of patriarchal, racist, misogynist, queerphobic, disablist, classist structures is an essential element of effective and transformative allyship.

It is not the endurance of human sin on the cross that characterizes God in Christ, but resistance through the cross and resurrection from it. Womanist theologian Karen Baker-Fletcher says, if 'God on the cross suffers with us in persecution and oppression ... This resurrected God rejoices with us in victory over evil and suffering' (Baker-Fletcher 2006, p. 151). The cross only becomes a story of Good News, where salvation (read: liberation, De La Torre 2017, p. 93) occurs, through the resurrection. That is, where there is no more violence. As Tombs comments, 'God's raising and restoring one who had been crucified was at the centre of the good news itself' (2023b, p. 75).

Though I argue elsewhere that readings of the resurrection encounters can help reimagine masculinities (Moore 2022a, pp. 171–4), I suggest here that the crucifixion can itself offer sufficient analysis of sin and masculinities. Crucifixion shows a dismantling of the gender binary and a queering of gender norms and expectations through the interplay of divine masculinities at the cross (Moore 2021, p. 91). Furthermore, crucifixion shows the reality of humanity's worst sin and the way in which it is historically tied to male dominance, power, control and violence. There is a tension here, then: in Jesus' death, the horrifying capacity of human sin is unveiled, yet the capacity for (human) resistance to the cross and its sin can also be discovered. The crucifixion is an act of useless and shocking violence, yet is still a generative site that reveals how God's goodness breaks open new possibilities. If sin is social and relational, then we have a collective obligation to impede such injustice from still occurring. We, too, can participate in the goodness of liberation.

Conclusion

Masculinities can be inflictors of, and inflicted by, sin, because of the various intersections found within the dynamics of heterogeneous masculinities. Even in Mark's crucifixion narrative, we noticed the presence of these interplays of masculinities. If the cross is a place of male-on-male violence and a site of oppression, Christ himself showed a resistance to patriarchal sin and the cross through a deep incarnational love and a final word of resurrection. This demands a resistance today to the oppression of others and the corruption of communal bonds. In other words, by questioning traditional ideas of redemption through the lens of masculinities and violence, I have shown that the cross pleads for a resistance to sin. If humanity put God on the cross once before, exposing the worst of human nature against the divine, let us not do it to each other again and again.

Attentiveness to the reality of sin and its intersectional social impact is essential. For those of us in faith communities, especially men, rather than being in collusion with violence and sin that we see around us on an individual as well as structural level, we must renounce it. Those who are oppressed must be helped down from their crosses. Power must be divested by giving amplification to those voices that society does not deem worthy of being heard. In doing so, we begin to recognize the violence done by men in the centuries of history that go before us – all the way back to the crucifixion of Christ. Then masculinity can be imagined in resistance to, rather than collaboration with, power and sin. In pursuing justice and liberation, sin is rejected as the 'defining truth about humanity' but instead welcomes God's grace (Robinson-Brown 2021, p. 30). For sin and grace are tied; they 'exist together in the complex matrix of violence' (Jones 2019, p. 38). Yet where 'sin [increases], grace [abounds] all the more' (Romans 5.20). It is God's grace and love that persists.

Writing as a Christian minister, among the reality of sin and violence today, and its entanglement with masculinities, I suggest we are called to bring about God's saving grace of *life* in the world. If sin is social, then salvation must also be (Coleman 2008, p. 86). We participate in this resistance of sin, and therefore saving work, by identifying and listening to those who are victims of such sin, helping them down from their crosses, and working to prevent anyone being nailed to the cross. In recognizing this reality and actively working against it, we turn closer to Christ who denounced sin through love and left the violent cross empty, a promise we hold onto for ourselves.

4.5 For reflection, conversation and action

1 How might men heal, or be helped to heal, their own 'broken and dis-eased bodies', and those of others?
2 How do you see men acting in solidarity with women, people of diverse genders and other bodies?
3 How might the story of Jesus' crucifixion be read in ways that reveal and confront violence?

4.6 Bibliography

Agius, Christine; Bergman Rosamond, Annika; and Kinnvall, Catarina, 2020, 'Populism, Ontological Insecurity and Gendered Nationalism: Masculinity, Climate Denial and Covid-19', *Politics, Religion & Ideology* 21(4), pp. 432–50.

Andrianos, Louk A. and Tomren, Tom Sverre (eds) (2021), *Contemporary Ecotheology, Climate Justice and Environmental Stewardship in World Religions*, Steinkjer: Embla Akdemisk.

Baker-Fletcher, Karen (2006), *Dancing With God: The Trinity from a Womanist Perspective*, St Louis MO: Chalice Press.

Bauman, Whitney (2003), 'Essentialism, Universalism, and Violence: Unpacking the Ideology of Patriarchy', *Journal of Women and Religion* 19(20), pp. 52–71.

Bird, Susan; Delgado, Rutilio; Madrigal, Larry; Bayron Ochoa, John; and Tejeda, Walberto (2007), 'Constructing an Alternative Masculine Identity: The Experience of the Centro Bartolomé de las Casas and Oxfam America in El Salvador', *Gender & Development* 15(1), pp. 111–21.

Bola, JJ (2019). *Mask Off: Masculinity Redefined*, London: Pluto Press.

Boonzaier, Floretta and van Niekerk, Taryn (2020), 'Discursive Trends in Research on Masculinities and Interpersonal Violence', in Lucas Gottzén, Ulf Mellström and Tamara Shefer (eds), *Routledge International Handbook of Masculinity Studies*, London: Routledge, pp. 457–66.

Coleman, Monica (2008), *Making a Way out of No Way: A Womanist Theology*, Minneapolis MI: Fortress Press.

Cone, James H. (2011), *The Cross and the Lynching Tree*, New York NY: Orbis Books.

Cone, James H. (2020), *A Black Theology of Liberation*, 50th anniversary edition, New York NY: Orbis Books.
Connell, R. W. (2005), *Masculinities*, 2nd edition, London: Polity Press.
Crysdale, Cynthia S. W. (2001), *Embracing Travail: Retrieving the Cross Today*, New York: Continuum.
Curry, Tommy J. (2017), *The Man-Not: Race, Class, Genre, and the Dilemmas of Black Manhood*, Philadelphia PA: Temple University Press.
De La Torre, Miguel A. (2017), *Embracing Hopelessness*, Minneapolis MI: Fortress Press.
Douglas, Kelly Brown (2015), *Stand Your Ground: Black Bodies and the Justice of God*, Maryknoll NY: Orbis Books.
Edley, Nigel (2017), *Men and Masculinity: The Basics*, Abingdon: Routledge.
Farley, Margaret A. (2006), *Just Love: A Framework for Christian Sexual Ethics*, New York: Continuum.
Galtung, Johan (1969), 'Violence, Peace and Peace Research', *Journal of Peace Research*, 6(3), pp. 167–91.
Galtung, Johan (1990), 'Cultural Violence', *Journal of Peace Research* 27(3), pp. 291–305.
Girard, René (1979), *Violence and the Sacred*, trans. Patrick Gregory, Baltimore MD: Johns Hopkins University Press.
Girard, René (1986), *The Scapegoat*, trans. Yvonne Freccero, Baltimore MD: Johns Hopkins University Press.
Greenough, Chris (2021), *The Bible and Sexual Violence Against Men*, Abingdon: Routledge.
Hultman, Martin and Pulé, Paul (2020), 'Ecological Masculinities. A Response to the Manthropocene Question?', in Lucas Gottzén, Ulf Mellström, and Tamara Shefer (eds), *Routledge International Handbook of Masculinity Studies*, London: Routledge, pp. 477–87.
Johnson, Elizabeth (2017), *She Who Is: The Mystery of God in Feminist Theological Discourse*, 25th anniversary edition, New York NY: Crossroad.
Johnson, Jessica (2017), 'Under Conviction: "Real Men" Reborn on Spiritual and Cinematic Battlefields', *Feminist Studies* 43(1), pp. 42–67.
Johnson, Keith L. and Lauber, David (eds) (2016), *T&T Clark Companion to the Doctrine of Sin*, London: T&T Clark.
Jones, Serene (2019), *Trauma and Grace: Theology in a Ruptured World*, 2nd edition, Louisville KT: Westminster John Knox Press.
Keenan, James F. (2016), 'Raising Expectations on Sin', *Theological Studies* 77(1), pp. 165–80.
Kelly, Conor M. (2019), 'The Nature and Operation of Structural Sin: Additional Insights from Theology and Moral Psychology', *Theological Studies* 80(2), pp. 293–327.
Longwood, W. Merle (2006), 'Theological and Ethical Reflections on Men and Violence: Toward a New Understanding of Masculinity', *Theology & Sexuality* 13(1), pp. 47–62.
Madrigal Rajo, Larry José and Tejeda Guardado, Walberto V. (2020), 'Hombres de cuidado ¡en emergencia! Los Cuidados y masculinidades en el actual contexto COVID-19 en Centroamérica', *Revista Punto Género* 13, pp. 109–30.

McCabe, Megan K. (2018), 'A Feminist Catholic Response to the Social Sin of Rape Culture', *Journal of Religious Ethics* 46(4), pp. 635-57.

Moltmann, Jürgen (2001), *The Crucified God*, SCM Classics, London: SCM Press.

Moore, Will (2021), 'A Godly Man and a Manly God: Resolving the Tension of Divine Masculinities in the Bible', *Journal for Interdisciplinary Biblical Studies* 2(2), pp. 71-94.

Moore, Will (2022a), *Boys Will Be Boys, and Other Myths: Unravelling Biblical Masculinities*, London: SCM Press.

Moore, Will (2022b), 'Gorifying the Gospels: The Treatment of Crucifixion Violence in Film', in Michael Spalione and Helen Paynter (eds), *Map or Compass? The Bible on Violence*, Sheffield: Sheffield Phoenix Press, pp. 193-205.

O'Donnell, Karen (2018), *Broken Bodies: The Eucharist, Mary, and the Body in Trauma Theology*, London: SCM Press.

Rambo, Shelly (2010), *Spirit and Trauma: A Theology of Remaining*, Louisville KT: Westminster John Knox Press.

Reaves, Jayme R. and Tombs, David (2020), '#MeToo Jesus: Naming Jesus as a Victim of Sexual Abuse', in Helen Paynter and Michael Spalione (eds), *The Bible on Violence: A Thick Description*, Sheffield: Sheffield Phoenix Press, pp. 282-308.

Reddie, Anthony G. (2020), *Is God Colour-Blind? Insights from Black theology for Christian faith and ministry*, 2nd edition, London: Society for Promoting Christian Knowledge.

Robinson-Brown, Jarel (2021), *Black, Gay, British, Christian, Queer*, London: SCM Press.

Robinson-Brown, Jarel (2022), 'Weeping Wounds: Queer Blacksculinity, Trauma and Grief', in Karen O'Donnell and Katie Cross (eds), *Bearing Witness: Intersectional Perspectives on Trauma Theology*, London: SCM Press, pp. 77-91.

Rose-Moore, Will (2024), 'Am I Kenough? (Barbie and) Ken's Masculinity in Process', *Theology & Sexuality* 30(1), pp. 1-14.

Ross, Susan A. (2019), 'Feminist Theology and the Clergy Sexual Abuse Crisis', *Theological Studies* 80(3), pp. 632-52.

Ruether, Rosemary Radford (1993), *Sexism and God-Talk: Towards a Feminist Theology*, Boston MA: Beacon Press.

Saiving Goldstein, Valerie (1960), 'The Human Situation: A Feminine View', *Journal of Religion* 40(2), pp. 100-12.

Smiler, Andrew M. (2019), *Is Masculinity Toxic? A Primer for the 21st Century*, London: Thames and Hudson.

Sobrino, Jon (1982), 'A Crucified People's Faith in the Son of God', *Concilium* 153, pp. 23-8.

Thomas, Charlotte (2022), 'The Lamb on Your Plate: Finding the Crucified God in the Violence of the Slaughterhouse', in Michael Spalione and Helen Paynter (eds), *Map or Compass? The Bible on Violence*, Sheffield: Sheffield Phoenix Press, pp. 227-42.

Thomas, Charlotte and Moore, Will (2022), 'Confronting Violence and the Bible', *Exploring Theology: Living with the Bible*, May, Sarum College, Salisbury.

Tombs, David (2021), 'Crucifixion and Sexual Abuse', in Jayme R. Reaves, David Tombs and Rocío Figueroa (eds), *When Did We See You Naked? Jesus as a Victim of Sexual Abuse*, London: SCM Press, pp. 15-27.

Tombs, David (2023a), 'Jon Sobrino and "the Crucified People"', *Religions* 14(2), 274, pp. 1–13.
Tombs, David (2023b), *The Crucifixion of Jesus: Torture, Sexual Abuse, and the Scandal of the Cross*, Abingdon: Routledge.
Weaver, J. Denny (2011), *The Nonviolent Atonement*, 2nd edition, Grand Rapids MI: William Eerdmans Publishing Co.
Williams, Delores S. (1993), *Sisters in the Wilderness: The Challenge of Womanist God-Talk*, Maryknoll NY: Orbis Books.
Wines, Megan (2023), 'Mas(c/k) of a Man: Masculinity and Jesus in Performance', *Religions* 14(9), 1162, pp. 1–16.

5

bodies of Christ I (the man Jesus)

5.1 Introduction

This chapter explores the changing body of Jesus and multiple bodies of Christ that we encounter in the church and wider society. In this introductory section, the focus is on the gospel Jesus. We ask how Jesus performed his masculinity in first-century CE occupied Palestine, before considering how Christian men today are invited to imitate Jesus the Christ.

In the second part of the chapter, Chris Greenough explores a range of contextual Christologies, developed in relation to the gospel accounts, but not bound by them: Jesus in solidarity with women, the queer Christ, the Black Christ, Jesus the healer of disabled people, and as a victim of sexual violence. Chris warns against the temptation to fix Jesus in our own image, calling for us to make space for an ever more expansive body of Christ, in which there is room for all. Chris identifies as a gay man, and writes as an academic interested in the use, function and impact of religion in contemporary society and culture.

Following Chris' contribution, Bee Scherer investigates the seductive nature of toxic masculinity and offers a reading of Jesus compared to the Buddha. A non-binary trans*person and survivor, Bee writes from a queer-feminist Buddhist and indecent theological perspective. In a challenging, profound and deeply personal reflection, Bee explores the crucified and resurrected body of Christ, asking how we see power and vulnerability in Jesus' male body, and questioning whether the resurrected Christ can be in solidarity with victim-survivors of abuse, or whether a different, queer Christ is needed.

The man Jesus

'Jesus is the most masculine man to walk the earth.' So claims Dale Partridge (2022). No more gentle Jesus – what men want, Partridge and other conservative Christians suggest, is a strong leader, a hero able to bear the pain of the cross. This Jesus is a success, even in death.

Kristin Kobes Du Mez's 2020 best-selling book, *Jesus and John Wayne*, traces the increasingly pronounced muscularization and militarization of Jesus within white US conservative evangelicalism. From 1950s' cowboy culture through the action-hero films of the 1980s and the post 9/11 desire for revenge, Jesus has been reimagined as the ultimate strong man. This is the lone warrior defending western civilization: 'a kind of muscular martyrdom of the white man played out against an apocalyptic background of otherness' (Krondorfer 2004, p. 18).

There are traces of the hero Jesus within British conservative evangelicalism – Bear Grylls' wilderness survival model of formation might serve as an example here – but Mel Gibson's William Wallace Jesus is more visible in US evangelicalism than in Scotland. And Jesus has yet to be recast as a World War II hero or 1966 English footballer. British popular culture is perhaps more comfortable with failure than success. In the *Manchester Passion*, Jesus is reimagined as 'a classic northern class warrior' sharing fish and chips with his mates before being pushed into a riot van and, ultimately, voted out by the public (Hatterstone, 2006).

Robert Beckford further notes how Jesus is reimagined within marginalized communities in ways that create connection to lived experiences and desires. In his book, *Duppy Conqueror* (2021), Beckford identifies three models of Jesus within African Caribbean Pentecostal communities in Britain: first, Jesus as one of the family, someone in whom to confide; second, especially in Rastafari, the rebel leader, the emancipatory Black messiah; and third, the dread Christ who is incarnate in the Black struggle against injustice.

But how far do these contemporary reimaginings of Jesus relate to the gospel accounts? Perhaps both more and less than we might expect.

In the gospels, we encounter Jesus as new-born baby, child migrant, cousin, friend, guest, prisoner. His Black-brown body is not constant: changing as he 'grew and became strong' (Luke 2.39); marked by circumcision; craving food, companionship and rest; bleeding and broken around the table and on the cross. It is a body transformed through life, death and resurrection.

Biblical scholars such as Peter-Ben Smit (2017) and Colleen Conway

(2018) have placed the gospel accounts in the context of first-century CE Jewish and Greco-Roman models of masculinity, asking whether Jesus conforms to or subverts such models. David J. A. Clines (2023) suggests that the gospel portrayal of Jesus generally conforms to dominant models of masculinity: physically strong, verbally aggressive, a leader of men. Yet while Jesus performs various roles that should confirm his status as a man – for example, as a skilled speaker and healer – he is often concerned to hide his power (van Klinken and Smit 2013), and his marginal status as a Galilean Jew would have meant he would be considered somewhat disreputable (Wilson 2016). Indeed, his masculinity cannot be understood apart from his ethnic and religious identity: a devout Jew, an Afro-Asiatic man (Felder 1993), a young man living under Roman occupation.

Moreover, Jesus appears to actively subvert social expectations of what it means to be a man. On becoming an adult, Jesus does not start a family but becomes an itinerant preacher, dependent on others for food and shelter (Wilson 2016). He calls his followers away from institutions that give power to men, especially those who are householders. Indeed, he asks them to be like children, like eunuchs (Moore 2022). Throughout his ministry, Jesus (mostly) challenges exclusion and hierarchy, gathering a diverse (often dishonourable) group of friends around him. As the *Che Jesus* image (Churches Advertising Network 1999) suggests, the gospel Jesus is better understood as an outsider, living life on the road with his band of merry men – and women, only entering the city to disrupt.

A man with many friends but no family; a man who the gospels explicitly describe as loving other men: How might we honour Jesus' friendships and desires (Martin 2009)? Instead of claiming Jesus as a model of celibacy and purity, or as a red-blooded heterosexual, perhaps it is Jesus' queerness – his subversion of social and sexual boundaries – that should be celebrated (Cheng 2012; Moore 2022). Indeed, Robert Beckford (1996) suggests that making visible Jesus' sexual identity is of itself transgressive, if and when Jesus is portrayed as a marginalized man. He sees images such as Robert Lentz's 'The Lion of Judah' icon in which Jesus is depicted as a Maasai warrior, his testicles visible through his robe, as a means of affirming the full identity of Black men, whose sexuality is often problematized.

That Jesus dies is an undeniable aspect of the gospel accounts. But should Jesus be understood as in control of his death – a muscular fighter, a sacrificial hero; or was his death something imposed upon him? In this second scenario, Jesus is no longer in control of his emotions, his body or his story; he is 'un-manned ... through a series of bodily invasions' (Wilson 2016, p. 31). Seeing Jesus as a possible victim of sexual violence disrupts dominant interpretations of the crucifixion (Tombs 1999). No longer the muscular hero confronting death, he becomes a feminized, bleeding victim, with all the ambiguity that results (Starr 2021). Even in resurrection, his wounds are visible.

Jesus' changing body

That the body of Jesus is assumed to be male has had a significant impact on cis women, whose lack of certain physical markers of male sex ('Do you have a penis?') has prevented them from becoming priests or leaders in much of the church. Feminist theologians have asked, in return, whether it is possible for a male saviour to save women, if femaleness is not assumed by Jesus (Ruether 1983). But such assumptions – that Jesus' body is exclusively, irredeemably male – have been challenged from a variety of perspectives.

Jesus crosses multiple borders, migrating between home and exile, land and sea, heaven and earth (Campese 2012). His body similarly transgresses boundaries, including those of gender. Candida Moss (2010) observes how Jesus' body is 'leaky'; power flows out of it. It is porous and unstable, surprising Jesus and others in its responses. Moss argues that Jesus' male body, therefore, sometimes appears feminine. Brittany E. Wilson (2016), noting how the gospels employ male and female imagery to explore Jesus' divine nature, further suggests Jesus' divine body is not confined to gender demarcations.

Such gender fluidity only increases as the man Jesus becomes the Christ figure who reconfigures identity and relationships (Galatians 3.28). Two British male theologians have called for theological discussion to focus less on the male body of Jesus and more on the multi-gendered body of Christ. Graham Ward (1999) traces multiple displacements – transfiguration, eucharist, crucifixion, resurrection, ascension – through which Jesus' male body is transformed into the body of the church. Ward argues, therefore, that to focus on Jesus' masculinity is somewhat of a distraction. Ward does not here, however, address concerns over how the maleness of Jesus' body continues to restrict women's roles within the church and society. For Gerard Loughlin (1998), the body of Christ is complex, containing the crucified and risen Christ, Jesus and Mary, Christ and the church. Therefore, Loughlin argues, there are multiple (although not unlimited) ways for men to be Christ-like.

Jesus the male saviour

The maleness of Jesus the saviour raises questions not only for women and non-binary people, but also for men. Dominant models of masculinity, centred around power, control and agency, are difficult to reconcile with the idea of being saved. Within conservative Christianity, we might identify two different (but interconnected) attempts to resolve this tension. First, Jesus is understood to lead other men to victory, success, that is, salvation. Christian men share in the task, fulfilling their roles as they might as members of a command unit, sports team, or corporation. In such models, all roles are honourable. Jesus may be the captain or CEO, but he needs his squad. And who knows, perhaps one day, they may have the chance to be the hero? Second, Christian men might embrace a more receptive role in relation to Jesus their saviour, singing 'Jesus boyfriend' songs as they wait for him to come down from heaven to save them. Yet rather than celebrate the possibility of male intimacy, male worshippers are encouraged to move from a potentially subordinate or dependent standpoint into their Christ-like role of preacher, husband or leader. So, we might ask, are these men singing to themselves? And how might Christian men be helped to develop authentic and vulnerable relationships with Jesus, without seeking to replace him?

It is especially important to challenge the notion of the white saviour. Jesus lived and died in a small, occupied land in south-west Asia. And as James Cone (1970) and other Black theologians have argued, in today's contexts of white violence, what is needed is a Black Christ. What might it mean for white men to be saved by a Black Christ?

Beyond any lone saviour, what might it mean to be communities of liberation and healing (Nakashima Brock 1988)? For Christian men, seeing Jesus as one of many companions on the road (Gebara 1999) might ease the pressure they experience to be the leader or saviour figure. After all, do we need another hero?

5.2 Contextualizing Christ – *Chris Greenough*

Jesus has been popularly portrayed as liberator of the marginalized in the gospel accounts (Bohache 2008). In Matthew 16.15, Jesus asks, 'But what about you? Who do you say I am?' This contribution attempts to respond to this question, providing, in broad brush strokes, a critical overview of contextual and constructive Christologies: liberation, feminist, LGBTQI+; as well as considering race, disability and sexual violence when thinking and talking about the person Jesus. Critical, contextual and constructive theologies place a burden of demand on the body of Jesus. In a move away from the traditional approach to Christology (grounded in New Testament writings, the early church and ecumenical councils from the second to eighth centuries CE), the focus here is on how social, cultural, political and activist tropes are found in contemporary interpretations of Jesus. What does Jesus look like through our eyes today? Christology literally means 'talk about Christ' and is the study of Jesus Christ. In this sense, it would be erroneous to imagine that there is a coherent disciplinary approach to the study of Jesus Christ, and therefore the plural term 'Christologies' is much more apt.

Based on experiences that combine identities, ideologies and locations, contextual Christologies are constructive and reparative. They move away from determinate readings of the person of Jesus to recreate Christological imaginations that are validated by and with groups of people who share the same understanding. Intrinsically, therefore, the figure of Jesus and of Christ is not created by Christian traditions, but through an encounter between Christ and contemporary contexts.

The body of Christ is the site on which social, cultural, political and ideological positions are conveyed. The image of Jesus' body is a screen onto which contemporary experiences, injustices, positionalities and identities are projected. Indeed, Christologies have the potential to validate local, national and global concerns. With its roots in Latin America in the 1960s, liberation theology brought the person Jesus into focus for those who lived under poverty and oppression. The gospel accounts of Jesus portray a ministry of liberating the oppressed. Liberation theologians sought to make visible both how Jesus communicated, worked with, healed and ministered to the marginalized, and therefore also the need for Christians to struggle against oppression.

Feminist Christs

The person of Jesus, as presented by traditional Christology, is problematic for a number of reasons: as maleness, whiteness and celibacy are given undue status. Feminist theologies have problematized Jesus' maleness and its inextricable connection with religious and cultural patriarchy; as Mary Daly famously asserts, 'if God is male then male is God' (1973, p. 19). Jesus Christ, through the figure of the male Godhead, has become the example *par excellence* of patriarchy. Robert Goss puts this poignantly, as he states, 'Jesus' asexual maleness continued to exercise a normative function, excluding from full ministerial participation in the church and continuing to legitimize antipleasure and misogynistic practices' (1993, p. 67). Following Daly, Rosemary Radford Ruether (1983) exposes how traditional theology is based on male experiences rather than human experiences. This is not only of concern for religious institutions such as the churches, but the Christian tradition has had a powerful influence in shaping society, culture, law and politics throughout its two millennia history. Whether one is non-religious or anti-religions, it is impossible to detangle patriarchal Christianity and its global impact through colonialism from the reality of the contemporary world.

Jesus' maleness is not only problematic for women, but it is also a stumbling block for men who may struggle to be in a relationship with a male deity. Howard Eilberg-Schwarz observes how 'Christ's body continues to generate a problem for Christian men – the same dilemma of homoerotic desire that a male God posed for Israelite men' (1994, p. 236). For Christians, entering into a private relationship with Jesus can be difficult given that the life narrated in the gospel accounts attest to Jesus' public ministry. Any privacy or personal life is erased. This is most transparent in the portrayal of Jesus as without sexuality. This is evident in iconographic portrayals of Jesus, as Robert Beckford notes: 'much of European church scholarship has tended to represent him as a celibate man and a model for a life of devotion … it is no surprise that … icons, paintings and sculptures of Jesus cover his genitals, inferring that he was or is non-sexual' (1996, p. 17). Moreover, religious homophobia fuelled by conservative and traditional teachings about homosexuality can increase male anxieties about homosexuality.

Queer Christs

The gospel accounts do not offer any detail of Jesus' life as a husband and father, a fact in itself that demonstrates a rupture and subversion with Jewish traditions. Indeed, Jesus' teaching on family life is countercultural for ancient settings. Mark Johnson (2014) draws parallels between the person Jesus and punk, examining Jesus' subversion of the national symbols of Israel, his relationship with Jewish authorities, his use of Scripture and his notion of the family. In Luke's gospel, we have an example of the radical subversion of familial relationships and vehement rhetoric; as Jesus speaks confrontationally, 'If anyone comes to me and does not hate father and mother, wife and children, brothers and sisters – yes, even their own life – such a person cannot be my disciple' (Luke 14.26). Jesus is portrayed as celibate or non-sexual, without consort and anti-family. And of course in much Christian doctrine, Jesus needs to be beyond sexuality, associated as it is with sin since the fall in Genesis. As I note elsewhere, this creates quite a dilemma for traditional Christian thought:

> On the one hand, if Jesus' being married is suggestive of Jesus having sex, the theological trope of celibacy is problematized. On the other hand, if Jesus is not married, this leads to contemporary interpretations that he may not be heterosexual, and likewise this troubles Christian theology. Both questions rupture traditional theological interpretations. (Greenough 2020, p. 74)

LGBTQI+ readings of the person Jesus have mobilized a gaydar to explore the hiddenness of Jesus' sexuality, just as non-normative sexuality is hidden until it is made public through the act of coming-out. Speculation on the lack of detail about Jesus' private life has allowed readings that permit queer-sensibilities. These may be homopositive or even homoerotic in nature. In John 2.1–11, we hear that Jesus attended a wedding in Cana, a known text popularized by the water-into-wine party trick. Gerard Loughlin considers how this wedding relates to biblical metaphors in which God is the husband to Israel (the wife) – and Christ is husband to the church. Loughlin's queer reading leads to the suggestion that Jesus marries his disciples in 'a queer kind of marriage – the bonding of men in matrimony' (2007, p. 2). Such readings can be seen as indecent, or 'queer' in the sense that they disturb and disrupt.

If one of the effects of queer Christologies is to provoke outrage or shock, then it reveals the degree to which the Christian tradition is saturated in homonegative and homophobic ideas. Robert Goss' compelling queer Christology, *Jesus Acted Up: A Gay and Lesbian Manifesto* (1993), is grounded in activism from the gay and lesbian liberation movement and the AIDS pandemic of the 1980s. Goss' queer Christ sees the person Jesus as identifying with LGBTQI+ experiences of injustice and discrimination, including violence. Goss reads the crucifixion story as one in which Jesus' experience can be understood in relation to the everyday lives of those who are marginalized and experience queer bashing. Jesus is queer because of his solidarity with queers who suffer (Goss 1993, p. 85).

Similar to Goss' queer Christ, Argentine theologian Marcella Althaus-Reid sees the disruptive potential of a Bi-Christ. Althaus-Reid says, 'In a

Christology of a Bi/Christ we are considering two things. First, the reality of people's identity outside heterosexualism and, second, a pattern of thought for a larger Christ outside binary boundaries' (2000, p. 117). The Bi-Christ is transgressive and disrupts categories of mono-relations, thereby providing a different way for Christians to understand Christ's divinity and humanity at the same time. Lisa Isherwood observes astutely how Christian life requires a solid base on which to build itself, but the fluidity of Christ's identities does not permit this. Instead, Bi-Christologies are boundaryless and empowering; as she comments, '[the Bi-Christ is] the Christ of ambiguity, fluidity and contradictions ... The Bi-Christ, moving us beyond the binary opposites embedded in hetero thinking that underpin the exploitative systems that we inhabit, is then supremely ethical and transgressive' (2018, p. 286).

Goss posits a transgender Christ arguing that 'Christology realizes its ultimate queer potential in a transgendered Christ – full of fluid identities' (2006, p. 637). A trans Christ enacts the same transgression to the presumed cisgender of Christ. A trans Christ is revealed through the multiple transformations the crucifixion entails. At the core of Christianity is a transgression between the stable concepts of life and death, human and divine, sin and salvation. Through Christ, binary positions are erased. Theologically, this is revealed in Paul's letters to the Galatians, 'There is neither Jew nor Gentile, neither slave nor free, nor is there male and female, for you are all one in Christ Jesus' (3.28). Susannah Cornwall reflects on the same transgression and ambiguity in relation to intersex people, as 'they already map onto the mixed-up, much-inscribed body of Christ. Jesus' body, too, is a complicated and unambiguous one' (2010, p. 91). The Christian tradition has sought to regulate bodies, relationships and sex through damaging and hurtful interpretations of scripture and positional statements. Conservative religious positions are prejudiced in opposition to same-sex marriage, to gay and lesbian parenting, to transgender reassignment and, therefore, the need for LGBTQI+ Christologies remains urgent. While injustices and inequalities exist, they will always be projected onto the person Jesus, the results of which are twofold. First, they expose the damage done by hostile, heteronormative, cisnormative, Christian positions. Second, they allow those on the margins to assert how Jesus knows and shares their suffering.

Black Christs

Western paintings of Christ, such as Warner Sallman's Head of Christ (1940), have tended to portray him with blue-eyes, light-coloured skin, effeminate features, undulating, curly hair and a beard with a light auburn tint. Such portrayals work to remove any depiction of Jesus' Jewish identity, resulting in the popular image of Jesus as 'a northern European saviour whose physical characteristics proclaim his distance from the despised race whom he has been sent to redeem' (Moore 2001, p. 108). The use, function and impact of a white Christ can be seen by tracing the centuries of colonization in Africa, Asia, Latin America and Oceania. The fact that Christ was made, inaccurately, in the image of the colonizers was simply no coincidence.

The writings of womanist scholar Kelly Brown Douglas brings *The Black Christ* (1994) into focus. She asks what the significance and vitality of a Black Christ is, noting how images of a Black Christ emerge from the 1960s. For Douglas, a Black Christ refers not only to Christ's physical appearance, but also to Christ's relationship to the Black struggle for freedom. The person Jesus is central also to the work of Robert Beckford in his book *Jesus is Dread* (1998), in which Black cultural analysis is interwoven with Black Christologies. Beckford's aim is towards equality and inclusion, as he positions Jesus alongside Rastafari dread culture and identity, a connection that explores Jesus' rebellion and continued mission for social justice. The significance of images of the Black Christ in the work of challenging racism is evident in the Black Lives Matter movement. Public outcry following the murder of George Floyd often connected the claim 'Black Lives Matter' with images of a Black Jesus – resulting in a Black Christology that testified to how both men died violently at the hands of the state, struggling for breath.

Disabled Christs

Contextual Christologies are therefore concerned with the person Jesus, but also how Jesus is represented visually in cultural and social contexts. Physical representations are connected to Jesus' humanity, as liberator and as someone who knows human injustices and suffering. The crucifixion depicts Jesus experiencing physical violence and pain, even if he was relieved quite quickly from this suffering through death and resurrection. Human pain, suffering and disability is also linked to Jesus' body in the formation of theologies concerned with disability. Just like other marginalized bodies, the disabled body too is marginalized in the Christian tradition. Nancy Eiesland's *The Disabled God* (1994) focuses on Christ's resurrected body as strong, but bearing the scars of the crucifixion. Such an image dispels myths about disabled bodies as weak, and highlights the hidden history of people with disability in the church and biblical interpretation.

The image of the disabled Christ challenges ableist thinking in theology and biblical studies. Moreover, there are numerous gospel stories that recount Jesus healing the suffering of others. Jesus exorcises demons, heals the sick and accepts the outcasts and, as Jürgen Moltmann observes, 'Jesus' power to heal lies in his power to suffer' (1998, p. 115). Yet, the traditional Christian focus on healing can be problematic when explored from a disabilities perspective, as it suggests that some bodies are in need of repair through divine powers and miracle cures. The impulse to see Jesus' actions as an attempt to normalize or repair bodies suggests that disabled bodies are less or lacking. Similarly, the eschatological notion that the resurrection offers hope to those who are disabled does not account for the diverse experiences of living disabled people today.

Jesus as a victim of sexual violence

The idea that Jesus shares in human suffering is encapsulated in the suggestion that Jesus was a victim of sexual violence. In the gospel accounts of the passion, Jesus is shamed, humiliated and disempowered. Jesus is stripped in Matthew 27.28. In John 19, Jesus is flogged, dressed in a purple robe and a crown of thorns is placed on his head as Pilate showcases him to the crowds, saying 'Behold the man!' (19.5). The biblical accounts clearly depict involuntary nudity, a strategy that would further shame Jesus through exposure.

Despite the gospel accounts, there has been an unwillingness to engage with Jesus' experience of sexual violence, and the images of Jesus on the cross that proliferate in Christian iconography are ones in which his physical abuse is immediately recognizable but his sexual abuse, not so. One of the contemporary myths around sexual violence that urgently needs challenging is that men cannot be victims – that ideal masculinity determines that men are strong and powerful, and that to be a victim denotes a weakness. To conceive Jesus as a victim follows previous contextual theologies that focus on Jesus as a co-sufferer, yet the idea of Jesus experiencing sexual violence has provoked outraged responses. In my book, *The Bible and Sexual Violence Against Men* (2020), I argue that 'if such respectable church members see a devaluation of Jesus because of his status as a victim of sexual abuse, then surely that reveals their distaste for all victims, as people who are damaged, sullied, and maybe even blameworthy' (Greenough 2020, p. 66). Resistance to the notion of Jesus as a victim of sexual assault reveals contemporary stigma around victims, something that needs addressing, particularly in light of the child sexual abuse scandals of the churches and the #MeToo movement. A broken Christ, bearing the wounds and scars of the crucifixion, challenges toxic notions of masculinity as dominant, complete and in control. A number of scholars argue that the naming of Jesus as a victim of sexual violence offers possibilities that encourage the churches to deal more effectively with the recent clergy sexual abuse scandals and their systematic failure to address the issue of sexual violence (Tombs 1999; Trainor 2014; Reaves and Tombs 2019; Reaves, Tombs and Figueroa 2020).

Concluding remarks

Contemporary Christologies focus on inequalities and injustices experienced by marginalized groups. They allow for explorations and challenges to the boundaries of theological thinking about the person Jesus, while simultaneously reflecting the social, cultural and political milieux in which they are produced. One word of warning, however, comes from Elizabeth Stuart who cautions that contextual Christologies risk turning God into a 'mirror-God simply reflecting our own image' (2003, p. 29). This problematizes the Christian idea of *imago Dei* – humankind made in the image of God, rather than God made in the image of humankind. A lot is therefore demanded of the figure of Jesus, used as he is to carry the burden of contemporary critical thinking, living realities, experiences of inequalities and injustices and radical political activism. Placing this burden onto Christ is, however, consistent with Christian biblical and theological teaching; as Jesus himself says, 'Come to me, all you who are weary and burdened, and I will give you rest' (Matthew 11.28). What remains a contentious issue, however, is the strategies of resistance that contextual Christologies may face. Many make claim to the one body of Christ. Yet, womanist Christologies provide a way forward that liberates Christ. Jacquelyn Grant (1989) points to the inadequacy of feminist Christology that focuses on one particular issue, and calls for multiple sites of oppression to be represented in the constructive formation of Christologies. Accordingly, the broken Christ is healed and offers healing to the marginalized and oppressed. Grant states:

> The analytical principle for determining the adequacy of inadequacy of White feminist Christology is twofold: (1) Because a single issue analysis has proven inadequate to eliminate oppression, a multi-issue analysis must be constructed. The race/sex/class analysis must be embraced as a representative corporate analysis for the destruction of oppressive structures; and (2) because Jesus located the Christ with the outcast, the least, Christology must emerge out of the condition at least. (1989, p. 6)

Christ's body is universal, reflecting the multiplicities of Christologies we have in contemporary settings (Isherwood 2007; Edwards 2012). Across the multiplicities, no one has the authority to fix Christ into a rigid, inflexible mould. In this way, human examples of Jesus the person are mobilized to reveal a more expansive Christ, unbound from the Christian tradition: a Christ who is just, unfixed, amorphous, creative and responsive to the struggles of the contemporary world.

5.3 The temptations of masculinity: a rude Buddhist-Christian theology of toxic seductions – *Bee Scherer*

Gender is a product of our societies, cultures and religion(s), and we are caught up in the day-to-day experience of a gendered world that apparently only knows two possibilities. The gendered binarism is a cultured analogue to sex, which is an interpretation of biology: but even with sex, if we look closer, the assumed certainty of binarism disappears: Genetic, chromosomal (not the same!), hormonal, gonadal, developmental and phenotypical multiplicities abound beyond the marginalized intersex umbrella and the seemingly certain sex dimorphism as male-female binary dissolves into the messy realities of embodiments beyond neat pigeonholes. In terms of contextually produced gender, the superimposed simplistic dualism reduces what is a colourful spectrum of subjectivities, expressions and performances to the *strai(gh)t*jackets of binary choices: the scripts of cisheteropatriarchy. The binary of man and woman, male and female, coerces us violently to portray to the outside world our own humanity according to simplistic and often badly suitable, or not at all fitting, templates. How we look, speak, show feelings, live intimacy and sexuality, tackle situations and conflicts, and how we build a future and construct meaning for ourselves: from the cradle to the grave, gender scripts provide us with a stifling framework of social expectations.

As a non-binary trans* person, assigned male at birth, gender has made me a freak; the barrage of verbal violence echoes threateningly in the inner labyrinths of my anxiety: *sissy, crybaby, mongo, bumboy, faggot, AIDS fucker, rentboy, whore, tranny, ladyboy* or simply *victim*. The traumata of my past experiences of assault and rape as a gender-non-conforming child, teenager and adult, are experiences of both cisheteropatriarchal and religious violence. My experience of deadly masculinity permeates all my social, academic and spiritual paths in life. In my past nightmares, the disgusting, first violent then drooping penis of the priestly rapist contrasts with the re-masculinization of Christ who is first queerly sagging on the cross and then brutally triumphantly re-erected. The risen, almighty Christus Victor smiles contentedly on the church wall over the whimpering heaps of sperm and blood, holy water and piss. The individual violence against the rejected, unworthy and oppressed is only possible because there is a systemic violence that accommodates, protects, empowers and encourages the individual violent perpetrators.

This edited volume highlights the questions of intersectional struggles with masculinity and faith. At the intersection of gender and religious belonging, we need to ask whereto for those believers who are disempowered by heritage, class, culture, race, ethnicity, language, education, 'disability' (vari/ability), physicality and neurodiversity – yet are, at the same time, privileged by hegemonic masculinity and cisheteropatriarchy? How to detox in praxis (i.e. thought and practice) (cis-hetero-)masculinities when their constant re-assertive performance remains the only reliable form of dominance available within the *theo-phallo*-tragedy of disenfranchisement? How to heal, the claim of phallic privilege divine where it is supported by religious patriarchal scripts, with its tragic manifestations among those cis-males that cannot reconcile their feeling of a God-given phallic superiority with the intersectional marginalization they encounter? Is it possible at all to successfully challenge masculinist religious scripts?

In these *a-phallo-sophical* reflections, I seek answers in a wisdom (*sophia*) aimed at *aphallia* as a state of non-domineering gender multiplicity: in an aphallic philosophy, i.e., a philosophy liberated from phal/logics. Coming from a queer-feminist perspective, I offer some *indecent* (Althaus-Reid 2003, p. 172 n. 1.1; Althaus-Reid 2000), even *rude* theologizing interspersed by phallo-focal *verbosturbations*, offering an irreverent paradox disruption of prevalent phal/logics that has rendered philosophy phallo-sophy.

Toxic masculinity

Hegemonic or toxic masculinity proves to be highly seductive and contagious by responding to and, rationalizing, the limbic need for security: the very act of neuro-cognition in the human brain appears as a battle for the reduction, selection and filtering of sense imprints to manageable data-bits for processing (interpretation) in aid of survival and pleasure. Hence, our incapability to deal with complexity, certainly on neuro-stem and limbic levels, gives rise to short-cut categories, delineations and concepts whence the monoliths of identity – subjectivities and belongings packaged into tidy and solid boxes – are erected. Like penises swelling up, these monoliths solidify by seduction: by the narcissistic, psychological feed-back loop of Othering (Scherer 2020, p. 20) we are tempted into readily available narratives of 'ontological security' (Giddens 1991); belonging appears to be a reward for adopting clearly delineated and essentialized types that play their specific and limited parts in societal scripts, be those roles counter-hegemonic or in aid of power and oppression.

The societal female-male, feminine-masculine binarism of sex and gender is particularity seductive: this binarism reduces the human sex and gender spectra into opposite yet complementary poles, eradicating the messy realities of intersex and trans* bodies in favour of the invitingly simple semiotics of erection and penetration, of dominance and submission. Theo-socially, the reductionist binary contraposition is synthesized and apotheosized into creation: the nuclear heteronorm and reproductive family structure are grounded in binaries of *thauma* and *trauma* that relate to, purportedly rational, philosophy and emotive intuition, to male and female, wonder and wound: the androcentric experience of wondrous penile tumescence and the wounding power of penetration that culminates in ejaculation which dialectically asserts dominion and reproduction.

Societal scripts of the gender-polar modes of being a human seduce with their ease of biopower distributions. Binary sexed and gendered belongings are scripted and policed by habitus in a constant echo loop with cultural systems of symbols: as long as human becoming- and *Dasein* (being-in-time) (Scherer 2018, p. 66) is only cropped and docked – mutilated and moulded into tidy and readable characters –

most people conform and pay for a feeling of cosy secureness with the tightening templates that govern and needlessly limit their expressions and performances of subjectivity, while ignoring individual agency and embodiment, complexity, muddiness and gaps (Sedgwick 2004, p. 8), in favour of straight lines and contours.

Religious phal/logics

Some regulatory cultural systems of symbols, e.g. some Abrahamic theologies, claim sex and gender binarism as the expression of a perfect complementarity (as discussed in Al Barrett's contribution in chapter 7), pre-postulating balance and equality. Yet, theological discourses and cultural realities struggle with the very core of such an equality; instead, the preponderance of (bio-)power swings to the male side, to the (Lacanian and de-Beauvoirian) *phallos*.

Just as the penis, the unsightly and odd penile appendage as a feature of external genitals in roughly 48% of humans, predominantly those assigned male at birth, often serves as a short-cut signifier for biological maleness, so does the *phallos* serve as a short-cut symbol of cultural masculinity. The semiotic power of the *phallos* lies in its extended signification of social power, dominance and threat. Cis-males, i.e., humans assigned male at birth who are content with such an assignment, often conflate penis and *phallos*, vesting anxieties into penile size and fertile prowess. Early evolutionary, limbic areas of the brain such as the hypothalamus and the amygdala house the neurons linked to both sexual arousal and violence. Sociobiologically, some primates show threatening behaviour by exposing erected penises and exposed fangs while also pacifying tense situations by switching aggressive with sexual activity. Masculine power is for no small part vested in the mystery of the *(r)e(sur)rection in the flesh* of the dangly appendage, usually serving as a urine tube – an abject conduit of waste liquid – to a redeemed, glorified *Rod*, pulsating and protruding, focused on sexual invasion and conquest.

Culturally and socio-biologically, masculinity and maleness are hence interpellated in the wonder of the hard-on, the *mysterium erectionis*: the privilege of, and obsession with, having the *phallos* and the anxiety of losing the *phallos* generate the cis-heteropatriarchal mechanisms of policing gender. (The pun points to 1 Timothy 3.9 in which deacons are exhorted to point out the 'the mystery of faith', God's mysterious manifestation in the world. When God became man – not woman – the wonder of male (r)e(sur)rection became divine: *mysterium erectionis*.)

Thus, the fear of losing the phallos – *aphallophobia* emerges as the overarching mechanism of oppression that expresses itself in misogyny and sexism and includes homo-, lesbo- and biphobia, as well as trans*-phobia and intersexism (Scherer 2018).

The patriarchal order is built on the *phallos* privilege wherein 'man' is actively human, while 'woman' is only an inferior, aphallic passivum; or, as Aristotle already put it: the woman (*gynē*) is 'like an impotent male thing' (*hōsper arren agonon GA* 178a): such is the symbolic order of prototype (Lakoff 1987) masculine power. (Note a subtle but crucial use of language that translators of Aristotle regularly miss: Aristotle uses the neuter form *arren agonon*; thus, a woman is dehumanized, since only man is truly human.)

As 'vestigial forms of governmentality' (Goldenberg 2015), cumulative traditions that we call *religions* including Christianities and Buddhisms are co-produced in cis-heteropatriarchal terms and they themselves co-produce the re-enforcing storyboards, narratives and myths that perpetuate the binarily male phenotypical exceptionalism and dominance while creating ever more restrictive forms of policing maleness and masculinities in exchange for hegemonic bio-power. The emasculative potential, the dysfunction and failure of both the penis and the *phallos*, appears as the very lynchpin of ontological masculine insecurity. Hence, when the *Creator Rod* is uselessly suspended in fleshy flaccidity, angsty images of emasculative deterrence are conjured that cajole and intimidate cis-males, the penile heirs to superior humanhood, into the toxicity of erective, rape-y and hegemonic performances.

How, then, to embody masculinities that are detoxed and de-hegemonized? How to embody queered, trans*ed, crip*ed, mad*ed, black*ed masculinities etc. when it is that very limbic phallocentrism that pervades the neocortical *logos* and *mythos* of cultural systems of symbols, Abrahamic and non-Abrahamic?

Rather than pretending to provide clear-cut answers to phalloreligious *Gretchenfragen*, the very highlighting of the often-irresolvable tensions and idiosyncrasies emerging from intersecting theo-social power negotiations already serves as a queer-feminist act of epiphanic defiance: shedding light on what has been rendered shadows, naming oppression and giving visibility and voice to the margin created by a toxic centre.

Hence, in the following I aim to delineate select indecent, rude theological comparative readings – for 'reciprocal illumination' (Sharma 2005) – of some religious narrative strategies in Christianity and Buddhism within the context of toxic cisheteropatriarchy.

Mysterium erectionis

The foundational mythic dimension of Christianity lies in the paradox of the auto-sacrificial male god-human whose limb submission, penetration and fatal dangling from the wood (-en T, *stauros*) transforms into glorified re-erection: the theodrama of Jesus of Nazareth as the 'Anointed One' (*chrīstós*) narrates within the framework of *aphallophobia* queer *phallic* loss and humiliation followed by cisheteropatriarchal glorification: Jesus' hands and feet are violently penetrated by the phallic nails: he becomes fixed in bondage (without safe word), his agency taken away. He is thus emasculated and has become an abject, abandoned by both his masculine followers and the spunky (creational, domineering and angry) God of the Israelites, i.e., the cisheteropatriarchal *Creator Rod*. Now, at the hight of the phallo-drama, in his last words (*ipsissma verba*) according to Mark 15.34 and Matthew 27.46, Jesus cries out in his *theo-phallic* abandonment (quoting the death Psalm 22 in Aramaic). Only three women are with him (John 19.25) among whom is his mother as well as his intimate demi-masculine (boy)friend John, 'the disciple he loved' (John 19.26). All Jesus can do is dangle, limp and flaccid, on the wood. The *Son of Rod* is queered and feminized: His hierarchical alpha role abandoned, he dies powerless, aphallically.

In death, his bodily core is sideways pierced by a lance (John 19.34): his very being, the core of his subjectivity and belonging, is in an act of necrophily penetrated by a spear (*lonchē*), a phallic war tool. The Romans are thus having their way with him. Indeed, Jesus' crucifixion can be read as sexual abuse (Tombs 1999) which makes Jesus a survivor of sexual abuse: he is depicted as surviving his sexualized killing wounds after three days of phal/logical darkness. But instead of awakening to post-gender transformation, Jesus, *Rod's Son*, de-queers, de-feminizes and claims the greatest *phallos* of all, infinite divine-phallic power: the resurrected Rod has atoned for its feminization and queerness and is, as *Christus Victor*, victorious over the evil of *aphallia*. The hallowed cry, *He has risen!* (or more accurately: *He has (been) woken up!* Mark 16.6 and Matthew 28.6: *ēgerthē*) – hails in the vital reinstatement of the dominant masculinist order: the cisheteropatriarchal father-god exerts his Viagra magic: he is made to rise again (*anestēsen* Acts 15.38).

The limb, dead flesh is resurrected – the Apostolic creed's 'resurrection in/of the flesh' (*carnis resurrectio / sarkos anastasis*), the ultimate *phallos* re-erected. As predicted the night before his death, the sacrificial queer god-human becomes the totalitarian über-male: the *Creator Rod* who is way, truth and life itself (John 14.6) to the exclusion of all other: one *phallos* to rule them all.

Hence, John (1.1) has the *Rod* ejaculating the Jesus-*logos* as the W/word of male theology (Althaus-Reid 2000, p. 54), a jizz produced from Stoic repression, smeared all over patristic theology by Justin the Martyr: the *logoi spermatikoi* as the fertilizing cum of male=divine reason.

In the face of über-maleness, Christ's followers are feminized; they become his bride (2 Corinthians 11.2) as does the assembly of the elected, the church (Ephesians 5.22–32; Revelation 19.7*seq et passim*). Indeed, in Early Christian writings (e.g. by Origen and Ambrose), interpreting the wedding imagery in the *shir ha-shirim* (the Hebrew Bible's *Song of Songs*), the essence in all humans, the soul (*psychē*) is destined to be (and made in baptism) the bride of Christ, the *(phal)logos*, the *Risen Rod*. In queer sacerdotal mysticism of the male clergy that often pursued ideals of spiritual castration and emasculation as celibates or 'eunuchs for the Kingdom of Heaven' (Matthew 19.12), the priest *in persona Christi* unites the phal/logic penetrator and the nuptial bride-penetree (Barrett 2017, p. 99). *May receive who can receive* ...

Mysterium retractionis

In contrast to the queered and redeemed hegemonic masculinity in the sacred biography and theodrama of the phallogocentric Christian foundation myth, the e- and re-masculinized *Saviour Rod*, the earlier sacred biography of the Buddha depicts the Siddhārtha Gautama paradoxically as endowed with both hypermasculine prowess and penile renunciation: The Buddha as 'highest among men' (*puruṣottama*) is addressed with the standard Epic patriarchal ornamental epithets (*epitheta ornantia*) of hypermasculinity, such as 'bull of a man; bull among men' (Powers 2009, pp. 26–7, 176–7, 241–3; Ciurtin 2013, pp. 341–5); yet he is also described with the mark of genital 'retraction': his penis is shielded ('sheathed'; see Powers 2009, p. 13) from sight even in nudeness. With all the imagery of hypermasculinity, the Buddha's crypto-genitalia shield the societal cisheteropatriachal oppression from sight, while, in reality, his 'chastity produces and accentuates his masculinity' (Langenberg 2018, p. 580). For example, in a homoerotic act of queering renunciation, the Woke One converts a young priestly upper-class man (Brahmin) by revealing to him the *mysterium retractionis*, his sheathed genitals (*kosohitaṃ vatthaguyhaṃ, Brahmāyu-sutta* MN 91 ii 135 PTS). The oppressive societal script, equally effective in Buddhist as in Christian civilizations, appears to take a subtler and less obvious *appearance* through the Buddhist foundational narratives: the shielded *phallos* elevates the Buddha above both the awkwardness of the dangling waste liquid conduit and the erect awe and threat of penetrative might. The Buddha's penis, neither dangling, nor erect, rests hidden by the docetic marks of his beyond-human realization of liberation and enlightenment.

Of course, the curious anatomical feature of the sheathed genital is part of the wider Classical South Asian myth of the *hyperman*, the 'Great Man' (*mahāpuruṣa*). The paradox of mythic hyperman and the retraction of the very power source of hypermasculinity points to the equal potential of Siddhārtha Gautama's birth to becoming *either* a world ruler (*cakravartin*) *or*, indeed, the highest spiritually accomplisher (Cp. Ambaṭṭha Sutta =DN 3 i 88-89 PTS and Nakamura 2000, p. 75). The bifurcated potential leads thus either to unlimited hypermasculine power – the revelation of the almighty phallos from its sheath – or to the highest meta-masculine spiritual realization – a gender-transcending, 'meta-gendered' (Scherer 2006) phallic disappearance.

Indeed, Siddhārtha Gautama the 'bull among the sages' (*munivṛṣa*, Avadānaśatakam 1.15 etc, nineteen times), despite the grooming attempts of his kin, chooses the later trajectory; like Jesus, he 'wakes up' (Mark 16.6; Matthew 28.6): the resurrective stirring of the *Saviour Rod* parallels the *Woke One's* retractive, post-genital relaxation into 'deathlessness' (*amṛta*). Resurrection and enlightenment as parallel central events in the founders' sacred biographies remain separated in crucial aspects of agency and experience (cf. Gethin 1996, p. 213). Unlike Jesus' divine rising, Gautama's metaphysical awakening experience comes on his own devices through countless karmic conditioning and gradually deeper insight into the complexities of conventional reality (Cp. Mahāsaccaka Sutta MN 36 I 247–249 PTS).

Despite the utilization of a fourfold sex/gender categorization on the monastic socio-legal level (see Scherer 2021), in early Buddhist psychology, the stubbornness of binary sex/gender categories of societal scripts is acknowledged, since the 'woman-man' (*strī-puruṣa*) binary is recognized among the ten 'signs' (*nimitta*) of falsely constructed reality that fall away in the absorption states (*samādhi*) of spiritual realization (e.g. Abhidharmakośa-Bhāṣya ad VIII, 28a, ed. Padhan 1967, p. 449).

Hence, just as is the case in Christianity, transcending the gender binary is part of Buddhist soteriology – with the noted differences in agency and example for the follower's *imitatio*. As the *samyak-saṃ-buddha*, the completely awakened one, the Buddha dispenses the *mysterium retractionis* of his shielded phallos, the renunciation of limbic emotions (the impulsive grasping at sensations) as the true transformation of his *mahāpuruṣa* hypermasculine potential into enlightened post-masculinity.

The temptation of toxic masculinity

The Woke One's ultimate abandonment of his cisheteropatriarchal world-ruling potential for the sake of *bodhi* (awakening) and the subsequent teaching of the Buddhist path to liberation, occurs directly after a temptation narrative that parallels the later Christian temptation narrative in the synoptic gospels after Jesus' baptism, during a 40-day fast in the desert, in the beginning of his revelatory and liberatory activities (Matthew 4.1–11; Luke 4.1–13; cp. Mark 1.12–13).

The Buddhist temptation narrative occurs in multiple forms found in Pāli, Sanskrit, Chinese and Tibetan canonical sources, the earlier canonical layers of which have been analysed by Hajime Nakamura (2000, pp. 155–69): Māra ('murderer'), the personification of Craving and Death (Bingenheimer 2007, p. 50), tempts Buddha with the (androcentric, heterosexual) sensual pleasure and threatens him with annihilation and death. In this 'battle' (*yuddha*), the 'Bull among the Śākyas' (*Śākyarṣabha*: Aśvaghoṣa, *Buddhacarita* 13.28) faces *erōs* and *thanatos*, sex and deadly aggression, and he stands – or better: sits – his ground; and he retracts (or: remains retracted) from afflicting emotions and the ego-illusion as the final hurdle before awakening (or in some versions: as first test just after awakening).

Jesus' temptation in the synoptic gospels after his baptism, during a forty-day fast in the desert sees him encounter the devil/Satan who tempts him (Matthew, Luke) also within the parameters of *erōs* and *thanatos*, the drive to live and the death-drive: Jesus should use his spiritual powers for selfish fast-breaking (stones into bread) or for thanatophobic, selfish display of spiritual superiority (leaping from the pinnacle of the temple). While sexual temptations and dominion are not the focus of the hedonic self-gratification part of the narrative, sexual hedonism, as part of the 'cravings of the flesh' (*epithymia tēs sarkos*), clearly features among the three worldly things to be avoided by the followers of God according to 1 John 2.16 – together with greed and boastful life-pride (*alazoneia tou biou*), i.e., the hegemonic bio-power that includes toxic masculinity. Indeed, the epitome of temptations in the Matthew-Luke narrative is the promise of unlimited power and wealth in exchange for submission – both the fullest extent of worldly *life* and spiritual *death*. Jesus, the

Saviour Rod, rejects this offer of unlimited worldly (bio-)power and hence the worldly phallic order in principle – while maintaining his penile privileges with serene phal/logics (Luke 4.12) or with apotropaic dick-swinging: *Hypage Satanā* – F*ck off Satan! (Matthew 4.10).

The phal/logics of cisheteropatriarchy in the Christian temptation narrative are also at the centre of the Brazilian *A Primeira Tentação de Cristo* – 'The First Temptation of Christ' (2019) directed by Roger van der Put and written by Fábio Porchat and Gustavo Martins of the comedy collaboration *Porta dos Fundos*. This Christmas special TV production drew the ire of conservative and fundamentalist Christians resulting in a Christmas Eve firebomb attack of the groups' headquarters and the removal of the film from Netflix Brazil (Stolworthy 2020); the reason for these events was the depiction of Jesus' homosexual attraction to 'Orlando' – i.e., devil, whom he met during his 40 days of fasting in the desert. The tempter's name appears to recall not only Ariosto's raging Orlando (*Orlando furioso*, 1591) and Shakespeare's handsome, chivalrous and ultimately successful lover of Rosalind in *As You Like It* (1600), but it also appears to anticipate the violent reaction to the filmscript by alluding to the horrific homophobic hate crime in Orlando, Florida: the fatal shooting at a LGBT nightclub on 12 June 2016, that resulted in 49, predominantly gay Latin*x*, casualties.

The culture war that rages around *A Primeira Tentação de Cristo* resembles in many ways the reception of Jo Clifford's play *The Gospel According to Jesus, Queen of Heaven* (2009) that has been performed with activist verve in Brazil since 2016 (Goh 2019). Yet, ironically – and in contrast to Clifford's liberatingly subversive play that depicts Jesus as a trans woman – the theology of *A Primeira Tentação de Cristo* is astonishingly cisheteropatriarchal and fundamentally reaffirms the Christian conservative condemnation of homosexuality and any trans-binary gender order. In *A Primeira Tentação de Cristo*, God is created in the stereotypical hypermasculine and macho image of men, flirting and trying to seduce Mary while her emasculated husband Joseph must look on impotently. When the stereotypically effeminate Orlando, Jesus' tempter, is revealed to be Satan who has tricked Jesus and God into inheriting the powers over the world, the mildly *femme*-performing Jesus accesses his true inner violent masculinity, penetrates Orlando in the form of divine light and explodes him from the inside out. Thus, Jesus masters his temptation and accepts his mission as the son of *Rod*. The only possible theological reading appears to be that homosexuality is to be equated with satanism which is overcome by Jesus finding his destructive theo-masculinity.

In the gospels, Jesus' theo-masculinity expresses itself in annoyance and rage. Unlike the crypto-phallically serene *Woke One*, however, prior to dangling – queered and powerless – on the wood, Jesus' own phallocity, his angry masculinity modelled after that of the patriarchal Israelite father-*Rod* (e.g. McCarthy 2009), is on display throughout the gospels (Mark 3.5, 10.14, etc.); it becomes post-first-century CE such an embarrassment in the Greco-Roman world that scribal editors proceeded to sanitize concerning gospel passages (Upson-Saia 2013, pp. 23–5). In contrast, the Buddha's genitally shielded, *bull-of-a-man* appearance expresses a pragmatic alliance with the cisheteropatriarchal societal context, yet points to the overcoming of sex/gender performances: the *Woke One's* penis, while constructed as a societal necessity, is still even physically invisible. The Buddha's actions are depicted as displaying serene sovereignty over any egotistic impulses, included sexed and gendered performances.

Conclusion

The intersectional struggles with toxic forms of masculinity and faith are unlikely to yield far-reaching liberatory success. More likely than not, the resolution of the tension between patriarchal oppression and religious paradigms of inclusiveness is straight (*pun intended*): the by and large maintenance of cisheteronormative and oppressive-patriarchal performance of bio-power. Theologies of constructive and inclusive masculinities are mainly futilely wrestling with the Rod that was created in Man's Image (*in imagine viri*). In the case of Christianity, liberation from toxic masculinity is interpellated with the wider trajectory of salvation and becomes deflected and bypassed as an eschatological project. In the case of Buddhism, the soteriological reality of metaphallic liberation can just as easily be bypassed by privileging centripetal, quietist forms of individual practice for awakening above the need for what the Fourteenth Dalai Lama termed the '*nirvāṇa* of society' (Brazier 2002, p. 97), or a 'Worldly Nibbāṇa' (Hu 2011) as an end to widespread collective suffering by means of an awakened society.

What hope, then, is there for healthy and positive masculinities? Can the penile-phallic exceptionalism be unlearnt? Can this be aided by the emptying of gender eschatology into radical, dephallic and dehegemonic immanence, always struggling to preserve rhizomatic inter-being against the domineering onslaughts of cisheteropatriarchy?

Reflecting on my own experiences, I cannot see how the *phonoïc traumata*, the murderous wounds, once inflicted by toxic masculinities, could ever be redeemed (Scherer 2019, pp. 145–7). Any Kierkegaardian leap of faith in masculinity failing, all I could imagine would be a continuous unlearning of masculinity itself as the only viable approach left: indeed, always wrestling with the *Rod*, never ceasing, never succeeding. What remains is a radical struggle for the degendering and the concomitant de-phallocizing of society.

For Buddhist traditions, could the Woke One's cryptophallocity be seen as a launch pad for truly aphallic embodiments? Can we experience post- and meta-phallic liberation as the result of overcoming of the three egoïc poisons (*triviṣa*) which are shaped to masculinist toxins: delusional displays (*ignorance*) of sex, violence and penetrative might (*sense-craving* and *hatred*)? Perhaps, but only when the Buddha's hidden phallus is continuously revealed and overcome. Since in Buddhist traditions, liberation and awakening is less an *eschaton*, a final point in a divine plan, but an immanent presence, the liberation from toxic masculinity requires such continuous unveiling of hidden penile powers, continuous re-embodiment through individual cultivation and, on the societal level, continuously wrestling liberation from cisheteropatriarchy by means of communal social justice activism.

A Christian post-gender ethic can emerge comparably, launching from the disavowing of gender in Galatians 3.27–28, which proclaims a mystical experience of unity, homecoming and healing of all opposites in the Christ Jesus; however, the New Testament corpus nowhere really questions the masculinity of the man Jesus and that of the God-Christ and binary gender images and symbols in many Christian denominations have oppressive consequences. Jesus' death as the emptying (*kenōsis*) of God in what Althaus-Reid theologizes as the *Messiah-in-progress* (Althaus-Reid 2000, p. 155; Gunnes 2020, pp. 222–3) can be seen with Thomas Altizer as a total emptying, as the death of God, the death of transcendence (Alitzer 1997, pp. 161–83). It is in our journeys that the kenotic God can unlearn his own toxic masculinity. In consequence, 'radical immanence' (Alitzer 1997, pp. 180–1) and presence with the oppressed calls for the transformative queering and gender-emptying of God here and now, not as a mystical eschatology, but as rhizomatic inclusiveness and solidarity. The emptied godhood can thus learn, absorb and represent the experience of all human facets – queer, trans, non-binary.

Can a kenotic post-male Jesus smile over the raped child? The queer kenotic Jesus doesn't rise again; God does not empty himself in the kingdom of heaven, but bleeds to death into radical presence with the raped and slain child; what remains is the abyss of the kenotic deity in the extinguished eyes of the oppressed.

5.4 For reflection, conversation and action

1 Is Jesus a manly man?
2 How do you see the crucifixion and resurrection shaping Jesus' masculinity?
3 What kind of Christ, if any, do you think is needed today?

5.5 Bibliography

Althaus-Reid, Marcella (2000), *Indecent Theology: Theological Perversions in Sex, Gender and Politics*, London and New York: Routledge.
Althaus-Reid, Marcella (2003), *The Queer God*, London and New York: Routledge.
Altizer, Thomas J. J. (1997), *The Contemporary Jesus*, London: SCM Press.
Barrett, Alistair D. (2017), *Interrupting the Church's Flow: Engaging Graham Ward and Romand Coles in a Radically Receptive Political Theology in the Urban Margins*, PhD thesis., Vrije Universiteit, Amsterdam.
Beckford, Robert (1996), 'Does Jesus have a Penis? Black Male Sexual Representation and Christology', *Theology and Sexuality* 5, pp. 10–21.
Beckford, Robert (1998), *Jesus is Dread: Black Theology and Black Culture in Britain*, London: Darton, Longman and Todd.
Beckford, Robert (2021), *Duppy Conqueror: My Theology*, London: Darton, Longman & Todd.
Bingenheimer, Marcus (2007), 'Māra in the Chinese *Saṃyuktāgama*s, with a Translation of the *Māra Saṃyukta* of the *Bieyi za ahan jing* (T.100)', *Buddhist Studies Review* 24(1), pp. 46–74.
Bohache, Thomas (2008), *Christology From The Margins*, London: SCM Press.
Brazier, David (2002), *The New Buddhism: A Rough Guide to a New Way of Life*, 2nd edition, New York NY: Palgrave.
Campese C. S., Gioacchino (2012), 'The Irruption of Migrants: Theology of Migration in the 21st Century', *Theological Studies* 73(1), pp. 3–32.
Cheng, Patrick S. (2012), *From Sin to Amazing Grace. Discovering the Queer Christ*, New York NY: Seabury Books.
Ciurtin, Eugen (2013), 'The Man with All Qualities: A Buddhist Suite', *Bulletin d'Études Indiennes* 28–29 (2010–2011) [2013], pp. 339–69.
Clines David J. A. (2023), *Play the Man! Biblical Imperatives to Masculinity*, Sheffield: Sheffield Phoenix Press.
Cone, James H. (1970), *A Black Theology of Liberation*, Philadelphia PA: Lippincott Press.

Conway, Colleen M. (2008), *Behold the Man: Jesus and Greco-Roman Masculinity*, Oxford: Oxford University Press.
Cornwall, Susannah (2010), *Sex and Uncertainty in the Body of Christ: Intersex Conditions and Christian Theology*, London: Equinox.
Daly, Mary (1973), *Beyond God the Father. Towards a Philosophy of Women's Liberation*, London: The Women's Press.
Douglas, Kelly Brown (1994), *The Black Christ*, New York NY: Orbis Books.
Du Mez, Kristin Kobes (2020), *Jesus and John Wayne: How White Evangelicals Corrupted a Faith and Fractured a Nation*, New York NY: Liveright Publishing Corporation.
Edwards, Katie (2012), 'Sporting Messiah: Hypermasculinity and Nationhood in Male-targeted Sports Imagery', in J. Cheryl Exum and David J. A. Clines (eds), *Biblical Reception*, Sheffield: Phoenix Press, pp. 323–46.
Eiesland, Nancy (1994), *The Disabled God: Toward a Liberatory Theology of Disability*, London: Abingdon Press.
Eilberg-Schwartz, Howard (1994), *God's Phallus and Other Problems for Men and Monotheism*, Boston MA: Beacon Press.
Felder, Cain Hope (1993), 'Cultural Ideology, Afrocentrism and Biblical Interpretation', in James H. Cone and Gayraud S. Wilmore (eds), *Black Theology: A Documentary History. Volume II 1980–92*, Maryknoll NY: Orbis Books, pp. 184–95.
Gebara, Ivone (1999), *Longing for Running Water: Ecofeminism and Liberation*, Minneapolis PA: Fortress Press.
Gethin, Rupert (1996), 'The Resurrection and Buddhism', in Gavin D'Costa (ed.), *Resurrection Reconsidered*, Oxford: Oneworld, pp. 201–16.
Giddens, Anthony (1991), *Modernity and Self-Identity: Self and Society in the Late-Modern Age*, Cambridge: Polity Press.
Goh, Katie (2019), 'The Revolutionary Play That Casts Jesus as a Trans Woman' *Dazed* 12 March 2019, https://www.dazeddigital.com/life-culture/article/43680/1/jo-clifford-the-gospel-according-to-jesus-queen-of-heaven-trans-lgbtq-play (accessed 26.10.24).
Goldenberg, Naomi R. (2015), 'The Category of Religion in the Technology of Governance: An Argument for Understanding Religions as Vestigial States', in Trevor Stack, Naomi Goldenberg and Timothy Fitzgerald (eds), *Religion as a Category of Governance and Sovereignty*. Leiden: Brill, pp. 280–92.
Goss, Robert (1993), *Jesus Acted Up: A Gay and Lesbian Manifesto*, New York: HarperCollins.
Goss, Robert (2006), 'Ephesians', in Deryn Guest, Robert E. Goss, Mona West and Thomas Bohache (eds), *The Queer Bible Commentary*, London, SCM Press, pp. 684–92.
Grant, Jacquelyn (1989), *White Women's Christ and Black Women's Jesus: Feminist Christology and Womanist Response*, Atlanta: AAR Scholars Press.
Greenough, Chris (2020), *The Bible and Sexual Violence Against Men*, London: Routledge.
Gunnes, Gyrid Kristine (2020), 'An Ecclesiology of a Queer Kenosis? Risk and Ambivalence at Our Lady, Trondheim, in Light of the Queer Theology on Kenosis of Marcella Althaus-Reid', *Feminist Theology* 28(2), pp. 216–30.
Hattenstone, Simon (2006), 'Day that Jesus came to the Arndale Centre', *The*

Guardian Saturday 15 April 2006, https://www.theguardian.com/uk/2006/apr/15/religion.arts (accessed 26.10.24).

Hu, Hsiao-Lan (2011), *This Worldly Nibbāna: A Buddhist-Feminist Social Ethic for Peacemaking in the Global Community*, Albany: SUNY Press.

Isherwood, Lisa (2007), *The Fat Jesus*, London: Darton, Longman and Todd.

Isherwood, Lisa (2018), 'Sexuality and the "person" of Christ', in Lisa Isherwood and Dirk von der Horst (eds), *Contemporary Theological Approaches to Sexuality*, Oxford: Routledge, pp. 277–288.

Johnson, Mark (2014), *Seditious Theology: Punk and the Ministry of Jesus*, London: Ashgate.

Krondorfer, Björn (2004), 'Mel Gibson's Alter Ego: A Male Passion for Violence', *CrossCurrents* 54(1), pp. 16–21.

Langenberg, Amy Paris (2018), 'Buddhism and Sexuality', in Daniel Cozort and James Mark Shields (eds), *The Oxford Handbook of Buddhist Ethics*, Oxford: Oxford University Press, pp. 567–91.

Loughlin, Gerard (1998), 'Refiguring Masculinity in Christ', in Michael A. Hayes, Wendy Porter and David Tombs (eds), *Religion and Sexuality: Studies in Theology and Sexuality 4*, Sheffield: Sheffield Academic Press, pp. 405–14.

Loughlin, Gerard (2007), 'Introduction', in Gerard Loughlin (ed.), *Queer Theology: Rethinking the Western Body*, London: Blackwell, pp. 1–34.

Martin, Dale B. (2009), 'Sex and the Single Savior', in Björn Krondorfer (ed.), *Men and Masculinities in Christianity and Judaism: A Critical Reader*, London: SCM Press, pp. 184–200.

McCarthy, Michael C. (2009), 'Divine Wrath and Human Anger: Embarrassment Ancient and New', *Theological Studies* 70(4), pp. 845–74.

Moltmann, Jürgen (1998), 'Liberate Yourselves by Accepting One Another', trans. Ulrike R. M. Guthrie, in Nancy L. Eiesland and Don E. Saliers (eds), *Human Disability and the Service of God: Reassessing Religious Practice*, Nashville: Abingdon Press, pp. 105–22.

Moore, Stephen D. (2001), *God's Beauty Parlor and other Queer Spaces in and around the Bible*, Stanford: Stanford University Press.

Moore, Will (2022), *Boys Will be Boys, and Other Myths. Unravelling Biblical Masculinities*, London: SCM Press.

Moss, Candida R. (2010), 'The Man with the Flow of Power: Porous Bodies in Mark 5:25–34', *Journal of Biblical Literature* 129(3), pp. 507–19.

Nakamura Hajime 中村 元 (2000), *Gotama Buddha: A Biography Based on the Most Reliable Texts*, Vol. 1., trans. Gaynor Sekimori, Tokyo: Kosei Publishing.

Nakashima Brock, Rita (1988), *Journeys by Heart: A Christology of Erotic Power*, New York: Crossroad.

Partridge, Dale (2022), *The Manliness of Christ: How the Masculinity of Jesus Eradicates Effeminate Christianity*, Relearn Press, https://relearn.org.

Powers, John (2009), *A Bull of a Man: Images of Masculinity, Sex and the Body in Indian Buddhism*, Cambridge: Harvard University Press.

Reaves, Jayme R. and Tombs, David (2019), '#MeToo Jesus: Naming Jesus as a Victim of Sexual Abuse', *International Journal of Public Theology* 13(4), pp. 387–412.

Reaves, Jayme R., Tombs, David and Figueroa, Rocio (eds) (2021), *When Did We See You Naked? Jesus as a Victim of Sexual Abuse*, London: SCM Press.

Ruether, Rosemary Radford (1983), *Sexism and God-Talk: Toward a Feminist Theology*, Boston MA: Beacon Press.
Scherer, Bee (2006), 'Gender Transformed and Meta-gendered Enlightenment: Reading Buddhist Narratives as Paradigms of Inclusiveness', *REVER* 6(3), pp. 65–76.
Scherer, Bee (2018), 'Beyond Heteropatriarchal Oppression: Inhabiting Aphallic Anthroposcapes', in Bee Scherer (ed.), *Queering Paradigms VII: Contested Bodies and Spaces*, Oxford: Peter Lang, pp. 65–81.
Scherer, Bee (2019), 'I am a Suicide Waiting to Happen: Reframing Self-Completed Murder and Death', in Ian Marsh and Mark E. Button (eds), *Suicide and Social Justice: New Perspectives on the Politics of Suicide and Suicide Prevention*, London: Routledge, pp. 141–51.
Scherer, Bee (2020), 'Atypical Bodies: Queer-Feminist and Buddhist Perspectives', in David T. Mitchell and Sharon L. Snyder (eds), *Cultural History of Disability in the Modern Age*, Vol. 6, London: Bloomsbury, pp. 19–28.
Scherer, Bee (2021), 'Queering Buddhist Traditions', in *The Oxford Research Encyclopedia of Religion*. Oxford University Press, doi:10.1093/acrefore/9780199340378.013.ORE_REL-00765.R1.
Sedgwick, Eve K. (2004), 'Queer and Now', in Eve K. Sedgwick, *Tendencies*, London and New York: Routledge, pp. 1–19.
Sharma, Arvind (2005), *Religious Studies and Comparative Methodology: The Case for Reciprocal Illumination*, Albany NY: State University of New York Press.
Smit, Peter-Ben (2017), *Masculinity and the Bible. Survey: Models, and Perspectives*, Leiden: Brill.
Starr, Rachel (2021), '"Not pictured": What Veronica Mars can teach us about the crucifixion', in Jayme Reaves, David Tombs and Rocio Figueroa Alvear (eds), *When Did We See You Naked?: Acknowledging Jesus as a Victim of Sexual Abuse*, London: SCM Press, pp. 165–77.
Stolworthy, Jacob (2020), 'The First Temptation of Christ: Brazil Forces Netflix to Remove Comedy Depicting Jesus as Gay', *The Independent* 9 January 2020, https://www.independent.co.uk/arts-entertainment/tv/news/netflix-jesus-gay-first-temptation-christ-brazil-judge-youtube-a9276226.html (accessed 26.10.24).
Stuart, Elizabeth (2003), *Gay and Lesbian Theologies: Repetitions and Critical Difference*, Aldershot: Ashgate.
Tombs, David (1999), 'Crucifixion, State Terror, and Sexual Abuse', *Union Seminary Quarterly Review* 53(1–2), pp. 89–109.
Trainor, Michael (2014), *The Body of Jesus and Sexual Abuse: How the Gospel Passion Narratives Inform a Pastoral Response*, Eugene: Wipf and Stock.
Upson-Saia, Kristi (2013), 'Holy Child or Holy Terror? Understanding Jesus' Anger in the Infancy Gospel of Thomas', *Church History* 82(1), pp. 1–39.
van Klinken, Adriaan S. and Smit, Peter-Ben (2013), 'Introduction: Jesus Traditions and Masculinities in World Christianity', *Exchange* 42, pp. 1–15.
Ward, Graham (1999), 'Bodies: The Displaced Body of Jesus Christ', in J. Milbank, C. Pickstock and G. Ward (eds), *Radical Orthodoxy: a New Theology*, London: Routledge, pp. 163–81.
Wilson, Brittany E. (2016), 'Gender Disrupted: Jesus as a "Man" in the Fourfold Gospel', *Word & World* 36(1), pp. 24–35.

6

healing bodies (seeking salvation)

6.1 Introduction

'He saved others; he cannot save himself.' (Matthew 27.42)

Men are taught to save others; as if they themselves do not need saving. In dominant western societies, men are repeatedly cast as the saviour, the hero. To be a man is to act, to take charge, to resolve a problem. This narrative shapes even how the crucifixion is understood. From failure and submission, from the passiveness of the passion, Jesus quickly emerges as a hero-saviour, battling the principalities and powers, tricking the devil and restoring justice and order. Even when Jesus' suffering is foregrounded, it is often in a way that celebrates the strength of Jesus, who carries the weight of the world on his shoulders. Yet, read carefully, the life, death and resurrection of Jesus has the potential to interrupt such heroic narratives, and to offer a different story of salvation.

The first part of this chapter asks what men need saving from, before exploring the intersection of models of salvation and masculinity. It notes shared patterns of control, violence, division and denial; and argues that, to be truly saving, Christian accounts of salvation need to challenge, rather than collude with, dominant models of masculinity. In the second part, Carlton Turner and Rachel Starr discuss aspects of this emerging conversation. Carlton is a priest and scholar serving in the Church of England. Originally from the Bahamas, Carlton is interested in postcolonial faith identities and accounts of sin and salvation (Turner, 2020). He has contributed to a workshop on men and masculinity as part of Tearfund's *Declaration 2022*. He is a trustee of USPG. Rachel is a feminist theologian, researching gender-based violence (Starr 2018). A poem by braveslave brings the chapter to a close.

What do men need saving from?

Formally, the church has taught that neither sin nor salvation is gendered. Men as well as women are understood to need saving from death, despair, decay and desire. Yet, early in the life of the church, a woman was made responsible for sin; and a man for salvation. Men, it would seem, need saving from women – whose bodies have long been considered more marked by sex and materiality. The man Jesus, perfect and without sin, saves other men from the temptation of their own and other bodies.

A second response to the question, what do men need saving from, centres on men's wellbeing. In this account, men need saving from social structures, cultural attitudes and patterns of behaviour that harm them – resulting in lower life expectancy and higher risks of encountering violence; and from intersecting oppressions that increase the risks and burdens for Black, Brown, queer, poor, differently-abled, old, young and undocumented men. Here salvation comes through the healing of bodies and souls, individual people and societies. And Jesus is the one who stands in solidarity with the lost, broken and dispossessed – a brother, with whom to share food and friendship.

A third response begins with the horror of male violence and patriarchal oppression. It names the sin of patriarchy (Ruether 1983). Men need saving from toxic forms of masculinity that do damage to men and others. Salvation requires a move away from the lone hero, and the pressures, power and privileges that accompany this role. This account breaks with the belief that salvation is men's gift – to give or take away. It disrupts the narrative that only men can save their wife, family or nation. Is there a place for Jesus here? Only alongside others, no more or less a saviour than his companions (Gebara 1999).

Critiquing models of salvation and masculinity

In their essay, 'For God so loved the world?', Joanne Carlson Brown and Rebecca Ann Parker (1989) consider key models of salvation, asking how each function for women facing violence. This next section begins to explore aspects of dominant models of salvation in relation to models of masculinity. What are the points of connection? What tensions and possibilities are revealed?

Christian accounts of salvation have tended to begin with recognition of God's power to save. God is righteous and in control. Humanity is helpless without this God, unable in their sinful state to even draw near without God's grace. While for many, belief in a just and all-powerful God is a source of comfort and reassurance, for others, the distance proves overwhelming, resulting in fear and despair. That God has tended to be described as male within dominant Christian traditions further complicates the dynamic. An all-powerful male God stands at a distance from sinful humanity. Such theology reinforces dominant models of masculinity that idealize superiority, control and independence.

Two of the earliest accounts of salvation underline the passivity of humanity. In the ransom model, sin holds humans captive to the devil. Jesus is offered to the devil as a ransom for humanity. But there's a twist – since Jesus is without sin, the devil has no authority over him, and Jesus is able to break free. In the Christus Victor model, through death, Jesus defeats the powers of death and evil (Aulén 1930). In both these models, humans remain bystanders, incapable of participating in their own salvation. Yet Jesus emerges as the swashbuckling hero, tricking the devil and breaking everybody out of hell. An Indiana Jones type of Jesus. Here then, the question might be as to the extent to which men are encouraged to imitate Jesus, through spiritual – or physical – warfare against a presumed enemy.

The satisfaction model of atonement, and even more so the later penal substitution theory, both serve to illustrate how God is often presented as overly concerned with due process. There is a rigidity to these accounts – God is unable to break free of the demands of justice that require satisfaction, or even punishment. So offended is God, so full of righteous anger at human sinfulness, God descends into violence. As Brown and Parker (1989) rightly point out, a father who demands the death of his son is an abusive father, not a loving one. Such understandings of how God saves have proved deeply problematic, serving to legitimate abuse within and beyond the home (Nakashima Brock and Parker 2001). In such accounts, men are framed as either abuser or victim; either way, they are encouraged to deny the truth of themselves, the goodness of their own and other's bodies, and the possibility of grace.

Dominant accounts of salvation share a language with dominant models of masculinity: both appear to give value and legitimacy to destructive power, violence, male heroism and sacrifice. In contrast, many (but not all) feminist and womanist theologians reject the belief that the death of Christ on the cross can be seen as part of God's saving work. They argue that God does not instigate or use violence and suffering to overcome violence and suffering. This represents a radical break with most dominant accounts of salvation, which assume that it is through the cross (on its own, or as part of the wider work of Jesus) that salvation comes (Nakashima Brock and Parker 2008). Such a critique requires also that models of masculinity engage honestly with the cost of violence, suffering and pain – for example through increased recognition of PTSD and other forms of trauma – rather than continue to glorify violence and thus deny its impact on men's bodies and other bodies.

Within dominant Christian traditions, salvation is often limited in its reach. It is presented as a scarce commodity, which only some will gain, through narrowly defined confessions or practices of faith. Similarly, what it means to achieve status as a man, according to dominant narratives, is achievable by only a select few: those who are wealthy enough, white enough, young enough and resolutely (hetero)sexual. What might it mean to understand both masculinity and salvation as spacious, with room for all in their diversity?

Finally, there is a connection in how dominant models of salvation have come to focus on heaven over earth, denying the value of one's own body and the bodies of others, including the body of the earth (Nakashima Brock and Parker 2008). As we have previously considered, such a denial of bodies (or at least, other bodies) is present in dominant models of masculinity. Indeed, the urgent task of protecting the earth is understood by some men as a threat, either because it requires them to practise caring, or because it limits their ability to consume, conquer or control the body of creation (Jennings 2019). Yet, there are alternative models. In *A Theology of Liberation*, Gustavo Gutiérrez (2001) draws together the sacred and profane, human acts of liberation and the gift of the kingdom. Here, salvation begins with attentive care of bodies, of self, community and of the earth.

6.2 Models of salvation and masculinities – *Carlton Turner, in conversation with Rachel Starr*

For a number of years, Carlton and Rachel have contributed to a course on theology and gender at the Queen's Foundation for Ecumenical Theological Education in Birmingham, where they are colleagues. This conversation emerges out of this work, and builds on a workshop at the *Behold the Men* conference in 2021. In the following text, the initial conversation is developed through further reflections and comment.

Saving men

Rachel: There's an overlap between dominant models of salvation and masculinity, primarily through the focus on violence. If violence is understood as necessary for salvation, it follows that we need a powerful, conquering saviour. It's the hero model of men, found in the muscular Christianity movement, the white saviour movement. It appears most strongly in the Christus Victor model. Dominant understandings of masculinity often centre around what have been traditional male heroes: firefighters, action heroes. What I would describe as the SAS model of salvation.

These sit alongside – are reliant on – models that focus on Jesus' suffering. Because the other way to save, it is suggested, is by receiving violence into yourself as a man. Such suffering is understood as noble, as we see in language around remembrance of war which is often sentimentalized as 'noble sacrifice'. There is a deep connection to dominant models of masculinity.

Further notes: Feminist theologians critique such hero worship, describing the 'search for a hero' as disempowering and distracting. Feminist and womanist theologians have widely rejected the claim that suffering saves, or that God desires the violent death of Christ (Brown and Parker, 1989).

Carlton: Either way is deeply problematic. The violence, whether a man or men are perpetuating violence, saving through force; or enduring violence as a test of masculinity. You can't come away from Scripture without a sense that violence is deeply part of any salvific attempt. And it's framed theologically in this way.

Further notes: Violence is assumed, legitimated, required and resisted in the biblical narrative. Violence shapes relationships and rituals. It is a mark of both faithfulness and betrayal. Because the Bible becomes understood as a sacred text, the violence within it comes to be seen as sacred. The denial of the sacred power of violence by feminist and womanist theologians is a fundamental break with dominant models of salvation – and perhaps of masculinity also.

Carlton: How does this relate to a society say like mine, in the Bahamas, that is patriarchal in its framing but matriarchal or matrifocal in reality? The place where divinity meets humanity often involves some kind of ritual, a dance. And the people who usually invoke the spirit or the divine are women. In such societies, the focus is no longer on violence as a means of encountering God and making everything right. But it is about encountering the other, the holy, the numinous, the overwhelming. It just shows how there's so much more to talk about when we talk about salvation.

Rachel: In that context, would the model of salvation be about pulling back the divide between heaven and Earth; a way of connecting to the sacred? Or a process of healing and restoration? Or both?

Carlton: I wouldn't differentiate because that's what it's ultimately always about for the healing of the community, the nations. This kind of trance is about drawing from someplace else. It is the kingdom come on earth as it is in heaven. It's the violence that I have an issue with. I'm trying to write about sin for a Caribbean theology textbook (Turner 2024). And I cannot escape René Girard's work on the scapegoat theory or from my point of view, when we're doing stuff like carnival, Mikhail Bakhtin and the carnivalesque tradition. You have these frolic moments and it releases tension. So, everything goes back to order, or ways of bringing things back to order.

Violence is so deeply ingrained within human societies, and we need to imagine another way. And often when we talk about sin, and salvation is always connected to sin, we think about the perpetrator, the one who sins. More recently, we think about the sinned against and the need for liberation and justice for marginalized, oppressed communities. But I think we need a deeper understanding of sin and salvation that looks at the process by which we determine sin itself.

Rachel: A question we've explored previously is who gets to name or define sin. Pamela Lightsey (2015) asks this question. Who gets to say someone, or something, is sinful? That can be an act of violence too. There is a theory that masculinity is shaped around the need for warriors and therefore most societies create a dominant or normative model of masculinity that claims being a man is ultimately about fighting because that is what is understood as needed from men. There's always been this belief in a need for soldiers and warriors. Perhaps that helps explain why salvation is framed through violence. Salvation becomes about enacting, receiving or witnessing violence. Although, as your example from the Caribbean reveals, salvation can be understood differently, but within dominant western traditions, it's hard to disentangle the process of salvation from the language of punishment, violence and fear.

Carlton: What do we make of this in relation to masculinities? The vision in Scripture is of the peaceable kingdom, where lion and lamb lie down together, predator and prey, and 'they will not hurt or destroy on all my holy mountain' (Isaiah 11.9). What does masculinity look like in the coming times, when violence is not the chief means of being?

Rachel: It must be unsettling for men for whom their sense of identity is rooted in the fight, whether that's the struggle for justice or the struggle to save. To be looking towards that vision of Isaiah – and to think that what ultimately you will be asked is to do nothing, to be asked to lie down next to the one who previously you were expected to protect or fight against. Is living at peace with each other disempowering for men, for those men whose identity is action hero?

It's interesting how, from a different perspective and set of commitments, feminist theologians have sought to retain agency within the process of salvation, and that strikes me as in some ways connected to masculinity. There's a fear of being passive, of being expected to receive salvation. So I do think that in both these quite different conversations, there is a concern that when everything's complete, there's nothing left to do.

Carlton: This need for men to fight, save or be strong is all about ego. But I wonder what it looks like when we read in Scripture that we are already the beloved of God. That we do not need to prove anything to anyone.

Rachel: This connects to how we see Jesus' work. The claim by some feminist and womanist theologies that Jesus' death does not achieve anything can feel quite disruptive. Everything's not done and dusted, there is no 'once for all' act of redemption. This again is central to many feminist and womanist theologies that see salvation as ongoing. For Ivone Gebara (2002), for example, there's no grand moment of salvation, but instead a series of small, often unnoticed moments. There's no climax. There's no salvation climax.

Carlton: The Christian tradition has wrestled with the notion of works versus faith. Where does my human effort fit into God's overall salvation? Whether we're talking individually or corporately. It's something we've always wrestled with; and if we look more deeply into it, we're wrestling with being versus doing. And we haven't done the hard work of trying to reframe salvation itself.

Male saviours, female sinners?

Rachel: Not only is masculinity often presented in salvific mode, as if (often) men can save the world, but within dominant Christian traditions, men are believed to save women. Men lead, teach and make holy; women are physically and morally weak. Women distract themselves and men, they are, in the words of Tertullian, the 'gateway to sin'. The belief in male headship in both church and home – and consequently the need for female obedience – persists even today in a variety of church denominations and traditions. I wonder if this gives us any clues to thinking about men and salvation, if men are presented as the saviours of sinful women.

Carlton: It's one of the ways that Christianity has been understood within the West, using hierarchy as a way of reading Scripture, constructing church. It seeps into who is constructed as right or holy. The dichotomies are an issue.

Rachel: There's the whiteness dichotomy as well, which makes some similar moves in categorizing some as right and holy, and others as sinful.

Carlton: There is no space for grey. But the idea of exclusively male leadership overlooks biblical characters such as Deborah (Judges 5). Men weren't the only leaders or even the most celebrated. When you have this kind of dichotomy, violence is perpetrated against those who are placed on the other side of right, normal or holy. I experienced that as a Black embodied person, even though I'm male. Who is on that other side, the barbarian, beyond-the-pale, unknown, illogical? What do we do with them? That's the issue, and that's deeper than just Christian traditions.

Rachel: There's the question of who we see as needing saving. As a white western woman, I'm conscious of how easy it is to slip into the familiar role of the saviour. In different ways, we are vulnerable to these narratives that suggest we need to save others, either because they're innocent or because they're wayward. These kinds of binaries – rationality or irrationality, culture or barbarism – are used to differentiate between different groups. And in terms of gender, men tend to be placed on the positive or more valued side and women on the lesser side.

Further notes: In the past decade, several church denominations have begun to investigate historic claims of abuse. Reports reveal that the vast majority of perpetrators of abuse – spiritual, sexual, economic – have been men who hold positions of power and authority. Other men and women have colluded with these men, sometimes out of fear. The notion of the male saviour has been used to justify abuse, presented as God-ordained teaching, spiritual guidance, mentoring or pastoral care. Theologies that encourage unquestioning obedience are further problematic in such contexts. Rather than men saving women, men are often those from whom women need saving. Women must be theologically empowered to see their own value, voice and wisdom – and to protect and celebrate their bodies and the bodies of others.

Can men be saved?

Rachel: It's important to make visible the ways in which dominant models of masculinity are problematic for men, the burden that they place on men and how they result in poor mental health, increased suicide rates, etc. At the same time, we need to recognize how men can collude with dominant models of masculinity – or seek to emulate them – in ways that are super problematic for women, non-binary people and other men, particularly those marginalized because of their ethnicity or sexuality, or because they are financially vulnerable. We had an example of that in the news this week (Davies 2023). Do men need saving from themselves, or more accurately, from their participation in toxic forms of masculinity? Where is the space for vulnerability, failure and transformation within these models of masculinity? Where's the space for grace and receptivity (Barrett and Harley 2020)?

Further notes: A study found that even when men were saved from a suicide attempt by the intervention of another, they found it difficult to acknowledge that someone else saved them. Instead, they would frame what happened in a way that foregrounded themselves, seeing the intervention as fate or a sign, rather than the actions of another (Oliffe et al. 2021).

Carlton: Men are vulnerable in many cases. As a father and a separated, almost divorced, person, I would argue that. The vulnerability of men goes very deep. Within family structures and systems, men can be in a vulnerable position. At the same time, we do live in a world in which the leaders of our world, who are disproportionately strong, white affluent men, are seen as representing masculinity. There are female leaders who stand out, for example, the Prime Minister of New Zealand or the President of Barbados. I am deeply impressed by these models of holistic leadership.

Rachel: With Jacinda Ardern there's a sense of her sitting more lightly to, not so much the task, but the position. There's a sense her role doesn't define her. Almost as if she is saying: I've taken it up for a moment. I've led as best as I can. I'm now recognizing that it's time to pass it on.

Carlton: Nothing to prove, just wanting to serve. In contrast, I watched Joe Biden give the State of the Union Address (February 2023). Here's this 80-year-old man who could hardly climb a flight of stairs, but he has to put on a show of strength for the American people. And the fact that he has to put on a show and prove that he is strong enough to lead is problematic.

Where is the space for vulnerability, failure and transformation within dominant models of masculinity?

Rachel: That connects to our next question: Where is the space for vulnerability, failure and transformation within the ways that we understand masculinity? The very concept of salvation suggests that we have failings and vulnerabilities (Clack 2013), that we need transforming.

Carlton: When we read the life of Jesus of Nazareth, how he is depicted in the New Testament, what resonates deeply with me is that you cannot just put Jesus in any one box. Jesus fights for justice, not to prove anything. Jesus dares to have an emotional breakdown somewhere in some garden. Jesus sheds tears. You know, Jesus is deeply human.

If we want a model of salvation, we need a model where we can be corrected. We don't have to have all the right answers. We can be simply loved. We can be human. We can cry. There's something about authenticity within this model of salvation. We can be deeply ourselves, complex as that might be.

Rachel: JJ Bola in *Mask Off* (2019) says something similar – performing expected ways of being a man is like wearing a mask. Authenticity is when you remove the mask and are just yourself. That's so much what we need, what we desire – to be able to be ourselves.

How can we speak of salvation?

Rachel: We've talked previously about how a lot of the language we use to speak of salvation – healed, freed, forgiven, justified – are quite passive and function as 'full stops' rather than suggesting an ongoing process of salvation.

Carlton: When I think about metaphors of salvation, particularly from the Scriptures, I am conscious how incomplete our language is. All of these terms are attempts at describing something that God does: alongside us, with us, within us, around us, through us, ahead of us, behind us. It's limiting when we just use one metaphor and say that's it, that's how we must describe God's saving work. And I agree, the language makes it seem so final. The maturing, ongoing process, that unveiling of who we truly are, that's not reflected.

Rachel: Justice, salvation, faith – it's all ongoing. We live each day *en la lucha* to cite Ada María Isasi-Díaz (2004): struggling for justice, for life, for ourselves and in solidarity with others.

Carlton: When I say getting somewhere, I think there's no full arrival point because what you're doing is going deeper and deeper into the infinite. That is how I tend to see it. To talk of salvation once upon a time, I'd be 'saved' from my ignorance, my Blackness, my Africanness … and I don't think we've gotten away from that type of thinking. We don't use that kind of language, but it's the way we frame it. I'm a Church of England minister and within my tradition, maybe even within myself, there is the idea that I am saved by what I know or how I have come to be, how I've been shaped. We do it all the time with other churches or traditions and they do it to us. For example, back home in the Bahamas, Pentecostals might say you're not saved as an Anglican because you haven't been baptized in the Spirit or manifested signs of the Spirit, and Anglicans would say you're not saved because you don't know enough.

Rachel: And in some Catholic traditions, what is important is participation in the sacramental life. Each tradition has its own way of drawing a line, between those who are seen as saved and those who are not. And to cross the line, you are told, you have to participate in something they've decided is the way in.

Carlton: Yeah, I usually challenge people: saved from what?

Rachel: In chapel today (at Queen's), I couldn't sing one of the hymns. It has a line about the best is saved for those who confess him first (Doerksen 2008). What a shocking boast – the idea that we've arrived and everybody else has to catch up with us! That there's a ranking. There is often such arrogance around discussion of salvation. Because nobody asked the question, 'Are you saved?' unless they think they are.

Carlton: Yes, it's the assumptions within these statements. As if salvation is a foregone conclusion.

Rachel: There's an internalization of what's being defined as problematic. Whether that's bodies or sexuality, or whatever it is. An obsession with saving ourselves from ourselves, rather than experiencing salvation as a coming back into communion with ourselves.

Carlton: I see how sin and salvation have been framed and how that's been played out in the lives of real people, often violently. But when you start talking about being as opposed to doing, what are the risks?

Rachel: I can see risks. 'I only have to be. I don't have to do' could be understood as 'I don't have to pay reparations for enslavement' or 'I don't have to say I'm sorry to someone I've wronged.'

Who are the people who make us feel better? They may point out the work we still have to do but more likely, they are the ones who see us, who see the real, authentic us.

Carlton: Can you even capture with language this idea that we call salvation? Can you really capture it in its fullness?

Rachel: We see from the Bible how many ways the writers attempt to speak of their relationship with God, of salvation. We get glimpses but no one ever grasps it. So perhaps we shouldn't try to come up with a perfect model.

What does it mean for men's bodies to be saved?

Rachel: Can we describe salvation as that which enables bodies that are healthy, flourishing, free, whole? Not in a body fascist way; but as appropriate to each body, in that particular moment. Authentic is a word we've come back to a lot in this conversation. There's something about being able to live with the authenticity of our bodies. Do any of these words feel helpful for you, Carlton?

Carlton: As a father, I'm so aware of the need to care for my health. That my body is important for my daughter's life, not just mine. This is where relationality comes in. I need to be the best me, beyond my baggage; to strive to be a better man, a healthier man. I don't know what's healthy in and of myself, but in relation to those around me. How does my male body help others feel safe and secure? Men's bodies aren't meant to sabotage our lives or the lives of those dependent on us.

Rachel: We need theological teaching that helps men value their bodies and all bodies as sacred. That moves beyond the binary of the valued soul, spirit or mind and the disgraced body. Or, among bodies, the valued and discarded.

Within dominant models of masculinity we can identify several attitudes towards the male body. One approach is for men to disregard their physical bodies. They are careless, reckless with it – punishing it, taking risks. 'I'm gonna drink too much. I'm gonna run across the road in front of traffic. I'm gonna do daredevil stunts.' The other is where the body is placed under intense scrutiny. The body is disciplined, shaped. Both of these attitudes to the body are, it seems to me, ways of distancing yourself from your body. You're either denying your dependence on it through physical risk, the bearing of pain. Or you're treating your body as a machine to enable you to perform sexually, or as an athlete. Both prevent men from having an integrated sense of self. Of course, these are extremes – most men muddle on, holding a range of feelings towards their bodies. What's needed is to be at peace with your body in whatever form that is.

An example – jiu jitsu

Rachel: Let's talk about the example we used at the *Behold the Men* conference (2021) of your experience of being part of the jiu jitsu community.

We talked about the importance of this embodied, community experience and began to explore some connections to a model of salvation that is focused on integration, authenticity and relationality of the body.

Carlton: So, I'm part of the jiu jitsu community. I'm two time British jiu jitsu champion in my age and weight category. I have a blue belt and now a purple belt. I find within this community a kind of consciousness. It is very much about figuring out who you are, what your body can do. Maybe you have a dodgy knee, so you have to find ways around it. The philosophy behind jiu jitsu or samurai martial arts originating from Japan is that you find the most efficient way to fight. A weaker opponent can outdo a much larger, stronger opponent. What it means is learning to fight from a vulnerable place. You learn about yourself, but you also learn about the other. You develop skills: balance, leverage. You learn new things at different angles. Most importantly, you learn how not to get in danger in the first place.

In this community, it's fascinating how people relate to each other. Men and women from all walks of life. One just out of prison, next one is a university professor. And there is such a profound respect. It's violent, yes. But what's going on between those two people is a profound respect for that person's life, helping that person know how to protect themselves, how to improve their skills. Your life is always in somebody else's hands. Your opponent could choke you or break an arm or leg but they don't. It's about learning how you should respond.

Rachel: So it's an approach that enables you to be in a physical encounter with others that isn't violent. I like what you said about knowing deeply your own vulnerabilities, and presumably also your own strengths.

Carlton: There's a level of unconsciousness within society – violence is so part of us we're not aware of it. We carry it out because we're not stopping to be conscious. But with jiu jitsu you are conscious of what you can do, what can happen. And so you safeguard against it. I'm a big strong guy. I think by now at this advanced stage of this martial art, I just know that if some young jock wants to kick off and carry on like this masculine über alpha, I wouldn't be threatened by that because I know it's not going to end well for them. Or harm could come to either of us and we don't need that. Let's take the pressure off. Let's approach this in a different way.

Rachel: So violence is a kind of immature way of being in the world, of claiming your identity. If we think instead about how we move deeper into the life of God – it's about being generous to ourselves and others, making space, holding things in tension, not to have to resolve everything.

Carlton: In psychoanalytic theory, problems arise when you try to cast something off. The goal is to try as far as possible to integrate, to be aware of the different parts of yourself. That's opening space for imagination and the creation of the new. Instead of a tendency to villainize, bastardize or marginalize a very real part of yourself. What's interesting, Rachel, is that any kind of martial art is deeply spiritual. In sparring or wrestling with somebody you can sense so much of who they are, how they are; even their deeper fears. And you learn about your own fears and responses in that interspace. It's transformative.

Rachel: The intimacy of bodies. Even though in church we talk about the body of Christ, we share the peace, the bread and wine. And we sing together. But we don't have that sense of being together in a way that is safe, that is authentic. Perhaps there are moments when we pray together. But knowing another person in their embodied self is hard to do.

In conclusion: Beginning with bodies rather than souls transforms the language of salvation. Rather than an individual, spiritualized process, salvation is understood as a collective work. The body participates in its own recovery but is often helped by the intervention and care of others, skilled and unskilled. Rather than a one-off event done to humanity, salvation is ongoing. Salvation does not protect the body from pain or trauma, but instead sees how caring for one's body and the bodies of others is saving work. Rather than dividing soul from body, salvation is understood as a process of integration and restoration.

6.3 Dinosaurs will roar and Eagles must soar – *braveslave* (April 2020)

Can man's healing come without stealing?
When he gets *that* feeling he wants
sexual healing baby, baby? Baby!

Does he, do we need to infantilize for *that*
feeling? That feeling of control demands
he compresses souls. 'Baby, do what you're told!'

BEHOLD THE MEN

Let us upturn earth and burrow to the source of the yearning,
the molten core of man furiously burning. The
energy emitted there is pure,
the problem is at the surface, for sure.

There is no order at man's border, he is freighted
with an albatross. He needs liberation, a cleansing
chaos. A cyclone to bring home, back home.

This cyclone will take him because,
to find healing he has to go to Oz.
Discover Dorothy is the key,
to unlock unbidden inner parts he,
is a plurality, living disassembled
needing harmony.

Frightened lions, heartless tin men, and
brainless scarecrows,
male archetypes, mere shadows,
punchlines out of time,
They are the shallows.

Without Dorothy to unite,
the hidden parts exist out of sight,
and out of control, to the disassembled man there is a
compression of soul.

Dorothy animates these other 'othered, unfathered
unmothered bastard sons, ever brittle,
arrested development stultifying growth
man-baby is little.

Man-babies screaming for satisfaction, want
sexual healing. Dorothy's magic is contextual
healing. As the frenzy and fear fade and grow still,
Dorothy unites man's archetypes into a guild.

But Oz has another mage, a powerful wizard
who dominates the stage.

The wizard is a blizzard, a natural disaster,
the Lord and Master. The wizard was a predator
a dinosaur who roared.

Dorothy shows us like the dinosaur
the wizard is already extinct,
Beyond frail, beyond the pail.
The Grim Reaper has long had his feast.
So how come dissembled man is still under the
curse of this putrefying jurassic beast?

The wizard is dead. The voice an
echo. Old tape, old script amplified in
stereo. Conditioning responses saying man
is one mode, 'bastard tough'.

As Dorothy lives she says man is
more than enough, already enough.
So man fly like a bird from the wizard's
words. Go in peace man you are healed and
are healing.

New masculinity is now unveiling,
Somewhere over the rainbow
ride the thermals, through the air
man you are sailing.

6.4 For reflection, conversation and action

1 What model or language for salvation is the one with which you are most familiar, in worship, prayer or study? What connections can you see to models of masculinity?
2 What do you think men need saving from, and for?
3 How might humans participate in the work of salvation?

6.5 Bibliography

Aulén, Gustaf (1930), *Christus Victor: An Historical Study of the Three Main Types of the Idea of the Atonement*, London: Society for Promoting Christian Knowledge.

Barrett, Al and Harley, Ruth (2020), *Being Interrupted: Re-Imagining the Church's Mission from the Outside In*, London: SCM Press.

Bola JJ (2019), *Mask Off: Masculinity Redefined*, London: Pluto Press.

Carlson Brown, Joanne and Parker, Rebecca (1989), 'For God So Loved the World?', in Joanne Carlson Brown and Carole R. Bohn (eds), *Christianity, Patriarchy, and Abuse: A Feminist Critique*, Cleveland OH: The Pilgrim Press, pp. 1–30.

Clack, Beverley (2013), 'Against the Pursuit of the Snazzy Life: A Feminist Theology of Failure and Loss', *Feminist Theology* 22(1), pp. 4–19.

Davies, Caroline (2023), 'Epsom College deaths being treated as homicide investigation, say police', *The Guardian* 8 February 2023, https://www.theguardian.com/uk-news/2023/feb/07/epsom-college-deaths-police-investigating-possible-murder-suicide (accessed 26.10.24).

Doerksen, Brian (2008), 'Come, Now is the Time to Worship'.

Gebara, Ivone (1999), *Longing for Running Water: Ecofeminism and Liberation*, Minneapolis MN: Fortress Press.

Gebara, Ivone (2002), *Out of the Depths: Women's Experience of Evil and Salvation*, Minneapolis: Fortress Press.

Gutiérrez, Gustavo (2001), *A Theology of Liberation*, London: SCM Press.

Holcomb, Justin S. (2017), *Christian Theologies of Salvation: A Comparative Introduction*, New York NY: New York University Press.

Isasi-Diáz, Ada María (2004), *En la Lucha/ In the Struggle Elaborating a Mujerista Theology*, 10th anniversary edition, Minneapolis MN: Fortress Press.

Jennings, Willie James (2019), *After Whiteness: An Education in Belonging*, Grand Rapids MI: William B. Eerdmans Publishing.

Lightsey, Pamela R. (2015), *Our Lives Matter: A Womanist Queer Theology*, Eugene OR: Pickwick Publications.

Nakashima Brock, Rita and Parker, Rebecca Ann (2001), *Proverbs of Ashes: Violence, Redemptive Suffering, and the Search for What Saves Us*, Boston MA: Beacon Press.

Nakashima Brock, Rita and Parker, Rebecca Ann (2008), *Saving Paradise: How Christianity Traded Love of This World for Crucifixion and Empire*, Boston MA: Beacon Press.

Oliffe, John L., Ferlatte, Olivier, Ogrodniczuk, John S., Seidler, Zac E., Kealy, David and Rice, Simon M. (2021), 'How to Save a Life: Vital Clues From Men Who Have Attempted Suicide', *Qualitative Health Research* 31(3), pp. 415–29.

Ruether, Rosemary Radford (1983), *Sexism and God-Talk: Toward a Feminist Theology*, Boston MA: Beacon Press.

Starr, Rachel (2018), *Reimagining Theologies of Marriage in Contexts of Domestic Violence: When Salvation is Survival*, Abingdon: Routledge.

Starr, Rachel (2023), 'Unbecoming: Reflections on the Work of a White Theologian', in Anthony Reddie and Carol Troupe (eds), *Deconstructing Whiteness, Empire and Mission*, London: SCM Press, pp. 225–44.

Turner, Carlton (2020), *Overcoming Self-Negation: Junkanoo and the Church in Contemporary Bahamian Society*, Eugene OR: Wipf and Stock.

Turner, Carlton (2024), *Caribbean Contextual Theology: An Introduction*, London: SCM Press.

7

bodies of Christ II (church)

7.1 Introduction

This chapter explores how the many bodies of Christian men gather: to worship and serve; as sacrament and sign; in unity, diversity and division. In the first section, we explore several ways of understanding the church, asking how each shapes the varied bodies of Christian men. We recognize how Black, queer men's bodies are often vulnerable in the church, and here we encourage engagement with two recent texts that make visible the harm done by the church, and that are themselves acts of healing and resistance: A. D. A. France-Williams' *Ghost ship: Institutional Racism and the Church of England* (2020) and Jarel Robinson-Brown's *Black, Gay, British, Christian, Queer: The Church and the Famine of Grace* (2021). We consider how, in many Christian traditions, the church has been divided along a gender binary: with men placed at the head of the church – as Christ's representative through their roles as priest, pastor, husband – in the process separating them from the feminized body. We ask how churches seek to discipline men's bodies, before considering what it means for men to be disciples of Christ.

In the second part of the chapter, Al Barrett critically examines three gendered ways of understanding the church as: penetrated body; penetrating body; and vulnerable and vulnerable-making body. In response, he offers a more fluid, receptive, grounded understanding, which invites the church to listen and learn from beyond its borders. Al is a white, middle-class, non-disabled(ish), straight(ish) cis-male priest, in full-time ministry within the Church of England. He is engaged in the ongoing pursuit – through embodied, conversational and written theological practice – of the intersectional, communal, coalitional and ensoiled work of 'decomposing mastery', in personal, ecclesial, political and ecological contexts.

To conclude the chapter, Donald Eadie reflects on weakness and vulnerability as a male disciple. Donald was a Methodist presbyter, spiritual director and writer based in Birmingham. He died in 2023, having keenly supported this project from the start. His gentle wisdom invites us to be similarly gentle with ourselves and others, in whatever journey of discipleship or discovery we might take.

Gathered bodies

Although early described as the body of Christ (1 Corinthians 12), the church has often turned its attention away from bodies, focusing on the cure of souls – in the process denying, dismissing and denigrating bodies. Ecclesiology, the study of the church, reveals a wide range of understandings of what it means to be church, each of which makes different demands of the bodies of men present. Below, we explore two such understandings: sanctuary and witness.

The church as sanctuary, an ancient understanding of sacred space (Numbers 35), has taken on renewed political significance in recent years. In Britain and elsewhere, migrant men, refugees and asylum seekers, men of many faiths, have sought out sanctuary and support from local churches, with mixed results. For some, the church has been a place in which their bodies are welcomed and restored, helping them become some-bodies (Groody 2017). For others, the boundaries of the church have been drawn tightly against them, and their bodies have not been welcomed. Arriving in 1940s and 1950s England, Windrush migrants from the Caribbean experienced repeated rejection from white churches (Reddie 2021). While some stayed within white majority churches, others formed their own worship communities that provided a Sunday sanctuary from white racist society (Adedibu 2013). For these and later migrants, Black Caribbean and African churches, mostly Pentecostal and Charismatic in tradition, have offered a rare space in which they might be leaders, preachers and pastors – where they might be celebrated as respectable, successful, faithful men (Adedibu 2013; Fesenmyer 2018).

While the church can be a place of affirmation and acceptance, it can also be a place of hurt and harm. Historic structures of inequality and theologically sanctioned sexism, racism and homophobia mean that the church continues to be an unsafe space for women, non-binary people and marginalized men. Many queer Christians are required by church teaching and practice to hide their identity and relationships. Yet, as Rachel Mann (2021) notes, discipleship is a process of becoming more fully and more truly oneself, which, she notes from her own experience, resonates with the process of transitioning as a trans woman. Both, she suggests, are about conforming the body to a more truthful form. To deny the value of any of the gathered bodies that make up the church results, Anthony Reddie (2021) argues, in the division of the church. Reddie and others call for truth-telling, justice-based reparations and reconciliation in order to rehabilitate a church marked by racism, sexism and homophobia, and thus restore the catholicity of the church.

A second model: the church as a place of witness, where truth-telling takes place, where stories are shared. Over many years, churches across Latin America, in South Africa and elsewhere have borne witness to violence and injustice, often at great cost. We can think of many prophets, martyrs and activists; those who speak out and those who listen to stories of trauma and sorrow. What might it mean for men to bear witness? To give testimony that does not grant status but places one at risk? In Britain, we might think of Inderjit Singh Bhogal, a Methodist presbyter deeply committed to the work of reconciliation, or Dan Woodhouse and Sam Walton, Methodist and Quaker activists who, in 2017, were arrested for attempting to damage British-made fighter jets expected to be used in attacks on Yemen.

And what might it mean for men to call the church to account? In the past few decades, many men have spoken out against abuse perpetrated within and by the church, either from their lived experience as survivors, or in solidarity with others. Once again, this bearing witness is costly and complex, as often the culture and structure of churches and denominations is intentionally or unintentionally complicit with the dynamics of abuse. The testimony of church leaders such as Matt Redman, who spoke about his and others' experiences of abuse during his time as a leader at Soul Survivor (in a statement on 13 July 2023, and in a documentary, *Let There Be Light*, April 2024), is revealing of the vulnerability of even men who have significant status, to being abused and silenced. The video, which Redman created with his wife Beth, and with theologian and activist, Amy Orr-Ewing, alongside a Church of England safeguarding investigation (concluded September 2023), make visible a lack of structures of accountability and appropriate boundaries in a culture that repeatedly ignored or excused coercive and controlling behaviour by Soul Survivor's charismatic leader Mike Pilavachi over four decades. Young male interns – often vulnerable financially and in terms of their own levels of emotional maturity – were repeatedly singled out by Pilavachi, resulting in spiritual and emotional manipulation, and inappropriate physical contact, including private wrestling sessions and semi-naked massages. What the video and report also reveal is the repeated unwillingness of leaders (and others) within the organization and wider church to respond appropriately to disclosures of abuse, choosing to protect 'somebody' over other bodies.

How then might the church be a place of sanctuary, welcome and witness for all bodies (Westfield 2001), a place of feast not famine (Robinson-Brown 2021)? Where all bodies are cared for and celebrated as sacred (Pinn 2006; Sheppard 2022)? Where every-body is recognized and respected? Where the truth of each other's lives is shared and honoured? Where the demands of the gospel: to bear witness, challenge injustice, seek healing and reconciliation – are heard and held? How might men be part of such a church?

Divided bodies

One of the ways in which men might help create a church where all are valued is to challenge the gender binary present within much of the church's self-understanding. Since New Testament times, the church has been divided along gendered lines. As the church came to be understood as a feminine or feminized body or bride, men were placed in contrast to the church – becoming representatives of Christ in their roles as priest, leader, husband or father. Men – most especially clerical men – became the head of the church, in the process losing their bodies. The 'mother church' lost her voice – and church fathers elected to speak for her. Thus, despite its claim, the 'one, holy, catholic and apostolic church' has been shaped and led, predominantly, by men alone.

Since, for much of the church, only men have been designated apostles, women have been prevented from taking up leadership. In Roman Catholicism and other traditions, only (celibate) men are ordained as priests, to preside at the Eucharist. As Natalie Knödel (1997) notes, this is a disembodied form of masculinity, which results in a denial of the reality of sexually active, desiring bodies of any gender in the church. The hierarchical clerical structures of many churches further work to feminize the laity, rendering them passive and voiceless in the decisions of the church. Such dynamics, as Stephen Burns (2019) and others note, are profoundly problematic in how they establish unequal power and control in the life of the church.

In conservative evangelical traditions, complementarianism, a belief in male headship and female subordination, also works to restrict women from leadership in the church (Fry 2020; Barr 2021). Ordained ministry (speaking, thinking, leading) has for most of the church's history been restricted to men. While in some traditions, women are now ordained priest and elected as bishops, within many churches, women continue to be given roles that are extensions of domestic responsibilities of caring, cleaning, child care. Women's leadership and activity is often hidden, but, as Valentina Alexander (1996) observes about Black churches in Britain, women may not formally hold leadership roles but may still be influential in shaping church life.

In order for men's bodies to be recognized as part of the body of the church, and women's voices to be heard, teaching from any tradition that limits participation in the church based on gender must be challenged.

Disciplined bodies

Within and beyond the church, men's bodies are disciplined for a range of purposes: punishment; purification; and preparation.

The church has a long, unfinished history of punishing bodies: women and men drowned and burned following accusations of witchcraft or heresy; Jewish and Muslim people and communities persecuted, expelled, murdered; African people enslaved, transported, raped, broken; local peoples colonized, slaughtered, forcibly converted. A deep prejudice against the body continues to haunt the church, making all bodies subject to scrutiny and mistrust, and certain bodies particularly vulnerable. As Anthony B. Pinn notes, the church has sought to tame and subordinate Black bodies through violence and intimidation in 'a death dealing economy of discipline' (2006, p. 25). Anti-body theologies continue to shape dominant Christian traditions. A starting point (although not a simple one) for men seeking to resist such teaching would be to recognize and value their body, and the bodies around them. It is important to note here that in some Christian traditions, long-standing connections between obedience, suffering and formation, remain unexamined, resulting in support for the physical disciplining of bodies, including, for some, corporal punishment of children. Christian men may need pastoral and psychological support to engage with childhood trauma, and to consider how this has impacted their own relationship with their bodies, and their relationships with partners and children.

Second, Christian men may be encouraged to purify their body as a sign or means of faith development. The church has sought to police sexual behaviour throughout the centuries, even as permitted practices have differed. The dominant church's imposition of heterosexual marriage; its practice of confession (often overly focused on sexual activity); and its resistance to women's access to sexual and reproductive health care, reveal a concern to control sexual desire and practice. In relation to spirituality, the sexual disciplining the body through periods of celibacy 'becomes the occasion for both suppression as well as a more robust union with God simultaneously' (Crawley 2008, p. 206). As well as abstaining from sex, Christian men may also choose – wholly or during certain days or seasons such as Lent – to fast and abstain from drink and drugs. They may discipline body and soul through: periods of intense prayer in the tradition of the Desert Fathers; silent retreats, often in the Ignatian tradition, following the example of Ignatius of Loyola who drew on his previous experience as a soldier in developing his spiritual exercises; or all-night Pentecostal and charismatic gatherings that may involve preaching, teaching and sharing spiritual signs such as speaking in tongues. While such practices are followed by people of all genders, some aspects intersect with dominant models of masculinity, especially the idea of training the body and spirit. Indeed, there are some claims that younger men are attracted to more rigorous forms of discipleship, with a recent report suggesting that some young Anglican men were drawn to the more demanding liturgy of the Book of Common Prayer because of the weight of tradition it carried (French 2023).

Third, Christian men might discipline their bodies in preparation for spiritual conflict or mission activity. Many men in Britain today regularly participate in physical training at the gym, seeking to shape their bodies into a particular form or achieve targets of weight, strength or endurance. They may talk about their bodies being disciplined – punished even – through acts of endurance. Another context for disciplining the body might be within the army or other military group, where groups of men are shaped into a unit. In some Christian traditions, men's groups provide a context for shared discipleship, often encouraging each other to be spiritually, morally and sexually pure, and often seeing leadership (in church and in the home) as the natural outcome of men's discipleship (Donovan 1998). This approach is visible in conservative evangelical Christian movements, for example, *The Code Bible for Men* (2013), produced in Britain by Christian Vision for Men and The Bible Society. Men are invited to discover in the Bible, 'the lives of assassins, murderers, cowards, adulterers, street fighters and dictators ... heroes and heroines, and ordinary blokes having a go'. This version of the Bible includes 'The Code, a rule of life for men that helps them live an uncompromising Christ-centred life.' The Code (supported by study group programmes) is a list of commitments men are invited to make. These include a commitment to Jesus as 'captain, brother, rescuer and friend' to whom absolute loyalty is due; to 'keep my body fit and free from any addictions'; to 'protect the weak'; and to 'not give up'. While The Code also encourages men to treat others equally and to care for creation, the emphasis is on a discipleship shaped around a dominant model of masculinity: physical and moral strength, purity of body and loyalty to other men.

Embodied discipleship

In this last section, we explore how in their discipleship, men may be attentive to the everyday, open to learning from unexpected people and places (Leith 2021), and willing to commit to long-term habits of faithful living (Jones 2023). Such models of discipleship are in contrast with those that present discipleship as heroic and spectacular, completed by self-sufficient believers.

Dietrich Bonhoeffer's *Discipleship*, written in 1930s Germany, continues to serve as a key text for many Christians in Britain today. Often, Kristopher Norris (2019) suggests, it is read in a way that promotes a model of discipleship focused on heroism and sacrifice, of masculine courage. Such a reading can be further strengthened by uncritical (and un-contextual) engagement with Bonhoeffer's *Life Together*, written about the process of being shaped with other men into a disciplined community. Norris suggests that a more helpful model of discipleship can be found through Bonhoeffer's real-life friendships which reveal mutual dependence and responsibility across differences, and which encourage openness and vulnerability among men.

For some, discipleship may be understood as being on a journey of faith, accompanied by fellow travellers, Jesus among them. A number of hymns explore the idea of being 'pilgrims on the journey', encouraging Christians to be willing to step out in faith and to seek to follow Jesus in the world. The Methodist Church in Britain describes being a disciple as 'taking an adventure through life, taking risks, growing and learning'.

Such understandings contrast with models of discipleship that centre on grand gestures, public acts of heroism and bravery. For Amy Laura Hall (2011), what matters is being present in the day-to-day stuff of life, the messy and mundane, cooking, cleaning and caring – activities, she notes, many men may be less involved in. 'Discipleship is boring' may be the tagline here. It doesn't require great gifts or great faith but simply turning up. But of course, turning up day-after-day is how faithfulness is practised. In Nick Hornby's *About A Boy* (1999), Hall observes, the character of Will comes to understand that what he is being asked to do is simply, yet not at all simply, be present to others, particularly those who are struggling and in need. And this, she suggests, functions as an example of discipleship.

There are some connections here to Sam E. Ewell's (2021) model of gardening as discipleship. Ewell, a Birmingham-based ecotheologian and community gardener, encourages Christians to see discipleship as a journey of conversion (return?) to the body of the earth. In his experience of community gardening in inner-city Birmingham, he notes how by connecting to the earth, people are helped to connect to their bodies and the embodied lives of those around them. He explores how gardening encourages friendship and hospitality as each responds to the other. For Ewell, discipleship involves a sustained commitment to community, openness to newness and surprise and, always, a willingness to learn.

Finally, we consider what insights might be learnt about being a male disciple from the original twelve. Although women were friends and followers of Jesus, and often display the key qualities of discipleship, in the gospels, only men are called disciples. Yet is it manly to be a disciple?

Susanna Asikainen (2018) explores how the Synoptic Gospels portray the disciples as often striving for honour and greatness as men, yet being taught to embody feminized qualities such as kindness, mercy and humility. Even more, the disciples are called to be like children, enslaved people and eunuchs, to align themselves with marginalized subordinated groups. To let go of masculine qualities of power and control, to serve, and to follow another man. Indeed, Robert J. Myles (2010) rereads various encounters between Jesus and his disciples in ways that make visible the potential queerness of these relationships. Jesus is portrayed in the gospels as 'cruising the seashores of Galilee' (p. 71), inviting young men to elope with him, to leave their homes and families and form a new community.

We might conclude that the primary characteristic of discipleship according to the gospels is that it is disruptive: of social hierarchies and boundaries, of notions of honour and shame. For men, and even more so for men with privilege and power, to be a disciple of Jesus might be understood to require a letting go of status and security, a willingness to be transformed by those on the margins, a commitment to kindness, generosity, honesty over failings, limitedness and relationality.

7.2 Penetration, prescription, appropriation: A risk assessment for (white, straight) male ecclesiologists – *Al Barrett*

Introduction

Doing ecclesiology is dangerous. Whatever we mean by it, the Church – whether as relational community, institutional structure, or mystical body – has great power to both form and deform human beings, the relationships between us (both internal and external to Church), and even the relationships between humans and non-human kin [and God]. When we do ecclesiology – in writing, in spoken word, in bodily gesture and in the unspoken assumptions that shape our acting and interacting – we participate in those processes of formation and deformation (Winner 2018). When the 'we' who 'do' ecclesiology is located in positions of structural privilege – of institutional position, or of race (i.e. whiteness), class, (non-)disability, (hetero)sexuality and, yes, when 'we' are cis-gendered men – that privilege risks combining structural *power* with structural *obliviousness*: what Mary McClintock Fulkerson identifies as a 'power-related willingness not-to-see' (McClintock Fulkerson 2007, p. 17).

As one such multiply privileged (white, middle-class, non-disabled, straight) man, I am both in a position of great power to shape a local church community's lived ecclesiology (as its incumbent priest), and someone who has published ecclesiological texts that have been (apparently) read by others. This is, accordingly, my first attempt at drafting a 'risk assessment' for my ongoing ecclesiological activity – conscious of its own limitations as an exercise. As preparation for that, I draw, with necessary brevity, on examples of dangerous ecclesiology written by other male theologians – much of which, by definition, makes for disturbing reading. But these examples are offered not as straw men to comfort us – 'at least we're not as extreme as them' – but rather to reveal the dangerous pitfalls of the terrain of ecclesiology, within which harmless innocence – at least while 'we' write with structural privilege – is impossible (see Rose's, critique of idealistic 'New Jerusalem' political philosophies that refuse to engage in the constant work of attending to power, 1996, p. 17).

In what follows I seek to pay attention not just to ecclesiological *texts* (the *logos* of ecclesiology), but also to the *authors* of those ecclesiologies and their locations, characters and relationships (*ethos*); and to their *audiences* (whether actual or imagined), which tell us a lot (explicitly or implicitly) about *who* is understood to make up the Church (i.e. ecclesiology's *pathos*) (Cunningham 1991, pp. 5–6). Where such ecclesiology has been clearly abusive, I have followed the feminist methodological principle of prioritizing the testimonies of resistance and critique, rather than giving space to the words of the perpetrators themselves.

Exhibit A: Church as penetrated body

In the writings of the Roman Catholic theologian, Hans Urs von Balthasar, feminist theologian Tina Beattie reads the complementarian strand of Christian theologies of sex, 'historically accumulated over two thousand years, internalized by countless men and women in their battle against their own sexuality', as 'reach[ing] an apotheosis', coming to a climax (Beattie 2005, p. 174). And von Balthasar's theology of sexual difference and his ecclesiology are intertwined. Depending on what Luce Irigaray terms a phallocentric model, God's creative power and initiative is equated with a limited subset of heteronormative, penetrative, male sexual activity, 'so that in von Balthasar's Christology (and indeed ecclesiology) it becomes important that only a male body can represent God' (Beattie 2005, p. 164). On the other hand, when he positions human beings in general (and the Church specifically) *in relation to God*, it is to the *female* body that he turns, and to what he describes as its 'active receptivity'. In so doing, he simultaneously fixes actual women in an essentialized femininity, and disappears them from his ecclesiology entirely, both insisting on an exclusively male priesthood (representing God to humanity), and appropriating the (idealized) female body for ecclesial purposes, as that which 'offers man the signifiers he needs in order to position himself before God' (Beattie 2005, pp. 162–4).

Von Balthasar goes further, however, in reclaiming the medieval idea of the Church as *casta meretrix*, the 'chaste whore'. Drawing on what biblical scholar Cheryl Exum terms the 'prophetic pornography' of Hebrew Bible imagery, von Balthasar chastises the Church's male office-holders using metaphors of 'wanton female sexuality' and a terrifying divine violence: 'his Christ', Beattie observes, 'humiliates sinful men by casting them in the role of whores who must be raped and conquered so that he can purify them' (Beattie 2005, pp. 172–4; Exum 1996, p. 102). In the extremity of von Balthasar's language, Beattie nevertheless glimpses a ray of hope: '[i]f his work manifests the poison, it might also provide the cure ... Von Balthasar's theology brings to light a flaw that runs through the Catholic theological tradition with regard to sex' – and, we might add, wider tendencies with regard to ecclesiology. Beattie herself has done more than most theologians both to highlight von Balthasar's theological genealogy, and to propose just such creative departures. Here, her analysis serves to alert us to the ways in which male ecclesiologists can project gendered characteristics – essentialized, fantasized, even violent – onto the ecclesial body, its internal relationships, and the relationships between the Church and God.

Exhibit B: Church as penetrating body

My own theological work has engaged in depth with Anglo-Catholic theologian – and co-founder of the Radical Orthodoxy strand of recent Anglophone theology – Graham Ward, his own theological development having been influenced significantly by – and in response to – von Balthasar. As Beattie comments of von Balthasar, Ward too is in some ways helpfully explicit about the dynamics of what he names as Christian desire, and we therefore catch glimpses of his own desires, as he re-reads the Christian tradition in intentionally persuasive theological rhetoric.

Ward's Church, then, is explicitly an 'erotic community' participating in the abundant economy of Christian desire. But in a creative departure from von Balthasar's essentialized gendering, Church here is a 'multi-dimensional, multigendered' body. While Ward acknowledges that the Church is far from free of 'mistakes', 'compromises' and 'blemish', the focus of his most intense frustrations is less on the Church itself (as von Balthasar), and more on the world beyond its doors. The economy of Christian desire is in stark contrast to the 'pathological', 'sadomasochistic' postmodern 'economy of lack', and we must look to the Church, as the body of Christ, to do the theological and practical work of 'safeguard[ing] the concreteness' of genuine bodiliness and nurturing 'what is most necessary for our well-being and cosmic flourishing' (Ward, quoted in Barrett 2020, pp. 96, 107).

Ward's approach becomes problematic, however, the more his description of the relationship between Church and world settles into a fixed opposition, with the Church as the one-way channel of divine love into a resistant world. Rooted in the divine overflow, the Church is in a permanently receptive relationship to God, in order to be active in sharing God's love with the world (Barrett 2020, pp. 89–90). As I have noted elsewhere, in this understanding of the flow of divine power and the channelling role of the Church, Ward exposes himself to be bound to what indecent theologian Marcella Althaus-Reid has identified as the dominant, patriarchal logic of theology, following 'models of spermatic flow, of ideas of male reproduction which defy modern science but are established firmly in the sexual symbolic of theology' (Althaus-Reid 2000, p. 155). Here von Balthasar's phallocentric theology reappears, and is extended in Ward's missionary Church. The 'erotic community' in Ward's work '"*overspills* defined places", "*expands* ever outward", "*disseminates*" the body of Christ "through a myriad of other bodies", and "*penetrates*" even the barren wastelands and violent "no-go zones" of the postmodern city'. Significantly, in the section of Ward's work where he explicitly uses the language of the Church penetrating certain urban places, he also insists that 'Christians in these places must be hospitable', revealing the implicit assumption of a (masculine, penetrative) Church centred outside such (feminized, abjected) places, presumably in white, middle-class suburbia – and alerting us to the possible risk, especially to urban, marginalized non-church others, of a Church acting in the heat of such a potentially violent passion (Barrett 2020, pp. 125–6).

Exhibit C: Church as 'vulnerable' – a universalizing prescription

How then, we might well ask with Althaus-Reid, 'can we cool down this erection of the *logos spermatikos*' in male ecclesiologies? Her own answer is to offer two strategies: '[o]ne way is by giving privilege to the subordinated part of binary compositions, what "leather" people would call the prevalence of "bottoms" (submissive partners) over "tops" (dominant partners). The other is by trying to find the different (not belonging to the binary pair in conceptual opposition)' (Althaus-Reid 2000, p. 155). In my own work I have paid more attention to the former, seeking to reverse the one-way missiological flow so prominent in Ward's work, and advocating instead for an ecclesiology shaped by a radical receptivity to both the gifts and the challenges of those who have been othered and marginalized by the Church. As much as possible, I have sought explicitly to ground such ecclesiological rhetoric 'in a careful, relationship-specific, context-specific analysis of the multiple (and not all one-sided) power imbalances within any particular encounter between people' (Barrett 2020, p. 235).

Until early 2020, an obvious theological resource for such radical receptivity was the written and spoken work of Jean Vanier, founder of the worldwide network of L'Arche communities, where people with and without intellectual disabilities live together in mutual care. Vanier over many years had articulated an ecclesiology of interdependence, where common ground was found in a shared brokenness and vulnerability, with those who are conventionally seen as strong needing to acknowledge their dependence on the gifts and personhood of those conventionally seen as weak (as well as vice versa).

On 22 February 2020, however, L'Arche International released the findings of an independent inquiry into Vanier's conduct over three decades, including the testimonies of six adult women 'assistants' in L'Arche communities, who each reported 'that Vanier had initiated sexual relations with them, usually in the context of spiritual accompaniment', and that these relationships were 'manipulative and emotionally abusive'. As the shockwaves of this revelation spread, many of us who had been profoundly influenced by Vanier's theology found ourselves asking whether the behaviour of the theologian (in the terms of rhetorical analysis, Vanier's *ethos*) could be disentangled from the theology he articulated (his *logos*) – or whether the two were, in fact, more consonant than we had wanted to believe.

An important early response from feminist theologian Jane Barter has argued for the latter, identifying three 'heresies' in and surrounding Vanier which together made up 'a theo-politics of coercion': an instrumentalizing and spiritualizing of 'the weak' (primarily referring to disabled people, but also, at times, to women); the cult of the (male) saint; and a (quasi-Thomist) 'baptizing [of] human desire with divine intention and purposefulness' with little acknowledgment of desire's shadow side (Barter 2020). The combination of these three left Vanier in a position of huge and unchecked power, and many people around him (women especially) in positions of coerced, unchosen and theologically-underwritten vulnerability.

Vanier's advocacy of vulnerability had turned from a particular, autobiographical discovery – a 'discovery' precisely because it was made from a position of multiple privilege and power – into a universalizing prescription, which he was able to put to abusive ends. Vanier's sanctified celebrity decontextualized his words as powerfully persuasive wisdom for all; and his framing of people with intellectual disabilities as the primary other aggregated everyone else (rhetoric's *pathos*, ecclesiology's 'Church') into an undifferentiated 'we' (what the poet Michael Rosen, in a Facebook post, 9 April 2021, has recently referred to, in the context of populist nationalism, as the 'coercive grammar' of 'we all'). Vanier's abuses stand as a warning to any of us (especially we who are straight, white, male and non-disabled) who argue for receptive, vulnerable ecclesiologies from a position of multiple privilege: on whom are we – intentionally or unintentionally – urging vulnerability as part of our constructions of Church? And who, in the process, is either excluded from the 'we' of our ecclesiologies, or put at risk within them?

Exhibit D: Appropriative ecclesiology

With Althaus-Reid, alongside developing a careful, contextual radical receptivity to those subordinated and othered by white hetero-patriarchy, my own ecclesiological work has, in some places, sought to reach beyond binary oppositions to 'find the different' (to use Althaus-Reid's phrase). Feminist, womanist and queer theologians are among those who have fired my imagination that, to tweak a well-used phrase, 'another Church is possible'. Among many possible resources for ecclesiological transformation, I have reached for Nelle Morton's (1986) description of the principles and practices of 'hearing one another to speech', Mayra Rivera's (2007) theological explorations of 'transcendent touch', Rita Nakashima Brock's (1988) Christology of 'erotic power' embodied in 'Christa-community', and Linn Marie Tonstad's (2016) sketching out of an alternative imaginary grounded in the non-penetrative 'surface touch' and 'copresence' of 'clitoral pleasure' (Barrett 2020, pp. 243–4, 247–9; Barrett and Harley 2020).

For a straight, white male like me, in the paid employment of a hetero-patriarchal, colonialist institution (the Church of England, in my case, part of the national establishment), such theological resources are attractive, precisely in the fecund suggestiveness of their alternatives to the status quo. They are exciting in their edginess – especially when articulated in the accent of a privileged male, into spaces where I know they will shock and unsettle. They are, if I'm ruthlessly honest, arousing: in the embodedness, the unashamed sexiness, of their language; in their otherness to the overwhelming weight of my lived experience (both in and out of church); and in their hopeful, passionate, enlivening possibility (here I am embracing Jo Ind's (2003, p. 33) broad definition of sexuality as 'whatever turns you on').

And in that confession is both the promise and the danger of what I am describing here. Promise, because these theologies *do* embody words of life, with an ultimate horizon of all humanity and all of creation. But danger too, because these theologies are not written for me. They are not 'resources' intended to be within my 'reach', for me to deploy tactically within my own ecclesiological projects, however radical or subversive I may hope those projects will be. They are written by women (*ethos*), first and foremost *for* women, seeking resources for survival and thriving in the face of ongoing patriarchal violence (*pathos*), worked out within the context of experimental, feminist, women-centred forms of community that sometimes (but certainly not always) want to name themselves Church.

And so all the risks I have already highlighted over the course of this chapter, of men writing Church, apply to my own engagements with feminist expressions of ecclesiology:

- The risk of appropriating female embodiment for ecclesial metaphors, while distorting them through the lens of patriarchy, and eclipsing the actual bodies of women in the Church (as per von Balthasar).
- The risk of taking women's words and re-speaking them with a man's voice, thus instrumentalizing them; and/or turning specific vulnerabilities into a universal prescription, thus masking my own structural power and privilege (as per Vanier).
- The risk of invading spaces of, and conversations among, women, thus re-inscribing phallocentric theological tendencies (as per Ward).
- The risk of avoiding facing up to my own identity and complicities by seeking to hide, or be absorbed, within 'other spaces', as has been highlighted by Rosemary Radford Ruether (1992, p. 17), Carter Heyward (1996, p. 266) and others.

Working with(in) the limits of (white, straight) male ecclesiologies

Having spent most of this essay identifying the risks of (white, straight) male-written ecclesiology, what – if anything – can a (white, straight) male ecclesiologist say? Space here permits little more than brief, tentative suggestions, offered in the hope they stimulate further conversation and development:

- Practising and prioritizing radically receptive and dialogical forms of theological engagement: listening to and learning from feminist, womanist and queer theologians doing, and critiquing, ecclesiology (Pryce 1996 is an excellent example of a man taking this approach).
- Unlearning the ecclesiological tendency to 'speak of/for the whole': recognizing and embracing our own particular locatedness, limited horizons (in smaller, sub-ecclesial spaces) and partial perspective.

- Practising a more apophatic ecclesiology: learning what we can't say, or know, about the Church from here, and when we should stop talking.
- More consciously, therefore, exploring what Marcella Althaus-Reid names as a fetishist theological methodology, an 'aesthetics of the fragment' (see Rivera 2010, p. 83).
- An immersion in the growing sub-discipline of ecclesial ethnography: paying careful and self-critical attention to what we see this particular, limited expression of church as doing – and experiencing – in its embodied life, here and now – but also being profoundly attentive and receptive to descriptions of 'our' ecclesial life offered by those from others situated differently to 'us' (Scharen and Vigen 2011).
- Exploring the positive value of limits and boundaries, not as obstacles to be transcended, but as means of safeguarding against the kinds of risk identified in this piece (for a further exploration of safeguarding in the context of power-imbalanced relationships, see Barrett and Harley 2020, pp. 184–7), and as ecotones or border-zones, sites of encounter, interaction and negotiation (see Muers 2021; Nausner 2004, p. 131; Nausner 2005, p. 277; Barrett 2020, pp. 179ff; Barrett and Harley 2020, pp. 142ff).

If those of us who are straight men seeking to do ecclesiology can begin to embrace this more limited vocation as border-dwellers, then there might indeed be a place for the passionate desire that has bubbled away under our explorations here. As in any relationship of desire across structural power differentials, such encounters at the borders – between white, straight male ecclesiologists and our diverse others – must surely involve the following:

- Both naming honestly, and listening attentively to, our differently positioned desires.
- Listening for resonances, and being receptive to challenges.
- Waiting patiently for expressions of not just consent, but invitation or initiative, and taking silences, non-engagement and articulated 'No's with the weighty seriousness they require.
- Acknowledging that 'love from across the border' will always – in the 'penultimate' – be a risky, power-imbalanced, but clear-sighted 'love of enemy' (as Karen Lebacqz puts it, with necessary starkness (1990).
- Embracing an honest, ongoing accountability – both across the border, and between men – for our desires and our behaviour, including our attempts at writing and practising ecclesiology.

- Discerning and evolving practices of repentance, resistance, responsibility and reparation for the ecclesial damage that patriarchy and our own entanglements in it have wrought.
- Experimenting with modest, peripheral and radically open sub-ecclesial spaces where we men can develop the disciplines of mutual accountability, consciousness-raising, self-critical learning, and anti-patriarchal, traitorly solidarity (akin, perhaps, to Alcoholics Anonymous – and closely aligned with gatherings of anti-racist critical white theologians. As my colleague Ruth Harley puts it: 'We are drawing aside to do this work; we're not expecting anyone else to help us with it, but we refuse to close the door behind us, to close out the possibility of interruption, challenge and critique' (personal communication)).

Engaging in something like this journey, we (white, straight) male ecclesiologists might begin to imagine the possibilities not just of learning from our feminist, womanist and queer theological siblings, but also of discovering opportunities for thinking, writing and living ecclesiologies together (Barrett 2023).

7.3 Weakness and strength: living within the paradox – *Donald Eadie*

> 'Must we break, crash, in order to understand the secret of our inner being and the strength of our weakness? Does something have to break to make the sky blue?' (Kjell Walfridsson)

We live within the scary and wondrous paradox of weakness and strength. It belongs within the story of our becoming human and is embedded within the diversity, inequality and interdependence of the human family. Signs of the paradox emerge like bruised, blood-stained watermarks in the wounds and blessings of our times.

The liminal place

Friends have introduced me to the imagery and language of the liminal place and it is within these rugged terrains I want us to begin our exploration. Both as communities and individuals, we are pilgrims within the in-between times living with incompleteness, unresolvedness, a turmoil from which we may seek to hide. The liminal place contains both the possibility of desolation and the potential for profound transformation. New patterns and forms may emerge within what feels like the end times, belonging to what some call resurrection. Embrace the chaos, seek the unfolding. To have faith is to trust enough to let go and to follow within what is unfolding. It is to trust the mysterious fertility that lies buried within powerlessness, transforming our tomb into our womb.

For each of us the journey within the weakness/strength paradox is different. For some the terrain is one of loss through bereavement; for others, a breakdown in significant relationships; redundancy into unemployment; living with cancer and the effects of treatment; living with ageing; or the slow progression into the world of dementia. I have been encouraged to explore the paradox in the context of my own experience of life and I trust that the insights offered will transcend our different circumstances and find recognizable resonance within our many layered stories.

In my youth I excelled in sport, playing for the Yorkshire Public Schools teams in both cricket and hockey. I captained the Kingswood School cricket team with a personal best batting score of 101 not out, and bowling figures, 9 wickets for 56 runs. I was tall, strong and competitive. My leadership style could be likened to that of the conductor of an orchestra. After teaching Pastoral Studies in Wesley College, Bristol I became Chairman of the Birmingham Methodist District in 1987. A few years later, aged 54, I was diagnosed as having a degenerative disc disease, three major spinal operations were required leading to early retirement. There have been further periods of hospitalization: a bypass in my left leg leading to a fasciotomy; a period in a dementia ward after becoming delirious during the onset of pneumonia; a triple heart bypass and most recently, heart failure.

I am an adopted person and chose to search for my birth parents during long periods of convalescence. It continues to be a huge journey, both inner and outer, emotional and physical, enabled by my close family and a few friends. I had no information about my origins. Woven within the texture of my being there is a slow awakening to the primal letting go by my birth mother, her handing me over at birth, entrusting me into the unknown. I was placed in a nursery hotel, waiting. Living within unknowing belongs to the core of who I am, imaginings that do not go away, questioning that increases. The seeking to know within the unknown was both exhilarating and terrifying, fears and fantasies swirled. A 'fat file' was discovered with correspondence from my birth mother. In time, I learned that both my birth parents were dead. During the years that followed, more information has emerged. There have been unanticipated encounters with members of my birth father's family, and the unfolding of surprising links and connections – the mystery some call synchronicity.

My world cracked open

Within a variety of circumstances, I have experienced anxiety, fear, rage, despair, being out of control and the questioning whether I possess the will and the energy to live through processes containing so many undercurrents, not knowing where they might lead. It was within this insecurity that my world cracked open, erupting within the depths of my being, a welling up that released an out-pouring, new life breaking through. In the stripping away of so much within us that seeks to control, contain, manipulate, I felt that I was being brought nearer to the core, the heart of things.

I saw vistas I had not seen before, saw things differently, sometimes shockingly so.

I experienced a process of inner realignment, entered new depths within my humanity.

I learned the power of 'being' and the 'being-ness' of things.

I reclaimed my name, my identity.

I discovered an inner freedom, playfulness, openness which surprised, embarrassed, shocked others and also myself.

I learned to fly and also to crash land!

I joined the truth seekers rather than the truth possessors.

I discovered fresh focus, directness, straightforwardness.

I began to learn the strength to be weak, to be gentle, to let the tears flow leaving their stains on my face.

I discovered that fear can be named, traced to its source, traced and faced, we need no longer be prisoners of fear.

I learned that vulnerability lies at the heart of transformation, the place of trembling and kneeling.

These encounters belong within the terrain I want to explore, to do so honestly, without clichés, naivety or retrospective romanticism. What is the nature of the emerging life that is breaking through? Each of us seeks our own images, clothes them with our own words. Within my increasing physical and emotional limitations, I am learning to let go of old ways of managing, slowly finding new strategies, establishing new 'default positions' (a term used by my physiotherapist at the Balance Clinic, Birmingham).

I encounter an unfamiliar solidarity, unexpected companionship, surprising communion.

I discover the God of life within life.

I am learning that my painful body is God's dwelling place and home.

I experience more wonder, curiosity, gratitude, joy and humour.

I gaze and ponder more, laugh and cry, cry and laugh more.

I am learning that the broken images of myself, of God, the shattered dreams, the false assumptions of weakness and strength can all be transformed into fragments within 'the yet more glorious mosaic' (Abel E. Hendricks, in conversation in Notting Hill).

I am learning to embrace the wounds in my life and, with God's help, their becoming part of a greater wholeness.

I am walking the bumpy road from resignation to reconciliation.

I am discovering that I am held but not protected.

I am learning to offer my messy liminal place toward God, with no strings attached.

I encounter angels, angels in many forms.

We are not alone in our weakness, we need each other's openness and love

In 2020, Kjell, whose words began this reflection, died. He was my wife's cousin, growing up in the same village in the forest and lakes area of central Sweden. For many years, Kjell has been a soul friend, a mentor within the weakness/strength paradox. We met every summer, shared in long conversations. He had been a social worker until, in his early forties, he learned he had Parkinson's disease and became unable to sustain his work. Great tiredness and angst belonged to Kjell's reality, his hands shook, he propped up his head and physical movement was limited. Slowly he learned to embrace both the wonders and terrors of his solitude. Through him, I learned that what is borne through weakness, what we can be reconciled to, can become a strength that deeply touches people. The doctor encouraged Kjell to paint, despite art having been of no interest to him in his youth. Learning to use his fingers to explore the language and possibilities of colour, painting became a creative, liberating process. Kjell also began to write poetry, compose his own songs and sing them. His wife asked: 'Why is it that Kjell only discovered his remarkable creativity when he became so ill?' He was a deeply spiritual man with a profound sense of God, yet was greatly disillusioned with the institutional Church. He had a deep antipathy towards people with 'slippery tongues', strong, certain people, too sure of being the possessors of the truth. In a poem entitled 'On leaving Church', written in the spring of 1997 Kjell vented his rage, concluding with these words:

> You have been
> cheated
> little career boy
> cheated of the water
> running
> between the stones
> on a barefoot walk.
> There you must
> bend down
> cupping your hands
> to be able to drink.

The consequences of Kjell's illness were not borne alone, it affected his whole family, most of all his wife. Together they learned the interplay of strength and weakness in their relationship, loving each other, honouring each other's needs, learning a complex interdependence. 'My wife is strong but there is an obvious risk that she always has to be the one who is strong and there is no space to acknowledge her own weakness', he shared. Through them, I learned that the mystery of our humanity lies not in weakness or strength but rather their essential interplay. We live with Kjell's question, 'Must we break, crash, in order to understand the secret of our inner being and the strength of our weakness? Does something have to break to make the sky blue?'

'Tis mystery all'

Within the erupting and outpouring in the liminal place there have been fragments of ancient wisdom, lines from poems, images, stories, phrases from the scriptures and liturgies. The interacting of the fragments continues to unsettle, realign, provoke fresh wondering. The fragments have become cathartic, thresholds of disclosure, unfolding, connecting, opening up messy mysteries to be entered and explored, not explained. Here are but a few glimpses.

The story of Hagar (Genesis 16, 21) emerged, awakening curiosity, requiring attention, during the summer of 2011 when, through a blood blockage, I nearly lost the use of my left leg. It tells of an Egyptian woman enslaved in the household of Abraham and Sarah, driven into the wilderness, abandoned, desolate, shielding herself from the sight of her son's death. In her overwhelming distress, she discovers a well of water that had always been there, but she had not seen. A friend, a refugee from Afghanistan, helped me to make the connections between Ishmael and Islam, Hagar and Hajj, the well of water in the wilderness transformed into a fountain, the place of annual pilgrimage to Mecca for Muslims. She spoke of Hagar with such warm affection, as of a sister. I wondered what it would mean to remember and give thanks for Hagar.

We met Father Aloysius Pieris, a Sri Lankan Jesuit priest in Colombo, during the cease fire in the Sri Lankan civil war in 2002. One of his books lies among my fragments. He writes of the poor, powerless and rejected being chosen by God, of the weak called to liberate the strong. We are drawn beyond the traditional image of the institutional Church as the Body of Christ toward a bodily communion integrated within the suffering, dying and being raised in the drama of our shared life on this polluted planet, all humanity, all creation. This is the threshold of the paschal mystery.

For over fifty years, I have visited Mount Saint Bernard Abbey, a Cistercian monastery in the folds of Leicestershire's hills. I encounter in the deep silence a mysterious sense of presence, not located in the tabernacle above the altar but in the huge crucifix suspended so high while remaining so intimate. It has become for me a sign of the mystery of the real presence of Christ, eternally transforming within the turbulence, glory, tragedy, wonder at the heart of everything. To be drawn into the paschal journey is to belong to those who:

> stumble, fall and are continually being lifted up
> liberated to be truth seekers
> shockingly inclusive, compassionate, counted among the pain bearers
> ridiculed as subversive trouble makers
> silenced, given up as finished
> raised through the mystery of divine fertility buried within every
>   circumstance.

We began this exploration into the weakness/strength paradox in the liminal place and conclude in the testimony to vulnerability at the heart of transformation, our being drawn into eternal paradox, 'Christ crucified, the power and the wisdom of God' (1 Corinthians 1.24). These reflections I now hand over, trusting that within their limitations there will be enough to provoke more wondering, more realignment, more following. May God help us embrace our weakness as our greatest strength.

7.4 For reflection, conversation and action

1 How are men's bodies present in the body of the church? Are they present in harmful or hopeful ways?
2 Which of the different ways of talking of discipleship resonates with you? Journeying, gardening, listening, questioning, befriending?
3 What has been your experience of power and vulnerability in the church, or other institutions?

7.5 Bibliography

Adedibu, Babatunde Aderemi (2013), 'Reverse Mission or Migrant Sanctuaries? Migration, Symbolic Mapping, and Missionary Challenges of Britain's Black Majority Churches', *Pneuma* 35, pp. 405–23.
Alexander, Valentina Elinor (1996), '"Breaking Every Fetter?": To What Extent has the Black-led Church in Britain Developed a Theology of Liberation?' PhD thesis, Coventery: University of Warwick, http://wrap.warwick.ac.uk/36220 (accessed 27.10.24).
Althaus-Reid, Marcella (2000), *Indecent Theology: Theological Perversions in Sex, Gender and Politics*, London: Routledge.
L'Arche (2020), 'Summary Report from L'Arche International', 22 February 2020, https://www.larche.org/documents/10181/2539004/Inquiry-Summary_Report-Final-2020_02_22-EN.pdf/6f25e92c-35fe-44e8-a80b-dd79ede4746b (accessed 27.10.24).
Asikainen, Susanna (2018), *Jesus and Other Men*, Leiden: Brill.
Barr, Beth Allison (2021), *The Making of Biblical Womanhood: How the Subjugation of Women Became Gospel Truth*, Grand Rapids MI: Brazos Press.
Barrett, Al (2020), *Interrupting the Church's Flow: A Radically Receptive Political Theology in the Urban Margins*, London: SCM Press.
Barrett, Al (2023), 'Praying Like a White, Straight Man: Reading Nicola Slee "Between the Lines"', in Ashley Cocksworth, Rachel Starr and Stephen Burns (eds), *From the Shores of Silence: Conversations in Feminist Practical Theology*, London: SCM Press, pp. 173–92.
Barrett, Al and Harley, Ruth (2020), *Being Interrupted: Re-imagining the Church's Mission from the Outside*, London: SCM Press.

Barter, Jane (2020), 'A Theo-Politics of Coercion – the Heresies of Jean Vanier', *rupert's land news blog*, 4 May 2020, https://rupertslandnews.ca/a-theo-politics-of-coercion-the-heresies-of-jean-vanier (accessed 27.10.24).

Beattie, Tina (2005), 'Sex, Death and Melodrama: A Feminist Critique of Hans Urs von Balthasar', *The Way* 44(4), pp. 160–76.

Cunningham, David (1991), *Faithful Persuasion: In Aid of a Rhetoric of Christian Theology*, Notre Dame: University of Notre Dame Press.

Donovan, Brian (1998), 'Political Consequences of Private Authority: Promise Keepers and the Transformation of Hegemonic Masculinity' *Theory and Society* 27(6), pp. 817–43.

Ewell III, Sam E. (2021), 'Discipleship as Gardening: Reflections on Ecological Conversion', in Andrew Hayes and Stephen Cherry (eds), *The Meanings of Discipleship: Being Disciples Then and Now* London: SCM Press.

Exum, J. Cheryl (1996), *Plotted, Shot, and Painted: Cultural Representations of Biblical Women*, Sheffield: Sheffield Academic Press.

Fesenmyer, Leslie (2018), 'Pentecostal Pastorhood as Calling and Career: Migration, Religion, and Masculinity Between Kenya and the United Kingdom', *Journal of the Royal Anthropological Institute* 24, pp. 749–66.

France-Williams, A. D. A. (2020), *Ghost ship: Institutional Racism and the Church of England*, London: SCM Press.

French, Daniel (2023), 'Why Millennial Men are Turning to the Book of Common Prayer', 2 May 2023, *Spectator Life*, https://www.spectator.co.uk/article/why-millennial-men-are-turning-to-the-book-of-common-prayer (accessed 26.10.24).

Fry, Alex (2020), 'Postfeminist, Engaged and Resistant: Evangelical Male Clergy Attitudes Towards Gender and Women's Ordination in the Church of England', *Critical Research on Religion* 9(1), pp. 65–83.

Groody, Daniel G. (2017), 'Cup of Suffering, Chalice of Salvation: Refugees, Lampedusa, and the Eucharist', *Theological Studies* 78(4), pp. 960–87.

Hall, Amy Laura (2011), 'Naming the Risen Lord: Embodied Discipleship and Masculinity', in Stanley Hauerwas and Samuel Wells (eds), *The Blackwell Companion to Christian Ethics*, Oxford: Blackwell, pp. 92–4.

Heyward, Carter (1996), 'Men Whose Lives I Trust, Almost', in Stephen B. Boyd, W. Merle Longwood and Mark W. Muesse (eds), *Redeeming Men: Religion and Masculinities*, Louisville: Westminster John Knox Press, pp. 263–72.

Ind, Jo (2003), *Memories of Bliss: God, Sex, and Us*, London: SCM Press.

Jones, Ian (2023), 'Five Time Perspectives on Christian Discipleship', *Practical Theology* 16 (1), pp. 55–68.

Lebacqz, Karen (1990), 'Love Your Enemy: Sex, Power, and Christian Ethics', *Annual of the Society of Christian Ethics* 10, pp. 3–23.

Leith, Jenny (2021), 'Radical Democratic Discipleship: Encountering the Spirit in Civic Life', *Political Theology* 22(6), pp. 510–26.

Mann, Rachel (2021), 'The Power of the Personal: The Promise and Challenge of Transgender Identities for Christian Discipleship', in Andrew Hayes and Stephen Cherry (eds), *The Meanings of Discipleship: Being Disciples Then and Now*, London: SCM Press.

McClintock Fulkerson, Mary (2007), *Places of Redemption: Theology for a Worldly Church*, Oxford: Oxford University Press.

Morton, Nelle (1986), *The Journey is Home*, Boston: Beacon Press.

Muers, Rachel (2021), 'Theology and (its) Borders: Hearing Shibboleth', unpublished paper, SST annual conference 2021.
Myles, Robert J. (2010), 'Dandy Discipleship: A Queering of Mark's Male Disciples', *Journal of Men, Masculinities and Spirituality* 4(2), pp. 66–81.
Nakashima Brock, Rita (1988), *Journeys by Heart: A Christology of Erotic Power*, Eugene: Wipf & Stock.
Nausner, Michael (2004), 'Homeland as Borderland: Territories of Christian Subjectivity', in Catherine Keller, Mayra Rivera and Michael Nausner (eds), *Postcolonial Theologies: Divinity and Empire*, St Louis: Chalice Press, pp. 118–33.
Nausner, Michael (2005), 'Subjects In-Between: A Theological Boundary Hermeneutic', unpublished PhD thesis, Madison NJ: Drew University.
Norris, Kristopher (2019), 'Toxic Masculinity and the Quest for Ecclesial Legitimation', *Journal of the Society of Christian Ethics* 39(2), pp. 319–38.
Pinn, Anthony B. (2006), 'Sweaty Bodies in a Circle: Thoughts on the Subtle Dimensions of Black Religion As Protest', *Black Theology. An International Journal* 4(1), pp. 11–26.
Pryce, Mark (1996), *Finding a Voice: Men, Women and the Community of the Church*, London: SCM Press.
Reddie, Anthony G. (2021), 'The Quest for Catholicity: An Anti-Racist Model of Discipleship', in Andrew Hayes and Stephen Cherry (eds), *The Meanings of Discipleship: Being Disciples Then and Now*, London: SCM Press.
Rivera, Mayra (2007), *The Touch of Transcendence: A Postcolonial Theology of God*, Louisville: Westminster John Knox Press.
Rivera, Mayra (2010), 'Corporeal Visions and Apparitions: The Narrative Strategies of an Indecent Theologian', in Lisa Isherwood and Mark D. Jordan (eds), *Dancing Theology in Fetish Boots: Essays in Honour of Marcella Althaus-Reid*, London: SCM Press, pp. 79–94.
Robinson-Brown, Jarel (2021), *Black, Gay, British, Christian, Queer: The Church and the Famine of Grace*, London: SCM Press.
Rose, Gillian (1996), *Mourning Becomes the Law: Philosophy and Representation*, Cambridge: Cambridge University Press.
Ruether, Rosemary Radford (1992), 'Patriarchy and the Men's Movement: Part of the Problem or Part of the Solution?', in Kay Leigh Hagan (ed.), *Women Respond to the Men's Movement: A Feminist Collection*, San Francisco CA: Pandora, pp. 13–18.
Scharen, Christian and Vigen, Anna Marie (2011), *Ethnography as Christian Theology and Ethics*, London: Continuum.
Sheppard, Phillis Isabella (2022), 'Reclaiming Incarnation in Black Life: Black Bodies and Healing Practices in Womanist Pastoral Care', *Journal of Pastoral Theology* 32(2–3), pp. 202–22.
Tonstad, Linn Marie (2016), *God and Difference: The Trinity, Sexuality, and the Transformation of Finitude*, London: Routledge.
Westfield, N. Lynne (2001), *Dear Sisters: A Womanist Practice of Hospitality*, Cleveland OH: Pilgrim Press.
Winner, Lauren (2018), *The Dangers of Christian Practice: On Wayward Gifts, Characteristic Damage, and Sin*, New Haven CT: Yale University Press.

8

resistant bodies (pastoral care)

8.1 Introduction

In this chapter, we consider how men within Christian communities might develop their capacity for healing and recovery in the face of trauma, illness and loss. By resistant bodies, we do not mean to encourage men to be resistant to change, pain or emotion. On the contrary, we hope the term might indicate resistance to unhelpful gender roles and relationships, to inauthenticity, inequality and injustice. In this introductory section, we explore what forms of pastoral care might help men practise self-care in solidarity with people of diverse genders. We ask how pastoral care might help men integrate diverse life experiences into their identity and journey of discipleship. As Armin M. Kummer observes, 'Pastoral care must ... help care seekers to deconstruct life-limiting gender codes, and create gentle opportunities for 'undoing gender" (2022, p. 116).

In the second part of the chapter, Raj Bharat Patta explores the intersection of caste, gender and other identity markers both in India and among British Indian communities from his Dalit perspectives, and calls for justice and solidarity within church and society. Currently serving as a recognized and regarded minister in the Methodist Church in Britain, Raj is interested in decolonial subaltern public theology and supporting multi-faith communities.

Following Raj, we hear from Karl Rutlidge, a Methodist Minister and trans man currently based in London. He has a PhD in Mathematical Physics and is currently studying for a second doctorate exploring God, physics and time. Karl reflects on the experiences of transmasculine people, suggesting that they offer a model of how to resist binaries and transgress barriers. He argues that transmasculine bodies reveal the diversity of human identity, offer insights into the work of solidarity, and bear witness to the struggle to be authentically oneself.

Developing a model of pastoral care for men

Within patriarchal societies, (certain) men's needs are prioritized, from being given more food or access to education when resources are short, to receiving higher pay, privilege and power. Yet, aspects of dominant models of masculinity threaten men's health and wellbeing. Men are encouraged to enact violence and participate in risk-taking behaviour. The same models discourage men from expressing and responding appropriately to a range of emotions; and from forming intimate relationships in which they can be vulnerable and receive support. It would seem that men are often ill practised at caring for themselves – and, as we explore in this and other chapters – are not encouraged to see caring as a task for men; despite the reality that many men are carers, both in professional and pastoral roles, and as informal carers of friends and family.

The World Council of Churches calls on churches to see health and healing as central to their mission, defining health as a 'dynamic state of wellbeing of the individual and society; of physical, mental, spiritual, economic, political, and social wellbeing; of being in harmony with each other, with the material world, and with God' (Makoka 2021, p. 2). It notes how churches can encourage people to care for themselves and others, to provide accurate health information, to work with health professionals to provide care, and to advocate for the transformation of unjust structures and practices that cause illness and suffering. Among the areas of healthy living that the WCC encourages local churches to support, a number are particularly relevant to pastoral care of men: eating well (more fruit and vegetables); active lifestyles; reducing alcohol and stopping smoking; and developing good mental health.

This introductory section draws on the work of Mark Pryce (1993, 1996) and Delroy Hall (2021), two British theologians who have sought to identify models of pastoral care for men which critically engage with shifting understandings of masculinity, bodies and power. It also makes use of the work of Emmanuel Lartey (2003 [1997]) and Bonnie Miller-McLemore (1999), both of whom extend understanding of pastoral care beyond the expected focus on healing, sustaining, guiding and reconciling, to include resisting, empowering and liberating. In the remainder of this introduction, we explore a series of transitions that such pastoral care might encourage men to make: deception to truth-telling; harm to healing; isolation to relationality; dominance to solidarity.

Deception to truth-telling

In his book, *Mask Off*, JJ Bola calls on the unmasking of a rigid, restricted masculinity that 'renders boys and men incapable of dealing with their emotions, and turns them into aggressors and dominators of other people, whether intentionally or otherwise' (2019, p. 9). For Bola, what is needed is a process of truth-telling. Suggesting that there is only one way to be a man results in deception; instead, Bola calls for recognition of the 'beautiful variations of manhood and masculinity' (2019, p. 73). In the 1990s, Riet Bons-Storm wrote how women's accounts of their experiences and feelings often went unheard because they did not fit within the accepted narrative. In the same way, many men are unable to share their experiences because they do not align with a dominant story of what it means to be a man. Telling the complex, changing truth about one's life takes courage and support. Pastoral care for men thus involves:

> making room for men and the realities of their lives. It means listening to them, patiently and attentively. It means listening to life narratives with a fine ear for cracks and discontinuities. It also means identifying life-limiting masculinity codes and deconstructing them jointly and gently. Finally, it means looking not only at the cracks, but also through the cracks – for the light. It means preparing the way for change and transformation. (Kummer 2022, p. 124)

Being able to be honest about hopes and fears, mistakes and misgivings, to share the reality of life, is fundamental to health and wellbeing. Indeed, Emmanuel Lartey (2003) suggests that the process of re-evaluating identity, belonging and relationships is empowering. While it may seem odd to suggest that men who already possess power need empowering, many men have been trained to silence their stories and hide their true selves. What such men need is the strength and support to step away from power gained through deception, towards the ability to live out a truer life story.

Delroy Hall notes the importance of retelling not only individual stories but those of marginalized communities also. Hall comments: 'Reclaiming history can, for the Black man, demonstrate the vitality and strength his ancestors possessed as a people' (2021, p. 133). For men from marginalized communities and contexts, to tell stories of collective struggle, resistance and achievement is significant for their own sense of wellbeing. Thus, Robert Beckford (2004) argues that churches need to recognize and celebrate the radical faith and struggle for freedom undertaken by African and Black people throughout history.

Harm to healing

Male violence takes place in public and private spaces, and is directed against people of all genders, including other men. Men often struggle to see themselves as victims, but men are more likely to experience violence, especially in public spaces. Men fight friends and strangers to establish social hierarchies, bond as a peer group, defend their own or the honour of others, to gain respect. In short, to perform dominant forms of masculinity.

Marginalized men are at increased risk of violence due to inequality and discrimination, directed at individual people or communities (UK Government 2023). In addition, they face increased risk of poor mental health, homelessness, drug and alcohol dependency. Despite significant legal and cultural changes over the past decades, homophobia and transphobia continues to impact on queer men's health and wellbeing, resulting in denial, discrimination and violence. In Britain, Black and Brown men are at risk of racially motivated violence. Writing in response to gang violence within Black communities in Birmingham, Robert Beckford (2004) noted a systemic lack of care for young Black people, who must negotiate everyday racism, economic exploitation, and an internalized sense of inferiority. Several decades later Delroy Hall (2021) observes similar patterns of discrimination and inequality. Hall notes how Black people carry the trauma of enslavement, colonialism and racism. 'Black men', Hall observes, 'are simultaneously sexualized and exoticized by White women and White gay men, and are the targets of extreme violence by White men' (2021, p. xii). Like Beckford, Hall notes how such violence spreads the '"dis-ease" of self loathing' among Black men (Hall 2021, p. xii).

How might the church help men move away from violence, directed against others or themselves? How might the church support male survivors of violence? Pastoral care can provide a supportive space for men to share emotions and explore generational and lived trauma. It can encourage men to find non-violent ways to express emotions and negotiate relationships. In addition, many local churches offer practical support to marginalized men (as well as women and non-binary people). Churches provide space for support groups designed to reduce drug and alcohol dependency, such as Alcoholics Anonymous. Churches and church members often are key to providing shelter and care for men and women who do not have secure housing, including through using church buildings as night shelters. Men are at higher risk of suicide than women and churches and church members are active in support of the Samaritans, CALM (Campaign Against Living Miserably) and other suicide prevention groups. In addition, the church must work to be in solidarity with marginalized men who experience violence due to their ethnicity, colour, sexuality, class or other identity marker. Here the church has often been part of the problem and will need to repent of its racism, homophobic and classist past and present, renounce toxic theologies and rediscover new ways of imagining all people. Men from evangelical traditions, might find helpful here Danny Brierley's recent book *To Inclusion and Beyond* (2024).

Isolation to relationality

Dominant models of masculinity serve to disconnect men from their emotions, resulting in a poor sense of self and lack of ability to form healthy relationships (Paterson and van Ommen 2022). Men and boys struggle with anxiety and depression, exacerbated by the belief that 'real men' do not experience such failings. The result is that they often suffer alone. How might churches help men recognize and explore their emotions? Summarizing the work of two German pastoral theologians, David Kuratle and Christoph Morgenthaler, Armin Kummer (2019) suggests that churches need to help men deconstruct dominant masculinity codes which encourage men's independence, strength and wildness. Many of the ways in which churches have sought to connect with men, have served to perpetuate models of masculinity that, while seeming to encourage emotion, do so in a restrictive, predetermined way. Men can express emotions of anger and pain, with other men, but only in order to become more 'manly' not in order to become more authentically themselves. It is therefore critical for churches to support men to be self-compassionate, to recognize the reality of their lives, to be open to emotions, and to be willing to work with others (Paterson and van Ommen 2022).

Second, churches can support men through encouraging critical friendships among men, perhaps through men's discipleship groups (Pryce 1993). Friendship is the quintessential model of male relationality. Honoured by Greco-Roman culture, friendship was seen as a good in itself by early Christian theologians such as Augustine. It was seen as a relationship between equals that was freely entered, open to growth and inclusive. However, the friendship model is not without limitations.

Men's friendship groups can result in uncritical support of each other and a failure to seek the well-being of people of other genders, or of men outside the friendship group. Authentic true friendship requires critical questioning, holding people to account and encouraging people to be their true self. JJ Bola argues that: 'Men ... must hold themselves and other men accountable for the ways in which they benefit from male privilege and patriarchy, and actively work to change that: ultimately, men must work to change other men' (2019, p. 112).

Dominance to solidarity

To bear witness to the truth of one's life is to come to see what needs to change. Pastoral support can help men acknowledge the ways in which they benefit from patriarchal structures and learn to resist and disrupt dominant patterns of masculinity and male privilege. Pryce (1993) and Yun (2016) note how much of the discourse within pastoral theology has been about the costs of masculinity and men's vulnerability, and insufficient attention has been given to critiquing male privilege and power. Over time, men have amassed economic, political, social, cultural power over the bodies of others, and control over institutions and discourse. Liberation for men who benefit from the status quo, can only emerge alongside liberation of others, including marginalized men.

Can a loss of power and privilege be liberating for men? Lartey (2003) describes the need for pastoral support to enable a person to be liberated from dependence (e.g. alcohol dependence) and oppression, including internalized oppression (self-hatred and ambivalence of self-worth). For Lartey, liberation begins with raising awareness of the causes of oppression. Thus, we suggest pastoral support should enable men to articulate male dominance and how they benefit from it, which will differ according to other aspects of their identity. It should enable men to see how they are already, and might further resist male dominance, in their own actions and relationships, and in challenging wider social structures and culture.

If men are to move from a position of dominance to one of solidarity, they must begin by listening to the experiences of women, people of diverse genders and other marginalized men (Pryce 1996). Where in the church might men be encouraged to step back and make space for others? How might men be helped to stand alongside other people and learn from them? We conclude this introductory section with a statement made by men gathered at the World Council of Churches Women's and Men's Pre-assembly in 2013:

There are many forms and practices of masculinity and we have not honoured the diversity of men. We express our solidarity with men who have been outcast because of their sexual orientation and suffer from the violence of homophobia ... We call on all the Churches to dare to work together towards just gender relations, promoting the life of peace and justice this will bring. Together as men and women we will play our part in being churches that are places of solidarity, affirmation and welcome of a new society of justice and life for all.

8.2 Conversations on Dalit masculinities –
Raj Bharat Patta

Having been born 'outside' the caste system, and living as a 'Dalit' male, my positionality in terms of my gender roles has oscillated between privilege and powerlessness. I have enjoyed a certain privilege because of my maleness, but at the same time have experienced powerlessness because of my 'outcaste' identity. Even in the UK, I am asked by members of the Indian diaspora to which caste I belong. Such inquiries are subtle yet revealing, for it is the dominant caste person whose obsession about caste identities result in persistent enquiries as to which place I come from and what my family name is. On establishing these details, they come to know that I am an 'outcaste' Dalit person. The conversation stops. My Dalit masculinity has always resulted in an experience of vulnerability.

Charu Gupta explains that in India, the high caste heterosexual Hindu male is considered to be at the top of religious and caste hierarchies, and thus this model of masculinity becomes the norm and is assumed to be natural (2016, p. 111). Gupta further explains that in the discourses around masculinity, Dalits are either invisible or othered. So, any examination of Dalit masculinities is an attempt to contest multiple hierarchical structures – particularly the hegemonic masculinity affirmed by the dominant caste male – for such an attempt exposes the nexus of masculinity and power. Patricia Hill Collins' exposition on hegemonic masculinity is helpful in understanding this notion in the context of caste dynamics. Collins observes that 'hegemonic masculinity reflects a cognitive framework of binary thinking that defines masculinity in terms of its difference from and dominance over multiple others. This dominance is the strength of hegemonic white masculinity' (2006, p. 82). So, in the context of caste systems, hegemonic masculinity is formed by the ideologies of caste as well as notions of gender, sexuality, class, age and race.

A discussion on Dalit masculinities must be about striving for dignity, rights and social justice for Dalit men, whose masculinity has been socially disempowered and dismantled by casteist ideologies. Caste ideologies have attributed inferiority, docility, stupidity, and emasculation to the construction of Dalit male bodies. But Dalits contest caste and gender dynamics by affirming their place in society through resistance of, and protest against, dominant narratives. Inter-caste marriages serve as an example of anti-caste assertions, offering resistance to the norm, though a number of Dalit men have become victims in the pursuit of such transgressive love.

The study of masculinity remains marginal within conversations of race and ethnicity (Edwards 2006, p. 64), even more so in the context of caste and Dalit-ness. Therefore, any serious engagement with Dalit masculinities must interrogate Dalit 'emasculation', Dalit feminism and the nexus of caste and patriarchy.

In the patriarchal societies of colonial and post-colonial India, although Dalit men have been seen negatively within dominant discussions of masculinity, at times they have colluded with such narratives, miming aspects of hegemonic masculinity in order to assert control over Dalit women in the domestic sphere. Dalit men's collusion with hegemonic masculinity has been visible also where Dalit men have been employed by dominant caste groups to participate in communal violence, fighting for their dominant caste landlord's interests. Gupta, on mapping the construction of Dalit masculinity in the context of colonial India comments:

> Theirs (Dalit masculinities) often became a non-conformist masculinity, acquiring a dynamic vitality that transformed the mundane into the sublime, and made the routine spectacular ... Dalit masculinity was not a stable category, but responsive to its cultural, historical, social and political embeddedness. Ultimately, its construction was neither fully cohesive nor entirely innocent, since gender identities were themselves immutable. (2016, p. 165)

Locating 'inferior' and 'excluded' Dalit masculinities within Christian theology requires investigation into complex dynamics of power: on the one hand, power exercised by casteist masculinities over Dalit masculinities and on the other, moments of collusion with 'hegemonic masculinities'.

Allow me to share a real-life incident of a young Dalit martyr, who was killed by the dominant caste community for falling in love with Divya, a girl from their community. 'Honour killings' of Dalit male bodies have become prevalent, with violence and torture serving as the tools of oppression. 4 July 2013 was a day stained with blood: the day of the brutal murder of Ilavarasan, a young Dalit man. It was a day when Ilavarasan and his love were defeated by the cruel forces of caste and patriarchy (Krishnan 2013). This young Dalit man was tortured and killed, all because he fell in love with a girl from a dominant caste. Dalit male bodies are routinely humiliated, mutilated and murdered in an attempt to diminish Dalit masculinity.

William Cavanaugh's explanation of torture as anti-liturgy in the context of an oppressive state regime in Chile is instructive. Cavanaugh observes:

> Torture may be considered a kind of perverse *liturgy*, for in torture the body of the victim is the ritual site where the state's power is manifested in its most awesome form. Torture is liturgy – or, perhaps better said, 'anti-liturgy' – because it involves bodies and bodily movements in an enacted drama which both makes real the power of state and constitutes an act of worship of that mysterious power ... The liturgy of the torture room is a *disciplina arcani*, a discipline of the secret, which is yet part of a larger state project which constitutes outside the torture chamber itself. (1998, p. 30)

In the Indian context, poor vulnerable Dalit male bodies are tortured. In their subalternity, exhibited as powerlessness, they become easy targets of oppressive state and caste regimes. Where is the space for Dalit male tortured bodies in the body of the Church? These bodies represent the crucified broken body of Christ. For in the tortured Dalit male bodies, the crucified body of Christ becomes visible, offering solidarity and hope for liberation.

For Cavanaugh, the tortured bodies of the victims challenge the Church's 'communal body', causing 'the disappearance of the visible body of Christ' (1998, p. 30). The anti-liturgy of torture pushes the body of Christ into spaces characterized by violence: the violation of human rights, humiliation, threat, exclusion and killings. In response, Cavanaugh proposes the Eucharist as the means by which the body of Christ is reimagined, re-envisioned, re-appropriated and re-enlivened.

Allow me to share the story from Genesis 4.1–16, where we read of the brothers Cain and Abel divided by their occupation, one as a tiller of land and the other as a keeper of sheep. According to an ancient story of creation told across India, humans were created to live as siblings but fell prey to the mischievous devices of Manu who classified communities based on their occupations, thus creating the caste system. In the biblical story, Cain could be seen to represent a certain dominant caste, for he was the keeper of sheep, an occupation that is placed higher up on the caste pyramid. Abel could be seen as an agricultural labourer, located way down the pyramid. When they both brought in their offerings, Abel's offering was accepted but Cain's was not. Cain therefore turned against his brother, taking him into his field and killing him.

Cain today represents the dominant caste community who cannot accept that their sibling community, the Dalits, celebrate love wherever it is to be found, including across the boundaries of caste. It was not that Cain's offering was not accepted but it was because Abel's offering was accepted that the saga of violence began. The same operating system works today in hegemonic masculinities of caste. Cain killed his brother Abel in the field but did not take responsibility for his violent actions. When God asked: 'Where is your brother Abel?' Cain replied: 'I do not know; am I my brother's keeper?' we hear this same reply today. In the context of Ilavarasan's murder, the dominant communities reply: 'I do not know; am I my brother's keeper?'

But God's response presents a challenge: 'What have you done? Listen, your brother's blood is crying out to me from the ground!' The blood of Ilavarasan and other Dalit men call out to God from the railway track. Like Abel, Ilavarasan could not speak aloud to bear witness to the truth that he was tortured because of caste prejudice, that he was murdered by casteist dominant forces. But his blood cried out to God. When so many Abels are still being slaughtered on the altars of caste, God speaks in judgement to Cain, and faith communities need also to demand justice.

Abel's male body represents Dalit male bodies. In contrast, Cain exhibits a hegemonic masculinity, in which occupation and power intersect, and which is expressed through violence. A transformative model of masculinity must address the anti-liturgy of torture by dismantling the power inequalities among those who were once siblings.

Elaine Graham says that 'public theology's objective must be to speak about God-in-the-world, *to* the world' (2004, p. 399). In the context of the torture of Dalit male bodies, public theology must speak about the crucified body of Christ and, in so doing, seek to redeem all tortured bodies. Unlike the anti-liturgy of torture, where identities and relationships are fixed through violence and control, in the Eucharist, all bodies are celebrated. The Eucharist therefore serves as a ground to celebrate transformative identities and to contest oppressive structures, which include hegemonic masculinity.

8.3 Transformative solidarity across people of diverse genders – *Karl Rutlidge*

In 2014, I had the joy of taking part in a panel discussion at the Greenbelt festival exploring how the Church (in the broadest sense) needs to recognize that LGBT+ people are not issues, but gifts. This theme has lost none of its urgency in the intervening period, as conversations around masculinity continue to develop. In particular, despite frequently being treated more like issues to be solved than real human beings to be loved, transmasculine people have particular gifts to bring to this table, not least in terms of solidarity across diverse gender identities.

From the outset, it is not hard to see why these gifts are too often overlooked by church and society. To use the language of gender identity is to set sail into choppy waters, in an environment and social context that is frequently hostile towards transmasculine people. The 'T' in LGBT+ stands for 'trans', which is an umbrella term used to describe those whose gender identity is not the same as, or does not sit comfortably with, the sex assigned to them at birth (usually based on their genitalia). To be a transmasculine person is to present oneself (through appearance, clothing, etc.) in a way that may generally be perceived as male, and it thus encompasses trans men (like me) and non-binary people who adopt a more 'stereotypically masculine' presentation.

To speak of gender identity at all and to accept that this could be in conflict with sex assigned to one at birth is to recognize, as the vast majority of feminist thinkers do, that despite how they are frequently used, the terms 'sex' and 'gender' are not in fact synonymous, and that the latter is multi-dimensional and complex. The *Genderbread Person* is one helpful model (Killermann 2017), which incorporates three interrelated factors that shape how a person might understand and express their gender. Here, we call these the biological, ontological and social dimensions of gender:

- Biological: includes both primary (genitals, chromosomes, hormones) and secondary (voice pitch, body shape and features, facial hair) sex characteristics.
- Ontological: a person's inner sense of their gender identity, which is not simply a feeling but, as Judith Butler describes it, an 'indispensable' existential reality (Jones 2021).
- Social: how one is perceived in social interactions, based upon secondary sex characteristics and presentation/behaviours in relation to gender norms in that historical and cultural context.

As the 2021 Census was the first to ask about trans identities, and as the question was voluntary, it is difficult to put a precise figure on the proportion of the UK population who experience, or have experienced, some degree of mismatch between the biological and ontological aspects of who they are, which in turn impacts profoundly on the social dimensions of life and one's ability to flourish and affirm oneself in the world (Jones 2021). However, estimates suggest this figure is around one per cent, and as the internationally recognized standards of care make clear, trans people cannot be 'cured' by psychological 'conversion therapies' (WPATH 2012). Instead, human flourishing in this context points towards a 'triangle of liberation':

- Ontological-Biological: Bringing a person's body into line with their gender identity, with the potential to impact both primary and secondary sex characteristics. This might involve access to hormonal and/or surgical interventions, but not necessarily.
- Biological-Social: Addressing social perceptions based on gender norms and expectations, and breaking down the gender binary to stop discrimination against anyone who is (or thought to be) gender non-conforming.
- Ontological-Social: Harmonization of how the person is perceived with their gender identity, which includes their presentation (name, clothes, hair, mannerisms) and requires overcoming the deeply problematic assumption that 'biology is destiny'.

Despite this, opposition to the validity of gender identity as a concept and to the authenticity of trans people's experiences has come from both self-defined 'gender critical feminists' (Pearce et al. 2020), and conservative Christian thinkers such as the political theologian Oliver O'Donovan. For the latter, to attempt to modify one's appearance or expression of gender is to deny the limitations that come with having sexed bodies: 'To know oneself as body is to know that there are only certain things that one can do and be, because one's freedom must be responsible to a given form' (O'Donovan 1982, p. 15). In short, then, 'biology is destiny' (Jones 2021).

Such perspectives arguably fall into the dual trap of treating appeals to human biology as if they are independent of a historical and cultural framework through which meaning is constructed, and failing to acknowledge the complexity and diversity that this subject illuminates. Claims that intersex people are in some way 'erroneous' or 'incomplete' for failing to fit neatly into a narrow binary understanding illustrate how this 'reading' of human bodies is not neutral (Carrera-Fernández and DePalma 2020). It also ignores inconvenient facts, such as how Greco-Roman culture saw gender as about social performance as much as, if not more than, physical anatomy (Loughlin 2007, pp. 115–17).

In this vein, as Carrera-Fernández and DePalma (2020) explain by drawing on Butler's seminal work *Gender Trouble* (1990), 'sex is normative, rather than simply descriptive', resulting in societal norms that determine which 'gestures and behaviours' are considered acceptable, and which are regarded as 'transgressive', based upon the sex assigned at birth. In particular, the notions of masculinity and femininity that prevail in western cultures are deeply intertwined with 'hegemonic heterosexuality', reinforced both through legal frameworks and policing by individual people and communities, including the Church – often in the name of defending the nuclear family.

What this means in practice is that 'society does in fact define gender by sexual orientation', so that masculinity is identified with 'male dominant heterosexuality' and femininity with 'passive submissive heterosexuality'. Fear of being branded homosexual or queer 'maintains rigid gender roles', in which distinctions are drawn between 'real men' and 'real woman', on the one hand, and deviants who risk censuring (and even violence) by not conforming to these categories, on the other (Mollenkott 2001, p. 72). I vividly remember first encountering this dynamic as an eleven-year-old, when I was called a 'dirty lesbian' by a younger boy who insisted that football was for boys only; another classmate of mine, who hated football, enjoyed sewing, and who was a sensitive soul, was subjected to merciless homophobic bullying simply for being himself.

To be trans within this framework is to be seen as dangerously subversive, by crossing the boundary between the two 'boxes' into which all people are supposed to fit, and pointing instead to a spectrum of possibilities for sex and gender. Misogyny, homophobia and transphobia are therefore symptoms of the same underlying disease, which severely limits the possibilities for human beings as embodied creatures. Into the mix, we might also add 'hegemonic masculinity', itself built upon an understanding of what it means to be a male which reinforces damaging binaries (Muesse 2002, pp. 4–5) harming men, women and non-binary people alike.

The net result for trans people has been the politicization, pathologization and problematizing of our bodies. Controversy over trans women's continued access to gendered spaces such as public toilets exemplifies how an 'emotive politics of fear' has sought to exclude, to minimize the very real danger to them in such spaces, and to uphold the relative privilege of those who conform to the above framework (Jones and Slater 2020, pp. 164–6). Moreover, only in very recent history has 'gender dysphoria' (the medical term used to identify mismatches between ontology and biology) ceased to be classified as a mental illness, and many of the same arguments made in the 1980s against gay men (including accusations of defying biological reality) are being dusted down and employed against trans people. We are hence viewed less as human beings made in God's image, and more as debatable 'issues'.

When transmasculine people are mentioned at all (we are usually rendered invisible in the repetitive 'debates' about trans lives), it is in notably misogynistic terms – as silly women, who cannot possibly know our own minds and hence need to be protected from ourselves, or as confused lesbians who are being 'erased' by predatory trans activists. However, despite this, transmasculine people are not issues for either church or society to 'solve', but gifts to both as interrupters to the flow and as embodied resisters of the pressure to conform to hegemonic masculinity.

For Barrett and Harley (2020), the Church needs to move beyond economies of 'counting', focused on growing that which can be quantified, and economies of 'giving out' that often fail to acknowledge power dynamics underlying the desire to provide, perform and/or possess. Instead, it needs to learn to embrace the interruption to its flow which comes from 'receiving from the outside', embracing gifts that are 'uncomfortable, unsettling, challenging' alongside the visibly 'beautiful, delightful, life-giving', so that the previously unnoticed might be revealed, treasured, and encouraged (pp. 128–31). This chimes with Baker's emphasis (2014) on the 'gift of not fitting in' to established approaches to church life that pioneers bring, and which it must learn to embrace in order to grow. Like the Syrophoenician woman whose feisty interruption expanded Jesus' horizons (Mark 7.24–30), so embracing the gift of transgressive transmasculinity has potential to be liberative across boundaries and to be part of building effective coalitions to work towards social justice for all (Faye 2021).

What does this mean in practice? Well, there isn't room to develop everything we might say in depth, but some of the uncomfortable gifts the Church and wider society might receive from transmasculine people if our resistive bodies and stories were valued relate to our 'triangle of liberation', as explored in the following paragraphs.

Transmasculine bodies, by virtue of the diversity of choices made in reconciling one's biology with ontology, defy straightforward classifications. In particular, as only a few trans men select to undergo phalloplasty, we challenge the reduction of what it means to be a man to his penis. Moreover, this diversity reminds us both of the beautiful kaleidoscope seen when the mystery of bearing the *imago Dei* is conceived in terms of relationship and community (rather than as offering theological justification for treating biology as destiny), and of the vitality of womanist theologian Jacquelyn Grant's observation in *White Women's Christ and Black Women's Jesus* (1989) that Christ's significance is in his 'ability to become universalized', and to 'empathize across borders' as God Incarnate (Bohache 2008, p. 134).

In no small part due to the lack of visible role models, many transmasculine people who grew up in the era of Section 28 transitioned (reconciled the ontological, biological and social) when they were older, and thus have experienced first-hand the forensic scrutiny to which women's and girl's bodies are subjected, and the realities of male privilege. Hence, they are well placed to stand in solidarity with feminist movements, alongside inspiring feminist allies to continually examine their own implicit assumptions and unconscious prejudices (Phipps 2021).

As Connell argues persuasively (2020), colonialism enforced gender hierarchies, and inflicted damaging models of masculinity on colonizer and colonized alike, manifesting themselves in the continuation of oppressive Victorian laws criminalizing homosexuality, for example. Given the racism also inherent in the anti-trans movement (Kayama 2020), we discover yet another instance of overlapping prejudice, and the need for solidarity across liberation movements. It isn't always easy to put this into practice, however, tensions between finding common ground and addressing community-specific issues can manifest themselves, and having experienced oppression oneself doesn't mean one cannot also be complicit in oppressing others.

Transmasculine bodies may carry scars from surgeries, such as mastectomies, that have led some to describe them as 'distorted' or 'mutilated'. However, Jordan's recognition that Christ's crucifixion body – which in apparent ugliness points towards the 'unspeakable beauty of God' and 'subverts our ordinary bodily aesthetic' (2007, pp. 288–9) – challenges conventional notions of beauty and wholeness, offering an intriguing possibility. Could transmasculine bodies open up an as-yet-underappreciated window onto the beauty of Christ on the cross? My scars remind me of the lifelong struggle for authenticity which characterizes human experience, but also of what it is to know oneself as an utterly beloved child of God, held in the loving embrace of the Christ whose vulnerability and powerlessness overcome evil, and liberate from shame.

In these senses and others, transmasculine bodies are resistant bodies, and thus gifts to the Church and society alike, even if both as yet find them uncomfortable.

8.4 For reflection, conversation and action

1 What is your experience of offering or receiving pastoral care or other forms of support? How might men be encouraged to see themselves as both care-givers and care-receivers?
2 How might people of diverse genders and identities be in solidarity with each other, both in the church and in wider society?
3 What scars do you carry, and how do they remind you of your struggle for authenticity?
4 How might you be attentive to your own need for self-care? Alongside your existing support networks, some organizations you may find helpful are: the Samaritans, the Campaign Against Living Miserably (CALM), Stonewall, HOPE not hate and the Open Table Network.

8.5 Bibliography

Baker, Jonny and Ross, Cathy (2014), *The Pioneer Gift*, London: Canterbury Press Norwich.
Barrett, Al and Harley, Ruth (2020), *Being Interrupted: Reimagining the Church's Mission from the Outside In*, London: SCM Press.
Beckford, Robert (2004), *God and the Gangs. An Urban Toolkit for Those Who Won't be Sold Out, Bought Out or Scared Out*, London: Darton, Longman and Todd.
Bohache, Thomas (2008), *Christology from the Margins*, London: SCM Press.
Bola, JJ (2019), *Mask Off. Masculinity Redefined*, London: Pluto Press.
Bons-Storm, Riet (1996), *The Incredible Woman: Listening to Women's Silences in Pastoral Care and Counseling*, Nashville TN: Abingdon Press.
Brierley, Danny (2024), *To Inclusion and Beyond: Evangelical and Affirming LGBTQ+ Relationships and Equal Marriage*, New York NY: Staten House.
Butler, Judith (1990), *Gender Trouble: Feminism and the Subversion of Identity*, New York NY: Routledge.
Carrera-Fernández, María Victoria and DePalma, Renée (2020), 'Feminism Will be Trans-inclusive or it Will Not Be: Why do Two Cis-hetero Woman Educators Support Transfeminism?', *The Sociological Review* 68(4), pp. 745–62.
Cavanaugh, William T. (1998), *Torture and Eucharist: Theology, Politics and the Body of Christ*, Oxford: Blackwell Publishing.

Collins, Patricia Hill (2006), 'A Telling Difference: Dominance, Strength and Black Masculinities', in Athena D. Mutua (ed.), *Progressive Black Masculinities*. New York NY: Routledge, pp. 73–98.

Connell, Raewyn (2020), 'Men, Masculinity, God: Can Social Science Help with the Theological Problem?', *Concilium* 2020/2, pp. 13–24.

Edwards, Tim (2006), *Cultures of Masculinity*, London: Routledge.

Faye, Shon (2021), *The Transgender Issue: An Argument for Justice*, London: Allen Lane.

Graham, Elaine (2004), 'Public Theology in an age of "Voter Apathy"', in William E. Storrar and Andrew Morton (eds), *Public Theology in the 21st Century*, Edinburgh: T&T Clark, pp. 385–403.

Gupta, Charu (2016), *The Gender of Caste*, Washington: University of Washington Press.

Hall, Delroy (2021), *A Redemption Song: Illuminations on Black British pastoral theology*, London: SCM Press.

Jones, Charlotte and Slater, Jen (2020), 'The Toilet Debate: Stalling Trans Possibilities and Defending "Women's Protected Spaces"', *The Sociological Review Monographs* 68(4), pp. 160–77.

Jones, Owen (2021), *Feminist Icon Judith Butler on JK Rowling, Trans Rights, Feminism and Intersectionality*; https://www.youtube.com/watch?v=tXJb2eLNJZE (accessed 27.10.24).

Jordan, Mark D. (2007), 'God's Body', in Gerard Loughlin (ed.), *Queer Theology: Rethinking the Western Body*, Oxford: Blackwell, pp. 281–92.

Kayama, Erni (2020), 'Whose Feminism is it Anyway? The Unspoken Racism of the Trans Inclusion Debate', *The Sociological Review Monographs* 68(4), pp. 61–70.

Killermann, Sam (2017), *Genderbread Person Version 4.0*, www.genderbread.org (accessed 27.10.24).

Krishnan, Rajan Kurai (2013), 'Ilavarasan: At a Deadly New Junction of Caste and Electoral Politics', Kafila, 16 July 2013, http://kafila.org/2013/07/16/ilavarasan-at-a-deadly-new-junction-of-caste-and-electoral-politics (accessed 26.10.24).

Kummer, Armin (2019), 'Reforming Pastoral Care: Male Pathologies, Spirituality, and Gender-Specific Pastoral Care', *Reforming Practical Theology: The Politics of Body and Space*, International Academy of Practical Theology, Conference Series 1, pp. 29–36.

Kummer, Armin M. (2022), 'Cracks and Care: Pastoral-theological Reflections on the Gender Implications of the Covid-19 Pandemic', *Journal of Pastoral Theology* 32(1), pp. 116–31.

Lartey, Emmanuel Y. (2003), *In Living Color: An Intercultural Approach to Pastoral Care and Counseling*. 2nd edition, London: Jessica Kingsley.

Loughlin, Gerald (2007), 'Omphalos', in Gerald Loughlin (ed.), *Queer Theology: Rethinking the Western Body*, Oxford: Blackwell Publishing, pp. 115–27.

Makoka, Mwai (ed.) (2021), *Health-Promoting Churches: A Handbook to Accompany Churches in Establishing and Running Sustainable Health Promotion Ministries*, Geneva: World Council of Churches Publications.

Miller-McLemore, Bonnie J. (1999), 'Feminist Theory in Pastoral Theology', in Bonnie J. Miller-McLemore and Brita L. Gill-Austern (eds), *Feminist and Womanist Pastoral Theology*, Nashville: Abingdon, pp. 77–94.

Mollenkott, Virginia Ramey (2001), *Omnigender: A Trans-Religious Approach*, Cleveland, Ohio: Pilgrim Press.
Monrose, Kenny (2020), *Black Men in Britain: An Ethnographic Portrait of the Post-Windrush Generation*, London: Routledge.
Muesse, Mark (2002), 'Don't Just Do Something, Sit There: Spiritual Practice and Men's Wholeness', in Philip L. Culbertson (ed.), *The Spirituality of Men*, Minneapolis MN: Augsburg Fortress.
O'Donovan, Oliver (1982), *Transsexualism and Christian Marriage*, Nottingham: Grove Books.
Paterson, Bill and Van Ommen, Leon (2022), 'Mindfulness, Masculinity and Liturgy: A Conversation Between Bill Paterson and Léon Van Ommen', *International Journal for the Study of the Christian Church* 22(3), pp. 230–51.
Pearce, Ruth, Erikainen, Sonja and Vincent, Ben (2020), 'TERF Wars: An Introduction', *The Sociological Review Monographs*, 68(4), pp. 3–24.
Phipps, Alison (2021), *Me, Not You: The Trouble with Mainstream Feminism*, Manchester: Manchester University Press.
Pryce, Mark (1993), *Men, Masculinity and Pastoral Care*, Edinburgh: Contact Pastoral Limited Trust.
UK Government (2023), 'Official Statistics Hate crime, England and Wales, 2022 to 2023 second edition', https://www.gov.uk/government/statistics/hate-crime-england-and-wales-2022-to-2023 (accessed 27.10.24).
World Council of Churches (2013), 'Statement From the Men Gathered for the WCC Women's and Men's Pre-assembly', 29 October 2013, Busan, Republic of Korea, https://www.oikoumene.org/resources/documents/statement-from-the-men-gathered-for-the-wcc-womens-and-mens-pre-assembly (accessed 27.10.24).
World Professional Association for Transgender Health (2012), *Standards of Care for the Health of Transsexual, Transgender, and Gender-Conforming People*, 7th edition, https://www.wpath.org/publications/soc (accessed 27.10.24).
Yun, Myounghun (2016), 'From Hegemonic to Post-Patriarchal Manhood in the Korean Context: A Theological and Psychological Analysis', PhD thesis, Nashville TN: Graduate School of Vanderbilt University.

9

receptive bodies (liturgy)

9.1 Introduction

In much Christian liturgical practice, men are assumed to be the ones who lead worship, even if changing gender identities mean that 'the Christian tradition has produced and been enriched by its own slippages and subversions of seemingly dominant scripts' (Berger 2011, p. 31). Within western influenced traditions, male preachers and presiders often perform masculinities marked by authority: directing and disciplining congregations. But such models of masculinity raise questions for men sitting in the pews, standing to praise. How do men listen to a sermon without appearing less knowledgeable? How are men led by the spirit to move, speak and pray in new ways? How are men able to receive the body of Christ and still retain their bodily integrity? In short, what does it mean for men to be receptive bodies in the worship space?

Lewis R. Gordon (1996) asks if it is even possible for men, especially white heterosexual men, to worship. If worship requires openness to God, is worship possible for men, whose bodies are often considered closed and complete? Gordon suggests that, through fear of being penetrated by God, white men have claimed divinity for themselves. How then might men recognize their incompleteness before God, and be open to receive the gifts of the spirit and be transformed?

This introductory section explores these questions in conversation with a number of male liturgists who have been shaped by feminist, queer and postcolonial perspectives. To help us in our explorations, we turn to the work of Brazilian Anglican liturgist, Jaci Maraschin. Maraschin indicates ways in which certain forms of worship might work to subvert dominant understandings of masculinity, which are interwoven in much white, western liturgical practice. Maraschin offers a vision of worship as fundamentally playful, embodied and emotional: 'it has no aim beside itself and it gives pleasure' (2009, p. 164). Worship should involve the body in all its fullness, and while not irrational, should be celebrated as a 'non-sense activity' (p. 165), with no instrumental logical use. As an embodied activity, worship should not be dominated by the word or text (as is true of dominant white Protestant traditions), a move that Maraschin suggests reveals a desire to control the liturgy. Understood in this way, worship appears to be profoundly at odds with dominant models of masculinity that emphasize reason, control and production. Maraschin's work makes visible some of the tensions explored in this chapter between different approaches to worship and different understandings of what it means to be a man today.

In the second part of the chapter, Simon Sutcliffe offers an imaginative reflection exploring ways of knowing, being and worshipping as a man. He considers how to make space for the voices, experiences and insights of others as a leader of worship, but even more than that, how to be transformed through the experience. Simon is a white cis heterosexual man. A Methodist presbyter, he is completing doctoral research exploring appropriate pedagogies for facilitating theological literacy among lay adults, particularly how commitment to environmental justice informs his pedagogical approach.

Men's bodies in worship

'If there is one underlying theme in the manifold and complex ways in which gender intersects with sacred space, it might be this: Anxieties and constraints surround the presence of gendered bodies across a whole range of sacred spaces' (Berger 2001, p. 65). While women's bodies have come under particular scrutiny, in dominant patriarchal Christian traditions – which honour minds not matter, souls not skin, bones and flesh – all bodies are suspect.

Within Roman Catholic worship, David Torevell observes a shift away from the body towards the mind. Writing from Liverpool, he argues that this reflects modernity's 'masculine' prioritization of rationality over 'the sensual and emotional dimensions of bodies' (1997, p. 383). According to dominant understandings of masculinity, Torevell suggests, to become a man is an ongoing and fragile process, which requires 'rising above' one's body. We might ask whether this observation holds true for Pentecostal forms of worship which are marked by embodied out-of-body experiences, but in ways that might be experienced as empowering of the worshipping body. Writing from the USA, Anthony B. Pinn (2006) explores how in Black church worship, unlike many white dominated spaces, Black bodies are visible and freed, Black voices shout out and are heard. This is a form of resistance. Moreover, Pinn argues that the intensity and power of the encounter between worshippers and God is revealed in bodies marked by sweat. For Pinn: 'Perspiration becomes a marker of engagement in the life of the spirit, demonstrated through, for example, dancing in the spirit or preaching hard' (2006, p. 21). To recognize the many moving bodies present in worship, the experiences, memories and desires they hold, and the relationships between them, is vital. Torevell calls for embodied worship, which makes space for mystery, even chaos. Writing from a Methodist perspective, Gary Hall similarly notes the need for 'congregated bodily presence and collective intention' in worship (2008, p. 289).

Leading as men

In a context of widespread clergy abuse, Stephen Burns (2020) argues that the dynamics of worship need to be reshaped and the authority of the worship leader revised. Worship is too often understood as a form of submission: to the moral demands of the preacher, the authority of the church, and, ultimately to God. Submission that results in domination, obedience that silences questions, order enforced through threat – such patterns of relationship need to be resisted (Cotter 2000; Carvalhaes 2015). Alongside feminist and postcolonial liturgists, Ash Cocksworth (2018) thus proposes a move from submissive postures of prayer, such as kneeling, to standing in prayer, as was often the practice in the early church. He describes this as a standing before God, against injustice, and in solidarity with others. Gary Hall (2008) argues that worshippers need to be enabled as collaborators rather than restricted to the passive role of audience. Worship and discipleship are shared responsibilities, which require mutual accountability and support. This requires worship leaders who are able to step back and make space for a more eclectic approach to worship, that reflects the diverse body of the church (Lyons 2008). In addition, Al Barrett (2010) calls for both presider and congregation to be open to interruption and improvisation, especially from those at the margins of the community. Indeed, as Cláudio Carvalhaes (2015) observes, the people have always interpreted liturgy in their own ways, subverting and expanding what is offered them.

Preaching and speaking as men

Alongside playing music, baking or flower-arranging, preaching is one of the few activities within the life of the church for which one can win a competition. The final three *'Times' Book of Best Sermons*, published annually from the mid-1990s to the early 2000s, each feature a picture of a man on the cover. This is unsurprising since, for a long time, preaching was very much a male activity. Even after many denominations allowed women to preach, high-profile politically influential preachers have tended to be men.

In many church traditions present in Britain, preaching is no longer an activity exclusively performed by men. Yet, in some ways, preaching continues to be informed by values and practices closely associated with dominant models of masculinity. A preacher is expected to speak authoritatively: offering a definitive interpretation of a biblical passage; or answer to a moral dilemma. A sermon may be described as powerful or hard-hitting. The ability to tell a joke, to captivate listeners with humour or conviction is praised. In many churches, the preacher occupies a dominant position – speaking from a pulpit high above the congregation, or mic'd up, prowling around the sanctuary. The preacher controls time and space, demanding the attention of the congregation. There is rarely an opportunity in the service for the congregation to question or challenge the preacher. Rather than perpetuate a model of preaching that colludes with dominant models of masculinity: authoritative, forceful (violent even), seeking influence and praise, men might work to develop more reflective, tentative, and invitational modes of preaching.

Beyond the sermon, we might also consider how God is named in worship. Here we note the contributions of several British male liturgists. Brian A. Wren (1989) suggests that exclusively male language for God is particularly problematic in worship settings since worshippers are invited to be open to God, and are not encouraged to offer critique. Wren sees the diversity of the biblical tradition, its playful, dialogical nature, as encouraging – demanding, even – of faith communities to, to quote one of his hymns, 'Bring Many Names'. Moreover, Wren argues for the constant subversion and unsettling of images of God – so that nothing is fixed or static. Jim Cotter's re-writing of liturgy and psalms offer new insights into familiar prayers; his version of the Lord's Prayer begins, 'Eternal Spirit: Life-Giver, Pain-Bearer, Love-Maker'. As part of the Wild Goose Worship group, John Bell (often with Graham Maule) has been a significant shaper of liturgy and hymnody in the Church of

Scotland. Bell's work is marked by honesty about the vulnerability and complexity of human life, the need to honour diversity, and a passion for justice. Despite such creative efforts, and the wider shift towards inclusive language for humans evident in some recent revisions to hymns and liturgical texts, Stephen Burns (2022) notes that male imagery for God persists in many official liturgies.

A further observation: in some traditions, the culture of worship does not allow for sorrow, doubt or failure. Under the influence of dominant models of masculinity, which prioritize self-control, lament may be seen as unmanly. The public expression of pain, sorrow, grief, often without a sense of agency or resolution, may be perceived as problematic. The lack of lament in many white middle-class churches is a denial of the reality of human experience (Brueggemann 1986). And, as Pauline E. Muir's (2018) research into a Black Pentecostal megachurch in London makes visible, praise and prosperity traditions in Black Pentecostalism can also work to prevent the expression of lament. In contrast to the polished performance of praise prevalent within certain church traditions, Gary Hall (2008) argues that worship must make space for complex, uncomfortable feelings. A challenge for men who lead worship, then, is to be attentive to the need for expansive language in speaking of God and the recognition of complex, diverse human lives. In addition, as Selina R. Stone (2023) explores, there is a need for churches to make space for anger and lament over social injustice, something that, Stone notes, is a feature of socially engaged Black Pentecostal churches, as they bring right worship and action together.

Presiding as men

How might we understand the bread and wine, the body and blood of Christ in relation to the bodies of men?

The question of who is able to preside at the Eucharist is deeply marked by gender. Roman Catholic and Eastern Orthodox churches do not permit women to be ordained to the priesthood. They argue that since the priest must represent Christ at the table, only men's bodies are able to preside over the body of Christ. Christ's maleness is seen as intrinsic to his priestliness and his sacrifice (Starr 2021). Hence it would seem that the question of how the bread and wine relate to the bodies of men has already been resolved: only men can preside over a ritual that is transformative of both the elements and the congregation. Even in those Protestant and reformed denominations where women preside, women's bodies continue to be understood by some as polluting, capable of nullifying the power of Christ's body (Jagger 2023).

Writing from an Episcopal tradition, Bryan Cones (2017) challenges such gender-based restrictions. He notes the continued insistence in some traditions that 'the gender of the presider, or at least the physical bodily characteristics that ground most male gender performance must match those presumed of Jesus' (Cones 2017, p. 129). The presider 'appears to "play" Jesus' – and this continues even with the ordination of women and non-binary people to presbyteral or priestly ministry, since they also are required to inhabit a role conceived of as male. Yet for Cones, it is not the presider but the whole assembly of worshippers who act as both Christ and the church. This is the body of Christ.

Beyond the question of presidency, eucharistic practices can function to either reinforce or interrupt dominant models of masculinity. Donald Eadie (2008) described the Eucharist as transforming the gathered people into the mysterious body of Christ. For Eadie, to receive the body of Christ requires being both physically open-handed, and spiritually open to gift, grace and generosity. Once again, the focus is on receptivity.

Following in the footsteps of Bartolomé de las Casas, liberation theologians from diverse contexts have connected the Eucharist with the hunger for justice (Jagessar 2015). In *My Faith as an African* (1988), Jean-Marc Éla questioned how the church can celebrate the Eucharist when many are hungry. To gather around the table requires attentiveness to the whole community; to share in the body of Christ generates questions about the sharing of resources. At the centre of the Eucharist are physical bodies and their physical hunger. Éla further questioned the requirement that the Eucharist must be celebrated with bread made of wheat and wine of grapes, even in contexts where local grains are uprooted in favour of cash crops and where alcohol consumption is culturally problematic. Éla's observations make visible how worship can replicate or disrupt unjust structures.

Beginning also from questions of violence and injustice, William T. Cavanaugh (1999, 2002) suggests that the Eucharist gathers and sustains community, in contrast with globalization, consumerism and repression which fragment and isolate. In times of injustice, members of the body of Christ suffer with each other and with Christ, and the reality of such solidarity is present in the Eucharist. For Cavanaugh, by consuming the Eucharist, the individual is consumed into the body of Christ. Such a focus on community is again at odds with the individualizing tendencies of dominant models of masculinity.

In contrast, Christopher Grundy argues that, rather than disrupt dominant models of masculinity, the Eucharist 'colludes with the social construction of masculinity and the maintenance of male privilege' (2003, p. 20). Drawing on the work of Marjorie Procter-Smith and Pamela Cooper-White, Grundy observes parallels between the symbolic violence of the Eucharist and the physical violence enacted against women's bodies. During the Eucharistic celebration, Jesus' body is 'torn, poured, handed out, and consumed' (Grundy 2003, p. 13). Each member of the congregation participates in this violence, but Grundy suggests that for men, such ritual violence reinforces a violent masculine identity and mode of being, whereby other people can be objectified and used for their benefit. Once again, then, we see the responsibility of both presider and people to shape just, inclusive, non-violent liturgies and to be similarly shaped by their work. As Cláudio Carvalhaes (2015) observes, liturgy must be the work of the people, not work not done on behalf of – or to – the people.

9.2 Worship: composting male epistemologies and other knowings – *Simon Sutcliffe*

This contribution is, what Donna Haraway calls, speculative fabulation, a term that develops Saidiya Hartman's (2008) concept of critical fabulation. It is not historically true. It's a verbatim account of a make-believe supervision session. Supervision in the Methodist Church is now a required component of being an ordained minister. It offers a space for a supervisee to reflect and explore a particular aspect of their ministry. After many attempts at writing this piece, I chose this form of presentation because I find it the most appropriate way of demonstrating my journey over the last few years. My hope is that it not only offers a commentary on how I understand the relationship between masculinity and worship, but also an insight into the emotional trajectories of a man trying to figure out what it means to be a man. This is not a record of a real conversation, it is fabulation and we 'fabulate, in order not to despair' (Haraway 2016, p. 130).

A FABULATED VERBATIM

Supervisor: Hi Simon, good to see you. Have you got everything you need for our session today?

Simon: Think so.

Supervisor: Good. How would you like to begin?

Simon: Maybe a time of silence?

Silence

Supervisor: Thanks Simon. Have you thought about what you would like to bring to supervision today?

Simon: I have. I've been thinking about my leading of worship recently and particularly what that means for me as a white, hetero, cis, ordained male.

Supervisor: OK, so why do you think this is important to bring to supervision? Why now?

Simon: Good question ... I've become painfully aware of my positionality and I'm not sure if that has a negative or positive impact on the worship I lead. As you know I've got plenty of teenage kids around me and during the covid lockdown they were ever present which gave lots of opportunity for chats (and arguments). I started to realize then that my inherited understandings of sex, sexuality and gender were out of sync with theirs. I'm a working-class northern kid thrust into a middle-class world. They were constantly challenging my inherited assumptions. I was already aware of these assumptions – I've worked in higher education and been exposed to a lot of feminist and queer theology and critique – but these conversations shifted it away from 'theory' into a grounded, personal experience. I went to bed on a night thinking: 'My kids hate me; they think I'm a dinosaur!' In fact, I'll be honest, it affected my mental health.

Supervisor: So, are you wanting this conversation to be about your relationship with your kids? You mentioned worship before.

Simon: No, it's about worship, but those conversations prompted it. There's also been a lot of stories in the news over the last few years too. The story that impacted me the most was the rape and killing of Sarah Everard. It renewed a wholescale movement of women protesting and demanding the safety of women in the streets and for society to take more seriously male violence towards women. That had a real impact on my daughter and stepdaughters. It also led to a twitter war between the #AllMen and the #NotAllMen keyboard warriors! Which prompted some deep thinking about many aspects of my life and ministry, especially worship. I'm struggling to work out if this was something that a few men did, and simply a question of re-education and punishment, or, if this was something I was complicit in. Is there something at a much deeper level at work here that I cannot see?

Supervisor: Do you think there is something deeper?

Simon: Yes – I do. I was appalled at the police treatment of the women who held a vigil for Sarah Everard in London. Particularly because this came less than a year after police officers abused the dead bodies of Bibaa Henry and Nicole Smallman who were murdered in June 2020. Despite everything that had been said about violence and misogynistic attitudes towards women, the police handled the vigil appallingly. At first, I thought this is just another case of men mistreating women and then I realized, in one of the news interviews, that at the time the head of the Metropolitan Police was a woman. It got me thinking …

I wondered if this wasn't simply about men's poor behaviour but a much more insidious problem that had to do with the way in which our public institutions are formed and held accountable. Is this not about behaviour (the way people act) but about epistemology (the way people think)? Was the problem with the police force less about what they did, and more about the principles and ethos of an institution that are derived from male (and probably white, cis, hetero male) ways of knowing and understanding the world? I then started to see it everywhere: my wife works for another public institution and often complains that it is an 'old boys' club'; and then there was the cabinet minister who was sacked because he breached covid rules and not because he was caught kissing a woman colleague he had seniority over.

Supervisor: I notice your tone of voice has changed. You began this session talking slowly and calmly. You now seem to be angry. Is that something you have noticed?

Simon: I do feel angry. Although I'm not sure what I'm angry at. Clearly the behaviour of these men and institutions makes me cross, but I think I'm angry at the hopelessness of it all. Maybe I feel guilty that I somehow, unwittingly, participate and contribute to this stuff.

Supervisor: So, you've explained how you got to feeling like this, but can I bring you back to your opening sentence – what has this to do with your leading of worship?

Simon: I'm worried that when I lead worship I embody the very thing that makes me angry. I'm worried that even though I try to say the right thing (I guess some might call that 'political correctness gone mad') those words are betrayed by my lack of awareness about my own epistemology. I read a book once by Donna Haraway where she wrote something that hasn't left me alone. She says that she learnt from a British social anthropologist called Marilyn Strathern that it 'matters what thoughts we use to think thoughts'.

> It matters what matters we use to think other matters with; it matters what stories we tell to tell other stories with; it matters what knots knot knots, what thoughts think thoughts, what descriptions describe descriptions, what ties tie ties. It matters what stories make worlds, what worlds make stories. (Haraway 2016, p. 12)

Do you see what I mean? I'm worried that I might be part of the problem when I want to be part of the solution, because of something so deep within me that I don't even know it's there. What if the thoughts I use to think thoughts with are helping to justify a society built on male epistemologies? What if the site of worship becomes another platform for a man to confirm the same prejudice and bias I'm so suspicious of?

Supervisor: It's starting to be a bit clearer now, but I think I still want to push you on 'why worship?' What is it about you, as a white, hetero, cis, ordained male, leading worship that troubles you?

Simon: I suppose it could be a problem in all aspects of my life, but I feel it more acutely when planning and leading worship. I try to lead worship as collaboratively as possible depending on the church, but I know, after nearly 30 years of preaching and leading worship, that for that hour on a Sunday I am seen as a leader and an influencer. I guess my question is 'how do I use that privileged position to challenge, rather than facilitate, a world built primarily on male epistemologies?'

Supervisor: So, do we have a question to work with? Is that the question you want to explore here?

Simon: Yes – I think it is.

Supervisor: So how do you want to explore that question?

Simon: Firstly, I want to run through some of my failed attempts at answering it over the last 12 months.

When I was a tutor at a theological college the staff team encouraged students to use inclusive language in worship. I remember reading Gail Ramshaw's brilliant essay on *The Gender of God* (1990) and recognized my own constrained use of metaphor and language about God and faith. She helpfully points out that by using only male language about God we lose a whole swathe of inferences about the character and nature of God that we might gain through using a broader spectrum of language. So, I remain attentive to my language – but it doesn't seem quite enough because it only addresses practice. Obviously, my practice is likely to flow from my epistemology, but it doesn't deal with the source. It doesn't deal with what I embody.

Supervisor: It sounds like you've read a lot of feminist theology, has that influenced your thinking about worship?

Simon: Actually, I've not read nearly as much feminist, queer, or Black theology as I should have. Most of my library is written by western males. But I have read enough to have my thinking challenged. Another strategy I use to try and help me plan and deliver worship is to bring in the voices of theologians who are not western males and allow them to speak into the worship themselves. So not only am I attentive to my language I am also attentive to my sources. I try and ask which voices I'm not hearing when I'm reading my Bible, preparing my sermon, choosing hymns and selecting prayers. But again, it doesn't seem to quite scratch where I'm itching. It doesn't deal with me – it just deals with my content.

Supervisor: Simon, I'm starting to sense an uncomfortable feeling here. Are you? whereabouts in your body are you holding all this? Where do you *feel* this?

Simon: ... I feel it in the pit of my stomach. It makes me feel nauseous. I feel guilty for being born a male and then I feel angry that the world pushes me to this. It's as if I'm fighting the #AllMen – #NotAllMen battle within myself. Maybe that's why I tried another strategy to deal with this that didn't quite work. I became really interested in the notion that gender is constructed. Years ago, I read a book by Israeli historian Yuval Noah Harari called *Sapiens: A brief history of humankind* (2015). His major theme throughout the book is that *myths* are what enable human society to operate and function. For him, gender is one of those myths. I began to wonder if part of my responsibility in worship is to debunk the myths of gender, but I ran into two problems. Firstly, for Harari, religion is also one of those myths that enables humans to cooperate and form society. It felt disingenuous to be trying to dismantle one myth while upholding another as truth. More importantly, his idea that gender was a constructed reality relied on the premise that *sex* was a fixed reality. From listening to my trans and intersex friends I now don't believe that determining sex is as simple as knowing your genetic makeup.

Supervisor: It sounds like you've been on quite a journey. Do you want to recap where you think we've got to?

Simon: I began by recognizing that my inherited assumptions about what it means to be a male have been challenged both by a younger generation and by events reported in the media. I came to a realization that what was at stake was the role of my 'male' epistemology and those masculine epistemologies that inform so much of our society. In worship I tried to offer something different by being attentive to my language, attentive to the voices I draw upon and by recognizing that my masculinity might be considered a myth worthy of discrediting – but in the end none of these strategies seemed to work.

Supervisor: That sums up your journey so far – so where do we go from here?

Simon: I'm not sure, I guess that's why I brought it into supervision ...

Supervisor: Do you mind if I make a suggestion?

Simon: Sure.

Supervisor: If we were to bring someone else into this conversation to help you reflect on it further, who would you invite? It can be anybody alive or from history, real or fictitious.

Simon: ... I'm not sure. The problem with inviting someone from the Bible or from the Christian tradition is that I fear that they might be bound up with the same epistemologies that I am trying to unearth. They might end up justifying my own bias.

Supervisor: Can I make another suggestion?
 I've noticed that the only person you have mentioned who has offered you an insight into what is going on here is Donna Haraway and her quote about it mattering what thoughts think thoughts. What would happen if we invited her into this supervisory space? Could she help?

Simon: She might well have something to contribute – although I don't think she'd appreciate the invite. She does not have much time for what she calls the 'sky gods and their minions'.

Supervision: Let's assume she accepts the invitation – what might she add to this conversation at this point?

Simon: Her book *Staying with the Trouble* (2016) is fascinating. She creates a whole new world to live in with new language and concepts (she calls it worlding). Her main argument is to think about the way in which humans and other-than-humans might live and die well together. I got the sense from the book that she isn't simply advocating a new ecological strategy but rather a new way to inhabit the world. It's what feminist scholar Karen Barad might call *Onto-epistemology* (a way of being and knowing).

Supervisor: Ok – and does this new way of inhabiting the world have anything to offer to this conversation?

Simon: It might ...
  She uses the word *sympoiesis* a lot. She often uses it as a corrective to the word *autopoiesis*. She's keen to emphasize the interconnectedness of life on this planet and that while we might think of ourselves as *autopoietic*, self-determining, self-making, and generally self-forming; we are only able to live because we work with other species to live and die on this planet. Bacteria are a classic example for humans: some bacteria need us to survive, but we also need them. I said earlier that I'm becoming much more aware of my positionality, especially in worship, but *sympoiesis* (the fact that I am not a work of my own making but a work of collaboration and participation) reminds me that my positionality is negotiated. Even though I embody my own sense of what it means to be a male, my maleness is not just of my own making.

Supervisor: So how might that help you in worship?

Simon: Another word Haraway uses a lot is *compost*. Which she relates to an old proto-Germanic and English word *guman* which is a predecessor, of sorts, of the word *human*. She never articulates why she prefers to call humans *guman*, but I sense it's because she wants to think of the human pre-myth, before we invented the imaginations of gender and sex. She reminds us that the biblical word *adam* finds its roots in the word *adamah* which means ground or earth and then she conflates all of this into the word *compost*.

> *adam, guman, adamah* become more a microbiome of fermenting critters of many genders and kinds, i.e., companion species, at table together, eating and being eaten, messmates, compost. (Haraway 2016, p. 170)

What I'm coming to understand is that worship is like a *compost bin!* I cannot help but embody my masculinity, I am *adam*, but in the habitat of worship I am eating and being eaten by a whole host of other epistemologies. My masculinity is not a problem to be solved (to be eaten) but nor is it a critter destined for the top of the food chain (to eat). I'm simply part of the whole decomposing/lifegiving mess of being.

Supervisor: How does this help you with your original question? 'How do I use that privileged position to challenge, rather than facilitate, a world built primarily on male epistemologies?'

Simon: Perhaps I'm coming to realize that the question itself germinates from male epistemologies. I started this session assuming there was a problem to fix. An issue to solve. Maybe what I am discovering here is that this is not mine to fix – but rather mine to intentionally live with. That is, of course, the name of Haraway's book *Staying with the Trouble*. What impresses me most about her writing is her shift away from many of the well-rehearsed lines in eco-ethics. She recognizes that some of what humans do in and to the world needs to stop, but some, even though they might be damaging, we might have to continue to do. Her point isn't about finding a list of things to stop doing, but to live differently and in relationship with other human beings and other-than-humans. She insists we find ways of collaborating and co-operating knowing sometimes this *sympoiesis* will benefit me and sometimes be my burden to carry. It mirrors my thinking about my place in worship. I thought that I could be a response-able man by doing the right things – being attentive to my language and my sources; but I seem to have ended by recognizing that as good as these things are, they are not enough. What is required of me is to allow myself to be fully immersed in the *compost* of worship. To rub up against ideas and ways of knowing the world that are not my own and be willing to decompose. At the same time, I hold on to the knowledge that I too am an agent of degradation – there is a place for me in the compost to nibble and reconstitute the epistemologies that are tossed in there with me.

Supervisor: I notice there is a lot of 'living' and 'dying' in that understanding ...

Simon: That's one of Haraway's key points – that we do all of this to learn to live and die well together, which, of course, are major Christian themes and in worship are exemplified in the Eucharist. I've noticed that I've been very Methodist in my thinking up until now. When I talk about worship I tend to think about the sermon and prayers. I'm wondering now if eucharist is the par excellence of compost. It is the place where we rehearse, and are invited to participate in, the life, death, and re-life of Jesus. In fact, this is all reminding me of some reading I did in ordination training. Orthodox theologian John Zizioulas wrote a book called *Being as Communion* where he makes connections between personhood and ecclesiology. His understanding is that a person can only be understood in relation. So, for him Christ isn't simply an historical figure, but a relational reality. The Eucharist, he argues, is an invitation into this truth. 'God's Word', he writes, does not reach us from an external source, 'but as "flesh" – from inside our own existence'.

> For this reason, the Word of God does not dwell in the human mind as rational knowledge or in the human soul as a mystical inner experience, but as communion within a community. (Zizioulas 1985, p. 115)

I'm beginning to imagine the Eucharist as a moment where I, a man, consume Christ, born a man, who in turn consumes me. Christ transforms me as I transform the elements of bread and wine, body and blood. As they become incorporated into my flesh, I am consumed into the Body of Christ. That sense of *compost* to be consumed and consuming, resonates with my sense of what is happening in Holy Communion.

Supervisor: We are coming to the end of our session, what might you do with the work you've done here? How is this going to help you in your planning and delivering of worship?

Simon: I'm going to have to use another word that Haraway uses. She uses the word *humus* to describe humans.

> Human as humus has potential, if we could chop and shred human as Homo, the detumescing project of a self-making and planet-destroying CEO. (Haraway 2016, p. 32)

I mentioned earlier that I see my role in worship as a 'leader and influencer', but what if I am neither of these things – what if I am to model *humus*. Humus is the black organic matter that is left over when all the constituent parts of soil, plant, and animal matter decay. You could say that it is the result of good composting. I noted earlier that I was more concerned with what I embodied than with my practice in worship. What I take from this supervision isn't necessarily a list of things to do, but rather a way to hold myself in worship. It's a reminder that my role in worship isn't to tell people what to think, how to believe or what to do but to create an ecosystem that invites people, and me, to nibble and be nibbled. To see ways of being and ways of knowing decompose together to bring about the possibility for new ways of being and knowing in the world.

Supervisor: That feels like a helpful place to stop, how would you like to end this session?

Simon: I think silence ... and then I am going to go and lie on the grass.

9.3 For reflection, conversation and action

1 How do you respond to the idea that worship is playful and unproductive – and therefore in contrast with dominant models of masculinity?
2 How might Christian worship celebrate diverse bodies and make room for different voices?
3 How might the experience of worship be one of collaboration and transformation, or, as Simon suggests, like a compost bin – both decomposing and renewing of identity and relationships?

9.4 Bibliography

Barrett, Alastair (2010), 'In Persona Christae: Towards a Feminist Political Christ-( )–logy of Presiding; or, How Presiding with Children Trains Us to Challenge 'the Powers That Be'', in Nicola Slee and Stephen Burns (eds), *Presiding Like a Woman: Feminist Gesture for Christian Assembly*, London: SPCK, pp. 166–17.
Berger, Teresa (2011), *Gender Differences and the Making of Liturgical History. Lifting a Veil on Liturgy's Past*, Farnham: Ashgate.
Brueggemann, Walter (1986), 'The Costly Loss of Lament', *Journal for the Study of the Old Testament* 11(36), pp. 57–71.

Burns, Stephen (2020), 'Liturgy After the Abuse', in Jione Havea (ed.), *Vulnerability and Resilience: Body and Liberating Theologies*, Lanham: Fortress Academic, pp. 173–85.

Burns, Stephen (2022), 'Liturgy, Gender, and Identity', in Gordon Jeanes and Bridget Nichols (eds), *Lively Oracles of God: Perspectives on the Bible and Liturgy*, Collegeville MN: Liturgical Press, pp. 227–50.

Carvalhaes, Cláudio (2015), 'Liturgy and Postcolonialism: An Introduction', in Cláudio Carvalhaes (ed.), *Liturgy in Postcolonial Perspectives: Only One Is Holy*, Basingstoke: Palgrave Macmillan, pp. 1–20.

Cavanaugh, William T. (1999), 'The World in a Wafer: A Geography of the Eucharist as Resistance to Globalization', *Modern Theology* 15(2), pp. 181–96.

Cavanaugh, William T. (2002), 'The Body of Christ: The Eucharist and Politics', *Word & World* 22(2), pp. 170–7.

Cocksworth, Ashley (2018), *Prayer: A Guide for the Perplexed*, London: Bloomsbury Publishing.

Cones, Bryan (2017), 'On Not Playing Jesus: The Gendered Liturgical Theology of Presiding', *Pacifica* 30(2), pp. 128–45.

Cotter, Jim (2000), 'You Can't Be Serious!', *Theology & Sexuality* 13, pp. 55–61.

Eadie, Donald (2008), 'More than Eucharistic Liturgies and Eucharistic Living', in Stephen Burns, Nicola Slee and Michael N. Jagessar (eds), *The Edge of God: New Liturgical Texts and Contexts in Conversation*, London: Epworth, pp. 11–20.

Éla, Jean-Marc (1988), *My Faith as an African*, Maryknoll NY: Orbis.

Gordon, Lewis R. (1996), 'Can Men Worship? Reflections on Male Bodies in Bad Faith and a Theology of Authenticity', in Björn Krondorfer (ed.), *Men's Bodies, Men's Gods: Male Identities in a (Post) Christian Culture*, New York NY: New York University Press, pp. 235–50.

Grundy, Christopher (2003), 'This Is My Body: Violence Against Women and the Ritual Formation of Men in Communion', *Chicago Theological Seminary Register* 93(1), pp. 13–24.

Hall, Gary (2008), '"I dreamed about Ray Charles last night": Reflections on Liturgy and the Machine', in Stephen Burns, Nicola Slee and Michael N Jagessar (eds), *The Edge of God: New Liturgical Texts and Contexts in Conversation*, London: Epworth, pp. 288–302.

Harari, Yuval Noah (2015), *Sapiens: A Brief History of Humankind*, London: Vintage.

Haraway, Donna J. (2016), *Staying with the Trouble: Making Kin in the Chthulucene*, Durham NC: Duke University Press.

Hartman, Saidiya (2008), 'Venus in Two Acts', *Small Axe* 12(2), pp. 1–14.

Jagessar, Michael N. (2015), 'Holy Crumbs, Table Habits, and (Dis)placing Conversations – Beyond "Only One is Holy"', in Cláudio Carvalhaes (ed.), *Liturgy in Postcolonial Perspectives: Only One Is Holy*, Basingstoke: Palgrave Macmillan, pp. 223–40.

Jagger, Sharon (2023), 'Presiding Like a Woman: Menstruating at the Altar', in Ashley Cocksworth, Rachel Starr and Stephen Burns (eds), *From the Shores of Silence: Conversations in Feminist Practical Theology*, London: SCM Press, pp. 144–60.

Lyons, Andy (2008), 'Participating in Public Worship', in Stephen Burns, Nicola Slee and Michael N Jagessar (eds), *The Edge of God: New Liturgical Texts and Contexts in Conversation*, London: Epworth, pp. 3–10.

Maraschin, Jaci (2009), 'Worship and the Excluded', in Marcella Althaus-Reid (ed.), *Liberation Theology and Sexuality*, London: SCM Press, pp. 163–77.

Muir, Pauline E. (2018), 'Sounds Mega: Musical Discourse in Black Majority Churches in London', PhD thesis, London: Birkbeck University of London.

Pinn, Anthony B. (2006), 'Sweaty Bodies in a Circle: Thoughts on the Subtle Dimensions of Black Religion as Protest', *Black Theology* 4(1), pp. 11–26.

Ramshaw, Gail (1990), 'The Gender of God', in Ann Loades (ed.), *In Feminist Theology: A Reader*, London: SPCK, pp. 168–80.

Starr, Rachel (2021), '"Not Pictured": What *Veronica Mars* Can Teach Us About the Crucifixion', in Jayme Reaves, David Tombs and Rocio Figueroa Alvear (eds), *'When Did We See You Naked?': Acknowledging Jesus as a Victim of Sexual Abuse*, London: SCM Press, pp. 165–77.

Stone, Selina R. (2023), *The Spirit and the Body. Towards a Womanist Pentecostal Social Justice Ethic*, Leiden: Brill.

Torevell, David (1997), Taming the Lion of Judah: Masculinity, the Body and Contemporary Christian liturgy, *Journal of Contemporary Religion* 12(3), pp. 383–400.

Wren, Brian (1989), *What Language Shall I Borrow?: God-Talk in Worship: A Male Response to Feminist Theology*, London: SCM Press.

Zizioulas, John (1985), *Being as Communion: Studies in Personhood and the Church*, New York NY: St Vladimir's Seminary Press.

10

created bodies (God)

10.1 Introduction

Rock, rainmaker, mother bear – the Bible offers a kaleidoscope of images of a nomadic God. Yet dominant Christian traditions have sought to contain and control God. A narrowing of names has taken place over the centuries, until only a handful remain: Lord, King and Father. Belief in this God has worked to legitimate a form of masculinity marked by power, self-sufficiency, and control.

In the first part of this chapter, we question the sacralization of male power, on earth and in heaven. We note how God is often portrayed as enacting violence and ask how such a God might be resisted. We then revisit three ways of imagining God: creator, father and friend; exploring each model in conversation with changing understandings of human identity and relationships. In the process, we consider a God who is deeply connected to creation, in ways that leave 'him' vulnerable.

In the second part, we hear from Michael J. Leyden, an Anglican priest and theological educator based in the North West of England. Michael explores what it means for men to be made in the image of God. While all things are present in God, Michael argues that masculinity is creaturely, part of human nature. He therefore challenges the connection between Jesus' masculinity and the nature of God, arguing that the incarnation does not reveal a male God. Weaving in his own lived experience and reflections on models of masculinity, Michael considers the implications of these insights for Christian men.

God alone

The dominant image of God in Jewish and Christian traditions is of a powerful, often violent, often white, male God who rules alone from on high. Yet the biblical text and later traditions offer a more complex portrayal of God.

So, we might ask: Is God male? Yes and no. David Clines (2021) argued that there is no sustainable evidence of female imagery being used for God in the Hebrew Bible. Even if some female metaphors are used to describe God's actions, God remains wholly male according to the text. Other biblical scholars disagree and argue that God is understood as female and in gender diverse ways (Gafney 2021). Yet it is clear that female consorts or rivals are visible only at the edges of the text, suggesting ancient traditions that honoured the sacred feminine came to be seen as problematic, even as the Bible was being formed. Alongside the removal of female goddess figures, Francesca Stavrakopoulou (2022) observes that later biblical editors favoured a less physical portrayal of the male God. Over time, and especially within a Christianity influenced by Greek philosophy, God's body disappeared from view. Despite this, Stavrakopoulou argues, in the Bible there remains a God who walks the earth, fights, eats, and even has children. This God has a large, powerful male body, in common with other divine figures across ancient South-West Asia. Indeed, Stephen Moore (1996) suggests that the biblical God is concerned he doesn't physically measure up to larger neighbouring gods.

But God is not unambiguously male according to the Bible. Both Moore and Nathan Carlin (2010) explore suggestions that the biblical God is androgynous. Carlin describes this God as intersex, having both breasts and male genitals. He suggests that, for God, this perceived gender confusion results in low self-esteem – which God seeks to remedy by demanding uninterrupted praise and affirmation. Exploring the potentially homoerotic relationship between a male God and the men who worship him, Howard Eilberg-Schwartz (1994) notes how the biblical texts hide God's face and especially his penis, allowing his male sex to pass unnoticed.

Exclusively masculine language for God suggests maleness is more holy than femaleness. Within western Christianity's orbit, moreover, God is imagined as not any man, but as an older, powerful white man. To apply Willie James Jennings' words, this is the God of 'white masculinist self-sufficiency, a way of being in the world that aspires to exhibit possession, mastery, and control of knowledge first, and of oneself second, and if possible of one's world' (2020, p. 29). It is vitally important to recognize that, in Chine McDonald's words, *God is Not a White Man* (2021), since to restrict the image of God in such a way has profoundly troubling spiritual and social consequences. Indeed, even within Hollywood culture, there is a recognition that to perpetuate this divinization of white masculinity is problematic, with increasing numbers of

Black men (and women) portraying God: Morgan Freeman, Whoopi Goldberg, Octavia Spencer, Dennis Haysbert. Within faith communities also, there is increased engagement with the many alternative images present in the biblical text and later traditions, for example in Margaret Moers Wenig's sermon (1999) which imagines God as an old woman sitting at the kitchen table, waiting for her children to visit.

Next, we might ask: Does God rule alone? Within most Christian traditions, God is routinely addressed as lord. In English translations of the Hebrew Bible, the title LORD functions as a stand-in for the divine name, which is understood within Judaism to be too holy to be spoken (Gafney 2017). The divine name, represented by four letters within the Hebrew text, suggests a God who is the source of life, who is being itself, who is more than words. Out of the biblical tradition, Wil Gafney (2021) offers over a hundred possible ways of addressing God, including: Fire of Sinai, Rock Who Gave Us Birth, She Who Is Holy. Yet, for the most part, Christians have settled on calling God Lord. Brian Wren argues that it is unsurprising that within patriarchal societies, God is portrayed as the ultimate mon-arch, ruling triumphantly from on high, untouched by creation (Wren 1989). To address God as lord or king invokes structures of power and control: enslaver and enslaved, master and servant, colonizer and colonized (Gafney 2021). Uncritical, sustained use of these titles for God results in an attitude of servitude being normative within most Christian services of worship. Indeed, we might ask if the very notion of worship sets up a problematic dynamic between God and creation.

Finally, we might ask: Is God violent? Yes, but perhaps not forever. In biblical and later traditions, God's power is often presented in violent ways. One of the most ancient ways in which God is imagined is as a warrior (Exodus 15.3), at home on the battlefield. While war and violent conflict impact on men, women and non-binary people, military contexts remain predominantly masculine spaces. War is seen as a space in which to prove masculinity, through aggression and the denigration of difference (Duncanson 2020). A further violent image is found in the prophetic texts, where God's actions are those of a domestic violence perpetrator, whose jealousy results in the sexual humiliation and violent punishment of his wife or partner (Weems 1995; Starr 2018). And in some Christian interpretations of the death of Jesus, we encounter an angry God who demands payment of debt and restoration of honour. In these models of atonement, God holds humans to meticulous standards, the transgressions of which result in endless torment. This is a despotic, tyrannical God. Such understandings of God's relationship with the world are used to justify violence and abuse (Nakashima Brock and Parker 2001). So yes, the image of God we encounter in the biblical text and later traditions is a violent one. But perhaps there is hope for him. For Walter Brueggemann (2019), God remains in recovery, wrestling with his anger and violence. And, as we have already noted, the diversity of ways in which God is imagined includes those in which God restores, sustains and heals, in just and peaceful ways. In the remainder of this introductory section, we reimagine three images of God which might offer more just and peaceful understandings of God.

Creating God

From Genesis to Revelation, the biblical writers offer a variety of understandings of God's creative work. Sometimes from a distance, sometimes kneeling in the mud, God imagines, shapes and delights in the world. For some believers, God completes the work of creation in an ordered and timely fashion, and then steps back and lets it go on its way; for others, God continues to breathe with the earth. For some, God's creative work is a solitary task; for others, it is shared by all.

Before we explore ways in which we might reimagine God as creator, we need to consider how this image of God functions in some dominant theologies.

First, in some theologies, God's act of creation is understood to establish God's power over and against rival gods. The Bible bears witness to the development of monotheism, as rival gods and powers are first conquered, then excluded from the story. Despite women's visible role in creating and bearing new life as mothers, Christian rejection of the feminine divine (goddess figures, mother earth, etc.) has resulted in creating being understood as a masculine activity. Today men's creativity is celebrated in still male-dominated spheres such as science and technology; entrepreneurship and expeditions. Dominant white men are seen as creators; and women and ethnically or economically marginalized men as the cleaners and carers of the world. As noted in earlier chapters, this has resulted in a failure of men to identify with creation and take seriously their environmental responsibilities.

Second, the doctrine of God as creator has focused on establishing God's otherness to creation. God is understood as immortal and unchanging, in direct contrast to the fragile, fleeting nature of creation. Since God created the world, God is understood to have absolute power over it. Indeed, early in the biblical story, God destroys most of the earth in an act of anger (Genesis 6–9). Such understandings of God as creator work to justify human exploitation of nature, and, in some conservative Christian traditions, result in the denial – or even celebration – of the climate crisis.

Building on ancient themes within text and traditions, ecofeminist and ecowomanist theologians suggest creation is a deeply collaborative process, which requires both humanity's and God's intimate and lasting engagement with creation (Baker-Fletcher 1998; Harris 2017). To understand the earth as God's body, offers us an image of a God both present and vulnerable to human activity (McFague 1987). To return to our earlier discussion about God's gendered body, we might then ask whether it is possible to imagine the earth as God's male body. To do so need not displace mother earth but may help us to recognize that bodies can be sacred, and that bodies can be male. In his paintings, Welsh artist Peter Prendergas depicted a landscape scarred by slate quarrying, yet still alive with colour. Such images might help us explore the exploited earth as God's body. This is a God whose body bears the marks of violence. This is a God who is met at the coal face. This is a God who is vulnerable to human activity and who seeks to collaborate with the earth in its healing.

God as father

Everyone has a father. Known or unknown; absent or present; adoptive, biological or step; one, two or more; alive or dead. Yet everyone's experience of having (and being) a father is different. This makes the metaphor of God as father both universal and unique.

For many people, their relationship with their father is irredeemably broken. For many of these people, to praise or ask forgiveness from God the father is retraumatizing. Criticism of God the father comes from both a recognition of the violence and abuse suffered by many at the hands of fathers, and from concern over how this model of God works to legitimate patriarchal structures.

While most feminist theologians have long encouraged a move *Beyond God the Father* (Daly 1973), other theologians argue the naming of God as father is foundational to Christian faith. To name God Father, Son and Spirit, they suggest, bears witness to the interrelatedness of the Trinity, in a way in which other names such as Creator, Redeemer and Sustainer do not (Hughes III 1985). For Katherine Sonderegger, the naming of God as father is an ecumenically 'settled matter', and is vital in enabling the Church to speak of the pattern of the Trinity in which humans are invited to participate (Meyers and Sonderegger 2021). A second argument is that since Jesus used father language for God, Christians should continue to do so, and to call God father does not need to limit God's identity (Bowes 2020). But other theologians argue that Jesus calling God father does not mean that his followers must also (Wren 1989). In 1997, the United Reformed Church offered an alternative statement of faith that recognized: 'We worship God, source and sustainer of creation, whom Jesus called Father, whose sons and daughters we are.' Third, a number of male theologians have sought to reimagine an 'intimate and grace-filled concept' of God the father (Anderson 2016, p. 247), who does not condemn or abandon his creation. Such moves towards a more nurturing, caring father God need to avoid suggesting that this is only possible through a feminization of God. Instead, as we have argued throughout this book, we need models of masculinity that encourage an attentive, caring and vulnerable approach to fatherhood. Perhaps surprisingly, if we look more closely at the biblical tradition, we might find such understandings of God as father there.

In the Bible, God is named the 'God of your father' (Genesis 26.24, Exodus 3.6) as a way of emphasizing the continuation of a community's relationship with God. The naming of God as father is strongly connected to God's protective and caring role (Hosea 11.1–3), especially for those without home and family (Psalm 68.5; see also James 1.27). In the New Testament, God is often named father, as a way of speaking of God's love (Romans 1.7, 2 Thessalonians 2.16), and the new familiar identity of believers (Romans 8.14–16). Jesus names God as his father in heaven (Matthew 12.47) as a way of reforming kinship bonds, and invites his disciples to call God 'our father' (Matthew 6.9). Jesus suggests God is a good father who will not provide stones instead of bread (Matthew 7.9–11). In the parable of the prodigal son, Jesus celebrates a generous father, who longs for his son (Luke 15). Elsewhere Jesus cries out to God as Abba (Mark 14.36), again invoking God's care and closeness.

Despite the rich biblical portrayal of God as father, within the history of the Church it does not take long for God to become an absent father, a threat held over believers ('wait till your father gets home'), whose primary concern is the respect owed to him. Yet in recent decades the social role of the father in western contexts has changed significantly (Hauari and Hollingworth 2009). Studies on fatherhood in Britain today suggest that a good father is one who is emotionally present for his children, who listens to them, who seeks to find a way of making decisions with them, who protects and provides for them, and who places the needs of the child at the centre of what he does. Fatherhood is a transformative event 'propelling men away from the routines of a more self centred life and into an entirely different orbit' (Edley 2017, p. 104). If we translate this to understandings of God as father, they represent a dramatic shift. From a disciplinary distant figure, we arrive at a caring playful God who seeks to listen to humanity, who does not demand obedience but longs to be invited into the life of the world. Such a suggestion is present in the biblical tradition, where in risky and vulnerable ways, God comes out to meet his children.

The image of God as father also allows for a changing relationship over time. How do we understand God as father when we are becoming the carer? If we are to speak out of the fullness of human experience, the image of God as father must be able to reflect the changing parent-child relationship. Out of her own experience, Rachel offers this reimagining of what it might mean to call God father:

> Father God. I will make you a cheese and pickle sandwich. I will cut up an apple and squeeze lemon on it to tempt you. I will find your glasses (many times) and your Mr Perfect mug. You will bring me cups of tea and a plate with biscuits (many times). We will walk over the playing fields and through the woods. Watch out for the tiger! You don't always remember but you always remember to ask me how I am. You believe in me without hesitation. You look for the swans and their cygnets, the blackberries, the robin. You tell me about when there was nothing here but trees and fields. Dogs (and bugs) rush to kiss you. You see the possibility of it all.

Befriending God

Our final image is that of God as friend. In the Bible, God makes friends with two men: Moses (Exodus 33.11) and Abraham (2 Chronicles 20.7; Isaiah 41.8; James 2.23). But God's friendship is available to all 'who fear him' (Psalm 25.14) – Wisdom makes new 'friends of God' in each generation (Wisdom 7.27); and in the New Testament, Jesus is keen to call his disciples friends (John 15.15). Building on Greco-Roman society, friendship became an important model of community for the early church. Friendship is a chosen relationship, and at best is marked by openness, integrity and solidarity. It can be both playful and painful. For marginalized people and communities, friends are chosen family, enabling survival in a hostile environment.

What might it mean then to imagine God as friend? It may offer believers a model which is more equal and flexible, in which joys and burdens are shared. Brazilian queer theologian André S. Musskopf (2009) reflects on the character of God explored in the film *God is Brazilian* (2003) in which God takes a holiday in Brazil but initially struggles to relax. He is helped by two strangers who, recognizing God's worries and loneliness, journey with him as he discovers more about the struggles of many in Brazil. With the help of his friends, God eventually is able to enjoy his holiday, and the film ends with a more playful God swimming in the sea.

We conclude then, with an encouragement to 'take the plunge' and explore the many ways in which God may be imagined, in ways that are life-giving, justice-seeking and befriending.

10.2 Masculinity and the *imago Dei*: learning how to be a man – *Michael J. Leyden*

I come to the topic of masculinity through the lens of doctrinal theology and in light of my formative experiences growing up in Liverpool at a time of social upheaval. My research sits at the interface of Christian doctrine and ethics with particular focus on Christology and anthropology. My approach is fideistic, and as such will be regarded by some with suspicion. This is compounded by other identity conferring factors: I am white, male, heterosexual, of working-class Irish immigrant heritage, and work as a church theologian and priest. I am receptive of the criticism of white male privilege and want to learn from it. Male systematic theologians have rightly been accused of ignoring issues of sex and gender when it comes to Christology, often collapsing Christ's maleness into the divine essence with difficult implications for masculinity. This is a theological mistake that has resulted in the alignment of doctrinal theology with patriarchy and structural sexism, and created an impossible account of masculinity for most men.

While it has long been the insight of feminist theologies that collapsing maleness into divinity is a false Christological step, the reasons given have not usually been doctrinal. Indeed, the tendency has been to reread doctrines in the light of their historical, patriarchal genesis and to offer correction from the insights of modern contextual and gender studies. However, Katherine Sonderegger, an American feminist systematic theologian and Episcopalian priest, suggests that there are good doctrinal reasons for coming to similar conclusions. In her two-volume

Systematic Theology (2015), she scrutinizes the role of understandings of biological sex and gender in God and critiques the reverse engineering of the doctrine of the incarnation by refocusing attention on the essential oneness of the Triune being. In so doing she liberates creaturely males to be exactly that – creatures. Her insights have shaped my thinking here.

I was very grateful for the robust and critical conversation with colleagues in response to my paper at the *Behold the Men* conference (2021). I still believe that Christian dogmatic theology (the umbrella term for doctrine, ethics, and spirituality) makes a valid contribution to wider theological discourse and, in turn, that dogmatics has lots to learn from practical and contextual theologies. I think this learning happens best when disciplines contribute on their own terms and invite robust conversation and scrutiny from neighbouring approaches. I have taken onboard the feedback to attend more fully to my own story in relation to masculinity and have expanded that here. I hope it is helpful and not indulgent to begin there.

Where did the questions come from? A brief personal narrative

I grew up in and around the city of Liverpool in the 1980s and '90s, and inherited a complex picture of masculinity that was shaped in that context. Mass unemployment caused by the nationwide recession meant that poverty was a common experience for many families, especially those who – like mine – were living on post-war council-housing estates. The steady decline of the port and docklands with the commercial turn towards Europe, and the seemingly never-ending stream of factory closures that followed, meant that by the mid '80s unemployment across Merseyside was twice that of anywhere else in the UK with 20% of eligible men out of work. The figure rose to over 30% for eligible Black men, with some electoral wards reporting unemployment among Black men as high as 70% (Gifford, Brown and Bundey 1989). It became normal for most people to depend on social security benefits most of the time.

That context did not *create* a crisis of masculinity, but given that working-class men historically 'made very explicit connections between their work and their gender identity as men' (Maynard 1989, p. 160) it sharpened the growing loss of identity felt by many living within it: a generation of older men out of work and unable to inhabit the traditional role of breadwinner, provider, and protector; a depressing sense of hopelessness for younger men inhabiting a different economic and socio-sexual space from their fathers but equally unable to work to lift themselves out of poverty and craft a different future.

Work and household dynamics are now widely reckoned to be the two most significant factors in the creation of male identity in post-war working-class communities (Ayers 2004). Men mostly worked manually and produced things that made a difference to society. But in the changing economic environment, society did not need (or want) what these men had to offer and did not know how to effectively re-deploy their skills. That impacted family life too. The money earned by working-class men was understood to be for those in their care – wives, children, parents – and they passed on this outlook to their sons. In the Liverpool in which I grew up, these two identity-conferring factors were upended: there was little work to be had, and men were thus unable to fulfil their responsibility to their families. Social breakdown followed close behind. What did it mean to be a man in that changing context?

With fewer and fewer opportunities for manual work or skills-based labour, working-class men often struggled to define themselves positively. At its worst this descended to civil unrest, as seen in Toxteth in 1981; but it also fed the militant left and gave rise to political radicals, such as city councillor Derek Hatton, whose anger had been stoked in the crucible of economic decline. An unexpected byproduct of the decline in working class employment opportunities for men was the rise of hypermasculinity, reinforcing stereotypically male characteristics. Hypermasculinity overemphasizes masculine ideals – bodily strength, provider-status, aggression, etc. – especially in contexts where it is perceived such ideals are under threat. I can vividly recall playing in the street with another boy who had been given an Action Man for his tenth birthday earlier that month, when his dad came round the corner from the bus stop. He stood over us, shook his head, snatched the Action Man up and threw it into a nearby bin. He then grabbed the boy by the scruff of his neck and shouted, 'Boys don't play with dolls!' His dad had been a labourer until just a month before and was returning from the dole office when he found us in the street, but it could just as easily have been my dad, or any of the dads on our street.

We were schoolboys looking up to a generation of men – our fathers – who were themselves struggling to know who they were and what they were for. How were we to know that for ourselves without their example? When I started to go to the local church in my early teens, coming from a family that didn't do religion, I expected to find an answer to that question. I'm not certain why, other than I expected to learn it from God. While friends and family assumed the church must be boring and patronizing (a widespread assumption, see Ahern and Davie 1987) I was captured by the fact that the male at the centre of church's narrative, Jesus Christ, did not fit either the vision of working-class masculinity – the family man providing for his wife and children and/or rebelling against the system as a political radical; or the weak, emotional, emasculated figure that some of my peers and family members imagined church-going men (singing semi-romantic hymns and listening to poetic liturgy) to be.

What could I learn about masculinity from the Jesus Christ I encountered in the New Testament and in the Church's teaching and proclamation? The question pervaded my religious imagination for much of my teens and twenties and was complexified by the theological description of Jesus' identity I encountered through various tiers of theological education. It's to this that I now turn.

Jesus' identity: the male imago Dei

According to the Chalcedonian definition (451 CE), Jesus Christ's identity consists of the union of two natures, human and divine, 'without confusion, without change, without division, and without separation'. The complicated language delineates the incarnation of divinity within the singular, historical, personal narrative of Jesus of Nazareth. The purpose of the definition was grammatical, clarifying the Church's position in the light of the anathematizing debates that preceded it and guarding priests and preachers from the pitfalls of one-sided readings of scripture that either overplayed Christ's divinity at the expense of full-humanity, or underplayed divinity to make space for a relatable human creature. The theological sweet spot was the overlapping tension between the two natures. The resultant definition therefore provided linguistic and grammatical boundaries, but not much by way of substance. It's not entirely clear what can be said positively about Christ's nature. It is a well-documented problem with the definition (see Coakley 2002).

One problematic attempt to say something substantial resulted in the collapse of Jesus' biological sex into divine essence, such that Jesus' maleness became equated with the *imago Dei* and vice versa. Human bodies are sexed bodies, and if God should choose a male-body at the incarnation then surely that indicates the status of men in relation to women? According to such readings, the historical Jesus shows that a fully-human human is a male human, and that male humanity is at its fullest when conjoined with divinity. So religious men are the best men. A woman's full humanity in this paradigm is always derivative (she was drawn from Adam's side, Genesis 2) and one step removed from the divine nature. This makes male incarnation ontologically necessary, while indicating that women can perform no representative function such as in priestly ministry. It's the paradigm that forced feminist theologians to ask: 'Can a male saviour save women?' (Ruether 1981).

But it's not only Jesus' biological maleness that gets projected into the Godhead this way; it is also masculinity. This is problematic because it divorces masculinity from context and perception, the realm of interpretation, and establishes a particular understanding of maleness as definitive. Masculinity is misdiagnosed not as 'the product of social power relations' but as 'nature' (Ruether 1981, p. 55). Once done, it makes what, in a given context, are thought to be 'male traits' become 'divine traits', universalizing them and adding moral weight to them. This is undoubtedly projectionism, but it is potent: the historical male Jesus of Nazareth reveals masculinity to be God-like.

When I first encountered this way of thinking, I wondered which kind of male creaturely traits were being affirmed? Those of the hypermasculinity I encountered growing up, or another set of masculine virtues that I hadn't yet seen? I certainly did not do masculinity like my dad did masculinity. And the Jesus of the New Testament didn't do it like either of us! How could we separate Christ's human nature from divine nature, and thus shed the (to us) burdensome task of being God, to learn how to be fully human? Katherine Sonderegger's recent work in systematic theology gives some indications of a way forward beyond this seeming impasse.

Sonderegger's critique of sex and gender in God

Sonderegger's approach to the question of sex and gender in God is to view Christology in the light of the essential unity of the triune God's inner life. In doing so she prioritizes the divine nature from Godself, making God's reality the Reality beyond everything that is created – including the creaturely traits of biological sex and gender. This is not to negate these creaturely distinctives, but it is to properly locate them in relation to divine being in ways that are consistent with the credal commitments of the Church, but which scrutinize and resist the usual doctrinal lean towards patriarchy and sexism.

Sonderegger's rationale for this rests in the event of the incarnation.

Unlike some feminist critiques of the masculine turn in Christology outlined above, Sonderegger resists the notion that the miracle of the incarnation was about male flesh only. She observes that when Christians describe God in Christ, 'we speak of the One God who took Mary's flesh for His own, the good God who breathed the air of Galilee and walked our pilgrim way' (Sonderegger 2015, p. 385). As such, Jesus of Nazareth, worshipped by Christians as the singular divine-human identity, is a man born of a woman. The idea that the incarnation is necessarily ontologically male is subverted by the fact that in Mary Christ is conjoined to female flesh, shares in her biology, and is subsequently nurtured by her. Whatever kind of prioritization of maleness has been drawn from this, it does not do justice to the reality of the female bodies and women's lives that are central to the incarnation narrative. If God does choose a male body, as masculine Christologies often suggest, God does not do so without choosing female bodies also.

In light of this, Sonderegger argues, we may think of God as encompassing male and female. But we must do so carefully. It is not because God is both male and female in Christ, nor because God's being negates biological sex. Instead, in the incarnation, divine being remains beyond biological sex while being intimately entwined with it. Or, in the words of Chalcedon, 'in two natures without confusion, without change, without division, without separation'. The second person of the Trinity remains divine without ontic change but also shares biology with Mary and with her son, and the impact is to affirm all human sexes as important and necessary.

This observation opens a door for Sonderegger to address the issues that emerge from what she calls grounding. This is the ideas that sex and gender, as creaturely realities, should of necessity belong to God too:

> To 'ground' something in God is to expect that a creaturely event or being, as such, has some foundation or primal origin in God: there is 'something' in God that gives rise to – causes – this creature ... under the shadow of this idea grows the conviction that whatever gives rise to the creature must *resemble* it in some way. Hence the notion of transcendent maleness. (Sonderegger 2015, p. 387)

While it is true that the Christian tradition understands that all creaturely life comes from God, and in that sense is grounded in God, the problem lurks in the shadows of that doctrinal commitment. If something is grounded in God, it must be akin to God. When it comes to masculinity and Christology, this way of thinking completes the projectionist circle: God is incarnate in male flesh, and masculinity as the enactment of maleness reveals or enacts divine nature. As such, we can learn masculinity from Jesus Christ who epitomizes it for us. As the only one whom the Church has described as fully human and fully divine, his masculine traits become the benchmark for the rest of us.

Sonderegger's objection to this is interesting. Rather than refute the logic of representation, she enquires as to the *nature* of Christological representation. Because we cannot dirempt Jesus Christ into divinity and humanity, yet we must read the New Testament narratives as describing a single narratable identity, we cannot know which of the behaviours is divine and which is human. In other words, God is seen and also hidden within Christ.

How can it be that God is both seen and not seen in the life and work of Jesus Christ? Sonderegger marshals key texts from John's gospel to make her case. For example, the phrase from the Johannine prologue, 'no-one has ever seen God' (John 1.18), indicates that even the earliest Christians did not equate Christ's maleness and masculinity with divine attributes. When they saw Jesus going about his daily business, they did not believe they were *seeing* God. They clearly believed that in Jesus' life and ministry 'the Word became flesh' (John 1.14), and thus that God was knowable and known in and through him, but they also resisted direct equation. For Sonderegger, that means the Johannine community could say that God is *known* but *unseen* in Christ: 'Holy Scripture teaches us that knowledge and sight cannot be identified, nor likeness and revelation collapsed one into another' (Sonderegger 2015, p. 391).

Sonderegger's thinking here is entirely in keeping with the Chalcedonian framework. Jesus Christ reveals God as God, but without losing his essential humanity. To see Jesus' face is to see the face of a biological human male. It is to see the face of a creature. But to encounter Christ, is to encounter God enfleshed. So, she argues that maleness and masculinity, as the enactment of maleness in a given socio-historical context, is entirely creaturely and not at all divine: they are the vehicles through which the divine encounter is enabled. The result of this thinking is both challenge and invitation: to figure masculinity as creatures in context and in dialogue with one another, both male and female, rather than to defer masculinity to Christ and then attempt to copy. Indeed, it is humanity rather than maleness or masculinity that Sonderegger sees at the heart of the incarnation narrative because of the presence of female and male bodies.

On not learning masculinity from Christ

What does this have to do with the question with which I started about how much can be learned about masculinity from Jesus Christ? If Sonderegger is correct, then to attempt to learn masculinity from Jesus Christ is a failure to understand the full extent of the doctrine of the incarnation, and masculinity as the contextual enactment of maleness. For those who argue that Jesus epitomizes masculinity, and indeed, demonstrates that overlap between masculinity and divinity, Sonderegger shows how they fail to properly attend to the two biological sexes involved in the incarnational narrative and the biblical witness to God's hidden-revealedness. You cannot learn masculinity from Jesus Christ. This is true not simply because as a historical figure he existed in a different time and context; it is true theologically, because masculinity is creaturely, not divine, and, as a particular human creature, Christ was free to be himself, and so too must we be.

Thinking this way should liberate men – whatever our class or context – to consider how we respond to each situation as men and as fellow-creatures. The alternative not only systemically relegates and undermines women, but, also despite the societal and historical advantages that have been afforded to men by that paradigm, undermines men too. Equating masculinity with Godliness sets unrealistic standards for men that will cause harm to themselves and others because they are impossible to achieve. Sonderegger's approach liberates us to see masculinity as a creaturely reality, and then challenges us to work it out and inhabit it with integrity.

For me, this is the ongoing challenge and invitation that Christian discipleship brings to being a human enfleshed in a male body. As a teenage convert, I was hoping church would show me a Jesus who would help me to practise maleness – a definitive manly-man and a role model in a context of crisis. And I did hear some teaching to that effect. But, perhaps because many of the Christians who nurtured and helped me to make sense of church and the life of faith were women, it was not as I expected. Those women taught me how to follow Jesus: their sex did not preclude or limit discipleship. They helped me to see that the gospel writers rarely present Jesus' maleness as identity defining. In his baptism, the voice recorded by the synoptic writers makes it clear that what was most important – and the clear foundation of all that Jesus would go on to say and do – was his status as one beloved of God. Matters of creaturely context were important, but in the baptismal proclamation they were re-ordered towards his primary identity and calling in relation to

God. And as Sonderegger strongly suggests, there are good theological reasons for declaring that this is true for all human beings.

The impact on me has been significant: I was and remain compelled by the gospels' witness to Christ who regularly eschewed expected male behaviours and established norms, and whose resistance to the prescribed social strata of his own day is reflected in nearly every recorded interaction he had with people. His identity was formed in healthy and loving relationships – with God, and with others.

In the church's ongoing sacrament of baptism, the priest proclaims that what was true for Jesus Christ is to be true for every Christian too. By virtue of our spiritual unity with Christ (Romans 6.5), our lives are reconfigured and the usual value-laden judgments we make about sex and gender are undermined. For me, this has meant recognizing that my male body is something to be inhabited in obedience to Christ's call to love others as God has loved me. And so, the question has become not 'what does Jesus teach me about maleness?' but 'what does Jesus show me about human life in all its fullness? And how can I live the same way?' It is the answers to these questions which I take to be the stuff of discipleship, instantiated in the particularities of my own life and context.

10.3 For reflection, conversation and action

1 How do you respond to the idea of creation as the body of God? What might this reveal about the vulnerability and interdependence of human bodies, the body of the earth and God?
2 How do you see your own experiences of fatherhood shaping your understanding of the image of God as father?
3 What might it mean for men to let go of the burden of being God?

10.4 Bibliography

Ahern, Geoffrey and Davie, Grace (1987), *Inner City God: The Nature of Belief in the Inner City*, London: Hodder and Stoughton.

Anderson, Tim L. (2016), 'God Our Father as a Script of Intimacy for Those Suffering Shame', *Journal of Spiritual Formation & Soul Care* 9(2), pp. 247–69.

Ayers, Pat (2004), 'Work, Culture, and Gender: The Making of Masculinities in Post-war Liverpool', *Labour History Review* 69(2), pp. 153–67.

Baker-Fletcher, Karen (1998), *Sisters of Dust, Sisters of Spirit: Womanist Wordings on God and Creation*, Minneapolis MN: Fortress Press.

Bowes, William B. (2020), 'The Fatherhood of God in Scripture: Theology, Gendered Language, Points of Reference, and Implications', *Puritan Reformed Journal* 12(2), pp. 17–28.

Brueggemann, Walter and Clover, R. Beal (2019), *An On-Going Imagination: A Conversation about Scripture, Faith, and the Thickness of Relationship*, Louisville KY: Westminster John Knox Press.

Carlin, Nathan (2010), 'God's Gender Confusion: Some Polymorphously Perverse Pastoral Theology', *Pastoral Psychology* 59, pp. 109–24.

Clines, David J. A. (2021), 'Alleged Female Language about the Deity in the Hebrew Bible', *Journal of Biblical Literature* 140(2), pp. 229–49.

Coakley, Sarah (2002), 'What does Chalcedon Solve and What Does It Not? Some Reflections on the Status and Meaning of the Chalcedonian "Definition"', in Stephen T. Davis, Daniel Kendall SJ and Gerald O'Collins SJ (eds), *The Incarnation*, Oxford: Oxford University Press, pp. 143–63.

Daly, Mary (1973), *Beyond God the Father: Toward a Philosophy of Women's Liberation*, Boston MA: Beacon Press.

Duncanson, Clarie (2020), 'Masculinities, War and Militarism', in Lucas Gottzén, Ulf Mellström and Tamara Shefer (eds), *Routledge International Handbook of Masculinity Studies*, London: Routledge, pp. 467–76.

Edley, Nigel (2017), *Men and masculinity: The Basics*, Abingdon: Routledge.

Eilberg-Schwartz, Howard (1994), *God's Phallus: And Other Problems for Men and Monotheism*, Boston MA: Farrar, Straus & Giroux.

Gafney, Wilda C. (2017), *Womanist Midrash: A Reintroduction to the Women of the Torah and the Throne*, Louisville KY: Westminster John Knox Press.

Gafney, Wilda C. (2021), *A Women's Lectionary for the Whole Church. Year A.* New York NY: Church Publishing.

Gifford, Tony; Brown, Wally and Bundey, Ruth (1989), *Loosen the Shackles: First Report of the Liverpool 8 Inquiry into Race Relations in Liverpool*, London: Karia Press.

Harris, Melanie L. (2017), *Ecowomanism, Religion, and Ecology*, Leiden: Brill.

Hauari, Hanan and Hollingworth, Katie (2009), *Understanding Fathering: Masculinity, Diversity and Change*, York: Joseph Rowntree Foundation.

Hughes III, Robert D. (1985), 'The Case for Inclusive Language by a White Male', *Religious Education* 80(4), pp. 616–33.

Jennings, Willie James (2020), *After Whiteness: An Education in Belonging*, Grand Rapids MI: William B. Eerdmans.

Marren, Brian (2016), 'Employment and Unemployment on Merseyside 1945–98', in Brian Marren (ed.), *We Shall Not Be Moved: How Liverpool's Working-class Fought Redundancies, Closures and Cuts in the Age of Thatcher*, Manchester: Manchester University Press, pp. 31–51.

Maynard, Steven (1989), 'Rough Work and Rugged Men: The Social Construction of Masculinity in Working-Class History', *Labour / Le Travail* 23, pp. 159–69.

McDonald, Chine (2021), *God is not a white man (and other revelations)*. London: Hodder & Stoughton.

McFague, Sallie (1987), *Models of God: Theology for an Ecological, Nuclear Age.* Philadelphia: Fortress Press.

Meyers, Ruth A. and Sonderegger, Katherine (2021), 'Jubilate: a conversation about Prayer Book revision and the language of our prayer', *Anglican Theological Review* 103 (1), pp. 6–26.

Moers Wenig, Margaret (1999), 'God Is a Woman and She Is Growing Older', in Eugenia Lee Hancock (ed.), *The Book of Women's Sermons: Hearing God in Each Other's Voices*, New York NY: Riverhead Books.

Moore, Stephen D. (1996), *God's Gym: Divine Male Bodies of the Bible*, New York NY: Routledge.

Musskopf, André Sidnei (2009), 'Ungraceful God: Masculinity and Images of God in Brazilian Popular Culture', *Theology & Sexuality* 15, pp. 145–57.

Nakashima Brock, Rita and Parker, Rebecca Ann (2001), *Proverbs of Ashes: Violence Redemptive Suffering and the Search for What Saves Us*, Boston MA: Beacon Press.

Neal, Ronald (2011), 'Engaging Abrahamic Masculinity: Race, Religion, and the Measure of Manhood', *Cross Currents* 61(4), pp. 557–64.

Ruether, Rosemary Radford (1981), *To Change the World: Christology and Cultural Criticism*, New York: Crossroad.

Sonderegger, Katherine (2015), *Systematic Theology Volume 1: The Doctrine of God*, Minneapolis MI: Fortress Press.

Starr, Rachel (2018), *Reimagining Theologies of Marriage in Contexts of Domestic Violence: When Salvation is Survival*, Abingdon: Routledge.

Stavrakopoulou, Francesca (2022), *God: An Anatomy*, London: Pan Macmillan.

Weems, Renita J. (1995), *Battered Love: Marriage Sex and Violence in the Hebrew Prophets*, Minneapolis MN: Fortress Press.

Wren, Brian (1989), *What Language Shall I Borrow?: God-talk in Worship: A Male Response to Feminist Theology*, London: SCM Press.

11

connected bodies (community)

11.1 Introduction

This final chapter serves as a conclusion to the book. There are many themes we might explore in a chapter focused on connection and community. We might consider how the Trinity offers a model of intimate, interdependent connection, in which all creation is invited to participate. We might explore further the need for human relationships to be shaped by authenticity, care and justice. We might acknowledge the importance of genuine friendship for men's health and wellbeing, and ask how the church might make space for careful, caring and critical friendships. We might engage with the work of James Nelson (1992), Joseph Gelfer (2009), Patrick Cheng (2013) and others on the need to connect body, soul and spirit in a deep, sustained and life-giving way.

As it is, we offer instead a space to pause and reflect on your experience of reading this book, perhaps on your own, perhaps in the company of others. We invite you to explore three final questions and to ask, what next in your own journey.

We hope the book has encouraged you to:

- Be attentive to the diversity of ways to be a man in Britain today, and to see how you, either within or beyond the church, might make space for authentic conversations about a variety of lived embodied experiences. By ending the book with a focused exploration of two north African men from early in the life of the church, we are reminded that diversity is made up of specific stories and bodies, and that there is no universal or normative experience of being a man.
- Develop new forms of relationships that challenge existing norms and work to overturn unjust power structures. What might it mean to challenge heteronormativity, white power and privilege, transphobia and misogyny in the spaces in which you are?
- Identify your next steps: developing reflection, exploring repentance, working for restoration, being open to new forms of reconciliation

with self, others, creation and, if a person of faith, with God. Again, we encourage you to seek out support and resources in this work, whether through friends, faith groups or some of the organizations we noted at the start of the book.
- Be hopeful about the possibilities of change, in yourself and in others.

Our final contribution comes from Jarel Robinson-Brown. It is a beautiful study of the friendship of two north African monks, living, loving and praying in the desert, in the early centuries of the church. With these and other saints, Jarel asks profound questions about the ways in which Black queer men's bodies and desires may be celebrated; and invites us to see the life-giving strength of connection. Jarel is Vicar of St German's Church, Cardiff, Honorary Canon of Bangor Cathedral, Visiting Scholar of Sarum College, Salisbury and Visiting Fellow at Regent's Park College, University of Oxford. He is a doctoral student at the University of Aberdeen and an Oblate of the Order of St Benedict.

11.2 'I have sought you and I have found you.' Queer African masculinity in the hagiography of Late Antique Egypt – *J. A. Robinson-Brown*

I

St Jerome's late fourth-century life of Paul is a queer text. Queer because as a 'Life' of a Saint it sits somewhere between the genres of history and romance, but queer too because it reveals the presence of intimate queer African masculinity which in the western world today would sit uncomfortably within our heteronormative understandings of the Black male body. The paraphrased words of Joseph Beam that 'Black men loving Black men is a revolutionary act' (1986, p. 9) were just as true of the North African desert in late antique Egypt as they are of an urban centre today. The queer bodies of Antony (often called the Father of Monasticism), a third-century Egyptian hermit, whose life was written by Athanasius of Alexandria, and that of his ascetical partner Paul trouble the heteronormative waters of Egyptian hagiography. The 'Life of Paul' by Jerome queers, certainly textually, the binaries of both hagiographical literature and gender roles in late antiquity. The text, most likely written in Antioch at the end of Jerome's own time in the desert (c.374–375 CE), is a window into the life of two African men whose connectedness one to the other had hitherto remained obscure in the Egyptian monastic oeuvre (Chadwick 2001, p. 435). It is queer too because, although entitled the 'Life of Paul', the text focuses primarily on Antony's journeying, longing and intimacy with Paul, rendering it not a typical 'Life', but a depiction of Paul's journey towards eternity under the watchful loving eye of Antony, culminating in the moment of Paul's apotheosis (the climax of his spiritual life). In his text, Jerome invites us to gaze upon his subjects, locating these African men along with their bodies, longings and desires into the myriad social, theological, anthropological and political contours of African, and therefore Roman Late Antiquity. In unearthing the nature of the relationship between Paul and Antony I will be, like Jerome, gazing upon their encounter and connectedness through Jerome's fourth-century lenses; relying largely on his text, and occasionally Athanasius's text on Antony.

Existing as they do as a tiny proportion of the population of the Roman Empire, the monks of the Egyptian desert hold great influence in certain Christian circles. Their bodies, and the views they held, are useful in the hands of powerful men, particularly bishops. While in much of the empire, the laws of the emperor are applied with brutal and relentless force, the desert simultaneously becomes an alternative city space through the inspiration of individuals such as Paul and Antony, and in particular the control of their bodies. As other men engage in the warfare of the empire, Antony and Paul spend their days in a different kind of battle where energy was invested in cultivating in the heart, the fruit that comes from the alternative laws laid down in the Gospel. Paul and Antony master the very same flesh which in other parts of the Empire is torn, tortured and regularly sacrificed in the exercise of brutal masculinity. It is Valerian, Decius and Diocletian who, through their persecutions, set the context for this period at a time when the desert monk and the Christian soldier cross themselves against the power of the demonic, while some other Christians refused 'manly' battle altogether, to the extent that they faced death (Chadwick 2001, p. 179). At the same time as Antony's birth (251 CE) an edict is published which meant that even upper-class Christians are not exempt from torture I and in which following Christ equalled treason. Anyone who refuses to offer sacrifices is put to death, and while some bishops seek to find a way to compromise, Antony and his desert siblings do not (Chadwick 2001, p. 181).

The rest of the empire then, stands in stark contrast to the intimate and gentle hospitality that exists between Paul and Antony, and in particular the equality, kinship and love evidenced in their meeting. Although totally unaware of each other in their shared North African landscape until 431 CE, it is clear that Antony found the isolation of the desert difficult, frequently seeking out others 'like a wise bee' and again in the words of Athanasius, not returning to his cell until setting his eyes on the longed for Paul; having 'obtained the gift of honey' (White 1998, p. 10). Antony's ascetic life involved the offering of hospitality to many visitors seeking advice, consolation, prayer and wisdom – but these are fleeting guests who visit the wise man not in a spirit of reciprocity but in a spirit of gain. Athanasius tells us that Antony's neighbours, and those he visited, 'loved him as a son, others as a brother' (White 1998, p. 11) yet none of these appear to be counted as friends nor do they share the level of intimacy with him as connected bodies that we see evidenced between Antony and Paul. It is a pattern of Antony's life that he yearns and seeks the presence of others, particularly older men – thereby setting a pattern that remains a key in monastic writing throughout the centuries: of a younger ascetic seeking an elder 'Amma' Mother or 'Abba' Father. Driven by his longing, Antony goes out into the desert to find one such guide to whom he can bear his soul and having found him he begs him that they might live together in the desert, only to be refused, leaving a lone Antony to occupy the mountain by himself. Antony exists in this way as a male African body both disconnected and 'cut off from the sight of men' while simultaneously drawing many to him 'in their desire' to live as he lived (White 1998, pp. 16–18). It is entirely possible, that, when read against the sanitizing tendency of a heteronormative, body-phobic and heteropatriarchal Christian perspective, we see an Antony afforded the freedom to be fully human in the diversity of humanity as understood in the modern mind. Is it, therefore, unrealistic to consider that alongside Antony's seeking of Christ, also lingers a secret longing for homoerotic male intimacy? Could Antony long to be touched, looked at, beheld, admired, dialogued with? Might in Paul, Antony be seeking the safety and solace he sought in God but could not physically find in the lone solitude and isolation of his Egyptian cave? Whatever the case, Antony exists in a time when the homoerotic functions as part and parcel of Roman society but which equally provokes visceral reactions in parts of the Egyptian desert (see the works of Shenoute of Atripe in Schroeder 2007).

II

In the depths of the arid desert, we discover two bodies, amidst satyrs, hippocentaurs, demons and sex workers. During a time of bloody and relentless persecution there is the story attributed to Jerome of two men whose bodies through long yearning, journeying and tenderness become connected (White 1998, pp. 76–9). So connected in fact, that we are only aware of the existence of Paul because Antony refuses to let him go. In a rather masochistic manner, the life of Paul begins with a scene in which men, amidst lilies and beside streams, are forced to lie down on thick feather beds and are tied up while being stroked; whose genitalia are caressed by beautiful women who, just at the point of arousal climb atop the bound men. One particular man, a soldier of Christ, bites off his tongue and spits it in the prostitute's face to defeat his lust by severe pain and deter the determined woman. So obsessed with sex is Jerome that this opening serves as a scene-setter that shows us that, despite what may follow, some soldiers of Christ did resist temptation and were not turned on by women. This is enough to suggest that not everyone who occupied the desert was queer.

From the very beginning, Paul is introduced as one who, although he flees into isolation because of Roman persecution, remains compassionate and loving. Jerome presents a rather enamoured Paul, one who falls in love with his surroundings, and this same Paul is quite literally the man of Antony's dreams. As a result of this vision, Antony goes in search of the man revealed to him 'although he did not know where'. Led on this journey solely by his longing, Antony is confident that he will not be abandoned by Christ. His night-long prayer vigil results in his being led by a panting she-wolf, perhaps symbolic of his own thirsty desire, which he follows with his eyes. At the entrance to the cave in which Paul's living body exists, Antony must be plunged into darkness just like the condition of the dream that beckoned him to begin his quest. Only once immersed in the darkness of the cave is he able to discern a distant light, the light of Paul's dwelling. It is in this darkness that the depths of desire are discerned.

Almost as if listening out for an intruder, Paul, on hearing a sound in the far distance, closes and bolts his door. Like a lover seeking a second chance, Antony falls to the ground and begs for hours to be let into Paul's home and hearth. 'I have sought you and I have found you' says Antony – echoing so clearly the words of Song of Songs 3.4. So committed to connecting to the physical body of Paul is Antony, that he threatens to die outside Paul's dwelling at which point Paul will be responsible for touching, holding, dressing and burying him. These are the responsibilities of attentive commitment, and therefore of love. As soon as Paul unbolts the door, the two bodies of Paul and Antony connect in embrace. They kiss one another (White 1998, p. 80), and sit down and begin to talk. In a gesture away from his desirability, Paul speaks of the untended nature of his own body. He is hairy, frail, made up of rotting limbs and will 'soon be dust'. Paul follows this by the statement, almost an aside before turning to 'current affairs' that, in the spirit of the apostle Paul in 1 Corinthians 13:'love endures all things'. In asking Antony about how the human race is doing, Paul enhances the intimacy of the moment – the real world is elsewhere, they exist now as African male bodies, breaking bread that is brought to them 'gently' by a raven whose gift Paul sees as a gift from the Lord who is both 'loving and merciful', who has sent 'us our supper'. Paul's gift from God has doubled: for the past 60 years he has only received half a loaf, but now, in Antony's presence, the Lord has doubled the portion. Life is now complete. For Paul and Antony 'Everything na double double' as the Nigerian Gospel song says. This doubling can be seen as God's approval of this encounter and its intimacy. Threefold, triune love then becomes part of this narrative: Antony in journeying, Paul in receiving, God in providing through a raven.

Between these two, truly queer characters, a dispute arises. Having decided that they will break the bread together, they argue while both holding the bread that has been brought to them. Without any clear outcome being recorded, we are left with the image of both men holding the loaf with a hand, bending over a spring, drinking a little water and offering praise to God. Whether they broke the bread and ate it we do not know, all that Jerome tells us is that they 'spent the night in prayer'. The concealed, mysterious and shrouded nature of the moment when the bread may or may not have been broken and consumed is perhaps telling of its importance – was the breaking of the bread a moment too intimate to be recorded, too queer an event for these two connected North African bodies to enjoy? And what are we, as readers, gazing upon this experience to make of its closeted nature?

When morning comes, Paul tells Antony that it was 'a long time since God promised that you would be my fellow servant'. Paul reads the night he spent with Antony as the fulfilment of God's promise of another connected body. Yet, this moment of intimacy and its intense nature is short-lived. Paul tells Antony in no uncertain terms that he is about to die, and will go to be with Christ as he has always longed for – it is there that his longings will be finally fulfilled. Antony, it appears now, was sent to Paul only to bury him. Like a lover, Antony is left in the position (a different one from whichever posture he took in the shrouded night) of losing one whom he has come to love and apart from whom he cannot live: 'When Antony heard this, he wept and groaned, and begged Paul not to leave him.' Paul, aware of Antony's reaction to the situation, sends him away and tells him to go back to his cave and bring the cloak of Athanasius so that Paul can be buried in it. Stricken with a grief that is too deep for words, Antony '[w]eeping in silence, kissed Paul's eyes and hands and returned to the monastery'. There he is asked where he has been, and he does not tell the exact truth: 'I have seen Elijah, I have seen John in the desert and now I have seen Paul in paradise'. When he is asked for more information, Antony evades the question and replies evoking Qoheleth 3: 'There is a time for silence and a time for speech.' The intimate encounter between Antony and Paul is subjugated into silence. Having collected the cloak, Antony makes his way back to his beloved Paul, he 'longed for Paul, desiring to see him and to contemplate him with his eyes and with his whole heart'. As Antony makes his way back to him, Paul dies. Antony sees him again only in a vision among the hosts of angels, among the prophets and apostles dazzling bright and ascending into the heavens. He is heartbroken and in tears, and declares to the heavens 'Why are you going away without saying goodbye? Are you leaving so soon, when I have only just got to know you?' Whether this knowledge is rooted in the biblical sense of 'know' is not made clear to us, but Antony is broken-hearted. He has now only one last thing to do – to embrace the dead body of Paul 'in a tearful embrace'. Antony wraps Paul's body up, and singing hymns and psalms tries to bury him. Without a spade to dig the dry earth of the desert, Antony realizes he is stuck and asks the Lord to let him die beside his beloved Paul. As he despairs, suddenly two lions come running from the depths of the desert with their manes flowing in the wind, roaring loudly like Antony's broken heart. The lions dig a grave for Antony's beloved, and once they have dug they lick Antony's hands and feet showing a public intimacy that Paul can no longer show or receive. Unable to say a final goodbye to his friend, Antony takes with him the tunic that Paul had made for himself out of palm leaves, a sign of the one he sought and longed for – and every Easter and Pentecost (feasts of life and consummation) he wore it, like a widow seeking to be close to one still loved but seen no longer.

III

There are ways, beyond the desert, in which understandings of masculinity land upon the African male body in modern times. That so few in some Christian contexts can speak of evil or sin without reference to 'black', 'dark' or 'homosexual' is testament to how Queer Blackness is configured in the Christian imagination. The defining characteristics of holiness can sometimes appear to be heterosexuality, whiteness, and a particular definition of the masculine. When such characteristics become synonymous with God / Holy / Pure / Acceptable, real bodies are not normative and suffer. Black male bodies in inner cities are separated regularly by the way they experience so often a premature death undeniably rooted in socioeconomic inequalities. Friends, like lovers, are parted by the brutal legacies of empire which position the Black body as inferior to those around it, and sees the Black male as inherently violent, as something to be feared in society. This induces a pain and grief rooted in ruptured intimacies which it is so often deemed unmanly, indeed 'un-African' to articulate. There are few places where Black men can express the longing for intimacy, or for safety that are a normal part of healthy human experience. An example of this is the lack of intimacy many Black males feel willing to show one another in public and in private, the kind of intimacy that would be totally normal for a father to show a son, but which due to the gaze of a particular kind of heteropatriachy is deemed effeminate and therefore not belonging to Black male communal spaces. In many studies around gang violence in the UK, more attention is given to 'absent fathers' as a cause of gang violence, but little to no attention is given to the trauma such fathers have experienced and endured. In her book *All About Love* bell hooks notes that M. Scott Peck begins his book *The Different Drum: Community Making and Peace* with the observation: 'In and through community lies the salvation of the world.' hooks elaborates:

> Peck defines community as the coming together of a group of individuals 'who have learned how to communicate honestly with each other, whose relationships go deeper than their masks of composure, and who have developed some significant commitment to 'rejoice together, mourn together', and to 'delight in each other, and make each others conditions our own'. (2000, p. 129)

For Black men to show the kind of honest communication and significant commitment that Peck speaks of means the deconstruction of the all-too-fixed Black male image as powerful, dominant, violent, unfeeling and heterosexual both in mass media but also in the human mind. It is this deconstruction that enables and makes more possible the kind of male intimacy we see between Antony and Paul, and so many other queer Black men.

In antiquity, the male body is equally burdened by a set of regulatory confines revealing to us that the restrictions on Black masculinity both then and now do not stop at the imagination, but bear upon real people and their bodies. St Augustine in his *City of God* shows us how a particular aesthetic applied to men's bodies: 'In regard to men's bodies it is surely better to be of moderate size, and to be healthy, than to reach the immense stature of a giant at the cost of unending disorders' (Book 3, Chapter 10). In a society in which men's bodies came under particular scrutiny and were often seen in public in battle and persecution the African male body was seen through both its gender and its ethnicity. While women in the Roman Empire's culture could gain approval by being hidden, it was deemed unmanly to be out of sight, such that public bodies (which even ascetic and monastic bodies become in the hagiographic gaze) were 'judged by body language as well as behaviour, educated to control gesture and stance as well as voice and language' (Clark 2020, p. 173). To be male was to be the opposite of effeminate, and effeminacy was defined by early church writers such as Clement of Alexandria by physical smoothness (*Pedagogus* 3.3, PG 8.581) such that the removal of facial hair was deemed a desecration of the body. Bodies within hagiographical literature must not only be unsexed, but they transgress and unmake masculinity when they show physical weakness, bodily smoothness, vulnerability, and ambiguous intimacy. When, we might say, they become the connected Antony and Paul.

JJ Bola tells the story of a Sunday during his teenage years of walking through North London with a group of older Black African men. At one point during their walk with him down a busy high street, he and another of the men are holding hands.

> It is a way for men to bond and show affinity, as well as affection towards each other. This is the culture I had grown up in. I had often watched my father holding hands while speaking with other men in the community, or as they walked. It was normal, and in those situations I did not think twice of it. However, outside of the cultural norms of this group, it took on an alien and embarrassing quality. (2019, p. 2)

For Bola, this level of Black male intimacy as a display of public bond, affinity and affection is both familiar and strange. He recognizes that such connectedness between Black men of various ages is an inherent part of one culture, but that in another is rendered as out of place. It is important to note that Black culture is not a homogenous entity – that differences exist, particularly in this regard between various African cultures and Caribbean cultures also. In his retelling of this event, Bola recalls how this moment becomes one of shame, but also contestation: he feels relief having turned off the high road (perhaps the equivalent of Paul's cave) where he is no longer under the all-pervasive gaze of those 'staring, pointing, and even laughing in the distance' (2019, p. 2). This mockery appears to be rooted in understandings of masculinity as something allied to respectability, street-cred, both of which are then allied to strength, or at least the perception of it. The Black African man is placed by those under whose gaze we exist, as bodies that are to inhabit a particular expression of masculinity which is usually interpreted as incapable of tenderness, fragility, and the opposite of weakness. Yet weakness is not what connects Bola's body to the older Black man with whom he is holding hands; rather it is the connectedness of bodies and cultures, both in which the gaze of the 'other' and the mechanisms of patriarchy and heteronormativity are operating on different levels. They are connected because in the mind of the older man, there is no external gaze that matters or intrudes here – and no understanding of intimacy that is threatened or scrutinized by societal pressures and strictures. It is hard to imagine, though we are not told by Bola, that the older man pays much attention to the gaze of others during this intimate moment, yet for Bola it is seeing those who focus on him with 'their faces portraying a range of negative expression, everything from confusion to disgust' that encapsulates a moment of reflection.

The playwright James Baldwin speaks in his essay 'Freaks and The American Ideal of Manhood' of how no love can be shown between two people without the risk of humiliation, and how the breaking of bread (like that between Antony and Paul) is akin to making love. He goes on to write about his own experience of discovering how the societal boundaries between masculinity, desire, gender and race are often transgressed in reality:

> These men looked like cops, football players, soldiers, sailors, Marines or bank presidents, admen, boxers, construction workers; they had wives, mistresses and children ... but I had first seen them in the men's room, sometimes on their knees, peering up into the stalls, or standing at the urinal stroking themselves, staring at another man, stroking, and with this miasma in their eyes. Sometimes, even, inevitably, I would find myself in bed with one of these men, a despairing and dreadful conjunction, since their need was as relentless as quicksand and as impersonal, and sexual rumour concerning blacks had preceded me. As for sexual roles, these were created by the imagination and limited

only by one's stamina. At bottom, what I had learned was the male desire for a male roams everywhere. (1998, p. 821)

African men living under and upholding heteropatriarchy exist often as disconnected bodies, subject to emotional neglect, low self-esteem and skin hunger (hooks 2004, pp. 66–7). If gender is performance, in the sense that it is there for comfort of the 'other' whose gaze is more powerful in society than the bodies being gazes upon – then, for the African body it is also a continued form of physical slavery, forcing the African body into modes of behaviour, public intimacy, and even forms of labour that are acceptable (or otherwise) to varying degrees on the basis of gender and gender stereotypes. Those who dare to transgress the boundaries of the established 'masculine' whatever that means, will always be perceived as 'queer', and deviant, and playing with the homo-erotic either by African diaspora cultures or by the lustful white gaze. It is the dismissal of this perception of queer desire as genuine, as appropriate, as sacred, as necessary, that phrases such as 'no homo' when Black male bodies connect in public, are designed to assuage. While many waters cannot quench love, language can deny desire.

For the connected bodies of African men to be freely connected, the connected bodies of African Late Antiquity will need to be recovered with a much more open mind, for there we see that our Black, queer intimacy, or our desire for it, is nothing new but an ancient way of feeling a natural longing for a holy love, and sacred friendship. The forming of the Black queer masculine as ancient and authentically African can only come from trusting in the nakedness of our bodies both past and present, surrendering to what they tell us and what they have told us. It is in reading the African bodies of late antiquity as both African and queer (or potentially queer) that we realize that as James Baldwin wrote:

> An identity is questioned only when it is menaced, as when the mighty begin to fall, or when the wretched begin to rise, or when the stranger enters the gates, never, thereafter, to be a stranger: the stranger's presence making you the stranger, less to the stranger than to yourself. Identity would seem to be the garment with which one covers the nakedness of the self: in which case, it is best that the garment be loose, a little like the robes of the desert, through which robes one's nakedness can always be felt, and, sometimes, discerned. This trust in one's nakedness is all that gives one the power to change one's robes. (1998, p. 537)

11.3 For reflection, conversation and action

1 What do you think is the importance of being part of a community of reflection, prayer and/or friendship?
2 How might diverse stories from the life of the church be celebrated, and what might be some of the barriers that prevent these stories being heard?
3 How might you continue the conversations, questions and actions that have emerged from your engagement with this book?

11.4 Bibliography

Baldwin, James (1998), 'Freaks and the American Ideal of Manhood', in Toni Morrison (ed), *James Baldwin Collected Essays*, New York NY: Library of America, pp. 814–29.
Baldwin, James (1998), 'The Devil Finds Work', in Toni Morrison, *James Baldwin Collected Essays*, New York NY: Library of America, pp. 477–572.
Beam, Joseph (1986), 'Caring for Each Other', *Black/Out* 1(1), p. 9.
Bettenson, Henry (trans.) (1972), *Augustine: The City of God*, London: Penguin Books.
Bola, JJ (2019), *Mask Off: Masculinity Redefined*, London: Pluto Press.
Chadwick, Henry (2001), *The Church in Ancient Society*, Oxford: Oxford University Press.
Cheng, Patrick S. (2013), *Rainbow Theology: Bridging Race, Sexuality, and Spirit*, New York NY: Seabury Books.
Clark, Gillian (2020), *Body and Gender, Soul and Reason in Late Antiquity*, Oxford: Routledge.
Gelfer, Joseph (2009), *Numen, Old Men: Contemporary Masculine Spiritualities and the Problem of Patriarchy*, London: Equinox.
hooks, bell (2000), *All About Love: New Visions*, New York NY: William Morrow.
hooks, bell (2004), *The Will to Change: Men, Masculinity, and Love*, New York NY: Washington Square Press.
Kelly, J. N. D. (2000), *Jerome, His Life, Writings and Controversies*, Peabody, MA: Hendrickson Publishers.
Nelson, James B. (1992), *The Intimate Connection: Male Sexuality, Masculine Spirituality*, London: SPCK.
Schroeder, Caroline T. (2007), *Monastic Bodies: Discipline and Salvation in Shenoute of Atripe*, Philadelphia PA: University of Pennsylvania Press
White, Carolinne (1998), *Early Christian Lives*, London: Penguin Books.

Index of Biblical References

Old Testament

Genesis	
1	24
2	12, 20, 187
3	23, 76
4	12, 148–9
6—9	179–80
16	135
19	25
21	135
26.24	181
34	25

Exodus	
3.6	181
15.3	178
33.11	182

Numbers	
35	116

Judges	
5	104

2 Chronicles	
20.7	182

Esther	25–6

Psalms	
22	86
25.14	182
68.5	181

Qoheleth	
3	200

Song of Songs	87
3.4	198

Isaiah	
11.9	103
41.8	182

Hosea	
11.1–3	181

Wisdom	
7.27	182

New Testament

Matthew	
4.1–11	89–90
6.9	181
7.9–11	181

11.28	80
12.47	181
16.15	73
19.12	87
27.28	79
27.42	97
27.46	86
28.6	86, 88

Mark

1.12–13	89
3.5	91
7.24–30	153
10.14	91
14.36	181
15	58–65
15.34	86
16.6	86, 88

Luke

2.39	70
4.1–13	89–90
14.26	76
15	181
23.34, 43	61

John

1.1	87
1.11	59
1.14, 18	189
2.1–11	76
8	26
14.6	87
15.15	182
19	79
19.25–6, 34	86

Romans

1.7	181
3.23	63
5.20	64
6.5	191
8.14–16	181

1 Corinthians

1.24	136
12	1, 116
13	199

2 Corinthians

11.2	87

Galatians

3.27–8	72, 77, 92

Ephesians

5.22–32	87

Philippians

2.7	62

2 Thessalonians

2.16	181

1 Timothy

3.9	84

James

1.27	181
2.23	182

1 John

2.16	89

Index of Names and Subjects

Adams, Carol J. 38
Africa, African 4, 22, 24, 34, 41, 58, 78, 107, 116, 117, 119, 135, 143, 163, 194, 195–204
  Egypt 135, 195–204
aging, older men 14, 38, 177, 184, 197
alcohol, alcoholism 14, 17, 36, 131, 141, 143, 145, 163
Alexander, Valentina 119
Alpha course 39–40
Althaus-Reid, Marcella 76–7, 82, 87, 92, 125–6, 128, 130
Anderson, Carver 32, 41–7
Anglican, Episcopalian 33, 34, 107, 158, 163, 183
Antony 195–203
Athanasius 195–7, 200
Augustine 50, 144, 202

Bailey, Randall C. 1
Baker-Fletcher, Garth Kasimu 20
Baker-Fletcher, Karen 63, 180
Baldwin, James 203–4
baptism 40, 87, 89, 190–1
Barrett, Al 52, 84, 87, 105, 115, 123–31, 153, 160
Beattie, Tina 124–5
Beckford, Robert 1–2, 4, 13, 20–8, 32, 33, 37, 41–7, 70, 71, 75, 78, 142–3

Behold the Men conference 2021 5, 100, 109, 184
Bell, John 161
Bhogal, Inderjit Singh 117
Black Lives Matter movement #BLM 78
Black Pentecostalism 2, 4, 23, 27, 32, 33, 34, 37, 41–7, 70, 107, 116, 119, 120, 159, 162
Black theologies 1–2, 19, 20–8, 33, 58, 60, 61, 70, 71, 73, 78, 104, 115, 119, 142–3, 159–60, 195–204
Bly, Robert 16–17
Bola, JJ 8, 55, 107, 142, 145, 202–3
Bonhoeffer, Dietrich 45, 121
boys and young men 32, 34, 36, 37, 43, 44, 55, 122, 142, 144, 152, 185
breadwinner as male role 16, 185
Brueggemann, Walter 162, 179
Buddhism, Buddhist 69, 81–92
Burns, Stephen 118, 160, 162
Butler, Judith 150, 152

Caribbean 4, 22, 24, 41, 70, 102, 116, 202
  Bahamas 97, 101, 107
  Jamaica 44
Carter, J. Kameron 22, 27

Carvalhaes, Cláudio 160, 164
Cavanaugh, William T. 148, 163
Centro Bartolomé de las Casas, El Salvador 55–6
Cheng, Patrick S. 71, 194
Church of England 4, 5, 15, 35, 38, 51, 97, 107, 115, 117–18, 120, 128, 176
Clines, David J. A. 71, 177
Cocksworth, Ash 160
Collins, Patricia Hill 146
colonialism 2, 32–3, 55, 75, 143, 147, 154
complementarianism 118, 124
Cone, James H. 61, 73
Cones, Bryan 163
Connell, Raewyn W. 7–8, 62, 63, 154
consumerism 33, 163
conversion 15, 40, 122
Conway, Colleen 70
Copeland, M. Shawn 19, 22, 23, 24
Cornwall, Susannah 77
corporal punishment 119
Cotter, Jim 160, 161
Covid-19 pandemic 16, 35, 52, 165, 166

Dalit people 140, 146–9
Daly, Mary 74, 180
death 12, 19, 89, 98, 119, 196, 201
disability theologies 4, 78–9
discipleship 15, 54, 116, 119–22 137, 144, 160, 190–1
Douglas, Kelly Brown 26, 27, 61, 62, 78
Driscoll, Mark 18, 53
Du Mez, Kristin Kobes 16, 17–18, 70

Dunbar, Ericka Shawndricka 25–6

Eadie, Donald 115–16, 131–7, 163
eating 17, 37, 70, 71, 141, 171, 199, 203
ecological destruction 50, 52, 170, 171, 180
Éla, Jean Marc 163
enslavement, enslaved people 24, 26, 32, 53, 77, 108, 119, 122, 136, 143, 178, 204
Eucharist 35, 72, 111, 118, 148, 149, 162–4, 172
Ewell, Sam E. 52, 122

family 12, 14, 15, 16, 17, 18, 33, 34, 35, 37, 38, 40, 42, 51, 55, 70, 71, 75, 83, 98, 106, 132, 141, 152, 181, 182, 185, 186
father, fatherhood 16, 46, 75, 106, 109, 118, 180–2, 191, 197, 201, 202
feminist theologies 2–4, 19, 28, 50, 54, 56, 60, 62, 69, 72–5, 80–1, 82, 85, 99, 101, 103, 124, 127–31, 158, 160, 168, 180, 183, 187
Figueroa Alvear, Rocio 80
food banks in church 36
France-Williams, A. D. A. 5–6, 56–8, 111–13, 115
friendship 3, 34, 38, 53, 56, 71, 98, 122, 131, 141, 143, 144–5, 169, 182–3, 195–204, 205

Gafney, Wilda C. 177, 178
gang culture, gang violence 36–7, 43–4, 143, 201

INDEX OF NAMES AND SUBJECTS

gardening, composting 122, 137, 170–3
Gelfer, Joseph 3, 9, 14, 17, 20, 34, 37, 38, 194
Genderbread Person 7, 150
God 1, 4, 20, 35, 45, 53, 59, 61, 63, 64, 80, 92, 98–9, 103, 107, 108, 111, 120, 123, 125, 134, 136–7, 141, 149, 154, 158, 160, 161–2, 176–91, 197, 199, 201
  God and violence 25, 35, 57, 86, 90, 99, 101–2, 176–9
  God as creator 12, 13, 20–1, 23–8, 80, 179–80
  God as father 86, 91, 99, 176, 180–2, 191
  God as friend 182–3
  God, gender of 52, 74–6, 86, 90, 92, 99, 124–5, 161–2, 168, 176–9, 183–91
Gordon, Lewis R. 158
Goss, Robert 74, 76, 77
Grant, Jacquelyn 26, 80–1, 154
Greenough, Chris 62, 69, 73–81
grief, lament 20, 162, 200–1
Grundy, Christopher 163–4
Grylls, Bear 39, 40, 70

Hall, Delroy 143
Hall, Gary P. 160, 162
Harley, Ruth 105, 128, 130, 131, 153
hegemonic masculinities, dominant models of masculinity 3, 7–8, 13–18, 33, 35, 37–41, 50–2, 56, 62, 71, 73, 82, 83, 87, 98–101, 105–7, 109, 120, 141, 144, 146–9, 152–3, 159, 161–4, 173

homophobia 75, 116–17, 146, 152
hooks, bell 27, 201, 204
hospitality 122, 196–7
Hultman, Martin 52
hypermasculinity 87–8, 185, 187

Ignatius of Loyola 120
Islam, Muslim 119, 136

Jennings, Willie James 33, 100, 177
Jerome, *Life of Paul* 195–203
Jesus Christ 1–2, 26–7, 45, 47, 58–65, 69–93, 97–101, 106, 111, 116, 118, 120, 121, 122, 124, 136, 148–9, 153, 154, 158, 162–4, 172, 176, 178, 181, 182, 183–91, 196–9
Judaism, Jewish 71, 75, 78, 119, 176, 178

Krondorfer, Björn 70
Kummer, Armin M. 14, 16, 140, 142, 144

Lartey, Emmanuel Y. 141, 142, 145
Leyden, Michael J. 176, 183–91
Loughlin, Gerard 72, 76, 152

Madrigal Rajo, Larry José 3, 52, 55
Maraschin, Jaci 158–9
marriage 15, 17, 53, 54, 76, 77, 120
McDonald, Chine 177
meat eating 37, 38
men's ministry movement, men's ministries 34, 37–9, 46

mental health 38, 105, 141, 143, 165
Methodist Church in Britain 4, 33, 36, 38, 116, 117, 121, 132, 140, 159, 160, 164, 172
MeToo movement #MeToo 21, 27, 57, 80
middle class 14, 15, 16, 17, 39, 115, 123, 126, 162, 165
migration, migrants 34, 37, 116
military 15, 55, 120, 178
misogyny 27, 59, 85, 152, 194
Moore, Darnell L. 19
Muir, Pauline E. 162
Muscular Christianity 34, 37, 70–2, 101
Musskopf, André Sidnei 183
mythopoetic men's movement 3, 17
Nakashima Brock, Rita 73, 99, 128, 179
nationalism 51, 127
Nelson, James B. 19, 194
neoliberalism 51
Nyhagen, Line 35

Parker, Rebecca Ann 98–101, 179
Patta, Raj Bharat 140, 146–9
Pinn, Anthony B. 19, 118, 119, 159–60
postcolonial 22, 97, 158, 160
prayer 34, 35, 39, 113, 120, 160, 161, 168, 197–9, 205
preaching 45, 120, 160, 161, 167
prison, prisoners 36, 39, 42, 43, 45, 53, 55, 70, 110
Pryce, Mark 17, 129, 141, 144, 145
Pulé, Paul 52

Quakers 117
Queen's Foundation for Ecumenical Theological Education, Birmingham 1, 3–5, 100, 108
queer theologies 3, 4, 19–20, 62, 69, 75–7, 81–92, 115, 116, 128, 129, 131, 152, 158, 183, 195–204

racism 5, 17, 24, 42, 55, 59, 78, 115, 116–18, 143, 154
rape, rape culture 21, 50, 53–4, 82, 85, 92, 119, 124, 165
Reaves, Jayme 60, 80
Reddie, Anthony G. 33, 61, 116, 117
Robinson-Brown, Jarel 19, 59, 64, 115, 118, 195–204
Roman Catholicism 2, 38, 51, 54, 108, 118, 124, 159, 162
Roman Empire, culture and society 60, 62, 71, 86, 91, 144, 152, 182, 196, 197, 198, 202
Rose-Moore, Will [Moore, Will] 3, 27, 50–1, 58–65, 71
Ruether, Rosemary Radford 60–1, 72, 75, 98, 129, 187
Rutlidge, Karl 140, 150–5

Scherer, Bee 69, 81–92
sexual activity 15, 17–18, 53, 54, 76, 77, 98, 120, 124, 197–9
sin 19, 23–7, 50–65, 76, 77, 97, 98–9, 102, 104, 108, 124, 200
Smit, Peter-Ben 3, 13, 70–1
Sonderegger, Katherine 180–1, 183–4, 187–91
Soul Survivor 117–18
Spirit, Holy Spirit 27, 39, 45, 107, 158, 160, 161, 180

INDEX OF NAMES AND SUBJECTS

Sport 34, 35, 37–8, 39, 40, 55, 70, 73, 132, 152, 203
Starr, Rachel 2–5, 16, 72, 97, 100, 162, 178, 182
Stavrakopoulou, Francesca 177
Stone, Selina R. 33, 37, 162
suicide 14, 17, 105, 144
Sutcliffe, Simon 52, 159, 164–73

Thatcher, Adrian 7
Tombs, David 5, 59–63, 72, 80, 86
Torevell, David 159–60
toxic masculinity 20–8, 53, 69, 83–4, 89–92
Trainor, Michael 80
transphobia 82, 143, 152, 194
trauma 19, 20, 25, 42, 43, 45, 46, 57, 82, 83, 92, 100, 111, 117, 119, 140, 143, 180, 201
Trible, Phyllis 12, 20
Trinity, triune God 21, 180–1, 184, 187, 188, 194, 199
Turner, Carlton 33, 97, 100–11

unemployment, insecure work 14, 15, 36, 37, 132, 184–5
United Reformed Church 181

van Klinken, Adriaan S. 71
Vanier, Jean 56–7, 126–7, 129
Vatican II 54
violence 12, 19, 20, 23, 32, 33, 37, 43, 50, 51, 73, 76, 78, 82, 97–104, 110–11, 117, 119, 124, 129, 146–9, 163–4, 176, 201
 gender based violence 2, 14, 21, 23, 25–7, 38, 40, 51, 53–5, 150–5, 165–6, 178–80

models of masculinity and violence 2–3, 17, 23, 40, 55–6, 58–65, 98, 101–2, 141, 143–4, 146–9
sexual violence 17, 21, 25–7, 40, 53–5, 69, 72, 73, 79–80, 81–92
von Balthasar, Hans Urs 124–6, 129

Ward, Graham 72, 125–6, 129
Weems, Renita J. 25–6, 178
white masculinities 33, 34, 146, 177
whiteness, white power and privilege, white violence 2, 4, 14, 15, 17, 19, 21, 22, 27, 33, 34, 38–40, 50, 51, 52, 55, 57, 70, 73, 74, 78, 81, 100, 104, 106, 116, 123–31, 143, 146, 158–9, 165–6, 176, 177, 179, 183, 194, 201, 204
Williams, Delores S. 61–2
womanist biblical interpretation 13, 23, 25–6, 178
womanist theologies 3, 4, 19, 21, 23, 24, 26, 27, 62, 63, 78, 80, 99, 101, 103, 128, 129, 131, 154, 180
working class 165, 183–6
World Council of Churches 13, 20, 32, 33, 52, 141, 145–6
Wren, Brian A. 161, 178, 181

Zizioulas, John 172

www.ingramcontent.com/pod-product-compliance
Lightning Source LLC
Chambersburg PA
CBHW022054290426
44109CB00014B/1094